The Bish

About David Bishop

"Bishop is the best player in the northern hemisphere... He is a team in his own right, and that says it all... He's magic."
  – **Brian Thomas, Neath and Wales**

"David Bishop is the best scrum half in Welsh rugby since World War Two. Surely there has never been a more dynamic and deadly attacker among scrum halves... the complete one-man army."
  – **John Billot,** *Western Mail*

"The best one-cap wonder in the history of Rugby Union or Rugby League. Or probably any other sport for that matter. His display against Gloucester in 1982 was the best example of a one-man team performance I have ever seen on a rugby field."
  – **Peter Jackson,** *Daily Mail*

"Genius sportsmen and women are often complicated individuals, and my friend David Bishop certainly comes under both those headings!"
  – **Craig Bellamy, Wales footballer and manager**

"There lurked throughout the land a horde of players guilty to a man of sins far more heinous than the punch thrown by David Bishop." – **Eddie Butler, Pontypool, Wales and Lions**

"Playing outside The Bish, you had the ultimate armchair ride... He was a comic book hero sort of player."
  – **Mark Ring, Cardiff, Pontypool and Wales**

"David Bishop is the greatest Welsh scrum half I ever saw at club level, and by a distance. He was better than Gareth [Edwards] at club level because he was brilliant all the time... The game was denied something special by the refusal of Wales to pick him."
  – **Bobby Windsor, Pontypool, Wales and Lions**

The Bish

It's All About Me

David J Bishop

with Brendan Gallagher

First impression: 2025

© Copyright David J Bishop, Brendan Gallagher
and Y Lolfa Cyf., 2025

The contents of this book are subject to copyright, and may
not be reproduced by any means, mechanical or electronic,
without the prior, written consent of the publishers.

The publishers wish to acknowledge the support of
The Books Council of Wales and Creative Wales

Cover design: Sion Ilar
Cover photograph © Mark Leech/Offside via Getty Images
All other photographs © David Bishop (from his
personal collection), unless otherwise stated.

We have made best efforts to contact the copyright
holders of all images. If we have failed to acknowledge
any copyright holder, we should be glad to receive
information to assist us.

ISBN: 978 1 912631 60 5

Published and printed in Wales
on paper from well-maintained forests by
Y Lolfa Cyf., Talybont, Ceredigion SY24 5HE
website www.ylolfa.com
e-mail ylolfa@ylolfa.com
tel 01970 832 304

Contents

Foreword by Craig Bellamy　　　　　　　　　　7

Introduction: Stolen Dreams　　　　　　　　　9

1　Irish Town　　　　　　　　　　　　　　　19
2　Rugby for Beginners　　　　　　　　　　33
3　Misspent Youth　　　　　　　　　　　　39
4　Mother and Baby Doing Fine　　　　　　52
5　Love at First Fight　　　　　　　　　　　58
6　Violence as a Way of Life　　　　　　　　68
7　Prisoner A79816　　　　　　　　　　　　85
8　Joining Pooler　　　　　　　　　　　　104
9　Lucky to Escape with a Broken Neck　　121
10　Cup Glory with Pontypool　　　　　　146
11　One-Cap Wonder　　　　　　　　　　163
12　The Punch That Ruined My Life　　　　181
13　The Crazy Gang　　　　　　　　　　　206
14　The One and Only Pross　　　　　　　222
15　Rugby Heaven with Ringo　　　　　　236
16　Tough Going Up North　　　　　　　258

17	Stormy Days with Rovers and Great Britain	274
18	Baseball	293
19	Return of the Prodigal Son	302
20	Coping with Charlie	324
21	Walking My Way Back to Fitness and Sanity	341
22	Absent Friends	351
23	In My Opinion…	358
24	It's All About Me	365
	Appendix 1: Mamma's Stew	371
	Appendix 2: Playing Record for Pontypool	372
	Appendix 3: Rugby League Club Appearances	374
	Appendix 4: Rugby League Career Summary	377
	Appendix 5: Sendings-Off – The Facts	379
	Acknowledgements	380

Foreword

GENIUS SPORTSMEN AND women are often complicated individuals, and my friend David Bishop certainly comes under both those headings! They see, feel and understand things differently.

A brilliant all-round sportsman who represented Wales in four sports – Rugby Union, Rugby League, baseball and boxing – I suspect The Bish would have excelled at almost any sporting activity. I wonder, what was he like at football?

He has that sporting chip in his brain. He gets it. Physically, he understood the need for practising repetitive skills and drilling that muscle memory into your system, but at the same time he also saw – and continues to see – the bigger picture. He understands tactics, but also the emotional dimension. When to dig deep, when the moment requires something special and instinctive.

He's unsparingly honest. When you talk sport with The Bish, he doesn't sugar-coat anything; he gives it to you straight, without fear or favour. He drills down instantly into the essentials. No dodging the issue.

That trait transfers to life in general. The Bish is a very loyal, warm-hearted and supportive friend, who willingly offers advice when you ask for it. He's always in your corner and frequently very thoughtful and wise... but he still gives it to you straight. Again, no dodging the issue. He's always been there for me, since the first day we met.

I'm aware that some people have a very different, not so favourable, perception of The Bish. His life's been complicated – as I say, genius can be complicated – but he leaves all that at the door whenever we meet up and I don't know any of the details. It's our continuing friendship that's important to both of us.

The Bish I know *was* a passionate, driven sportsman, and *is* someone who cares deeply about those he loves and befriends. Yes, he can be stubborn and can get a little cranky – to use his own word – at times, but he's also humble, he owns up to his own flaws, he's generous, great fun to be with and very human.

He can be very amusing with his one-liners and observations, and to this day has a presence about him. You know when The Bish has walked into the room, and when he phones you up, it's often like a blast of energy and good vibes coming down the line. You feel all the better for it.

Being friends with The Bish is for life, not a short-term thing. It's like pets at Christmas!

So, well done with the book, Bish – I can imagine you've sweated blood over it, but I'm hoping the sporting public get a real insight into the Bish I know and value as a friend.

Craig Bellamy
Summer 2025

INTRODUCTION
Stolen Dreams

So why now? Why tell my story close on 30 years after retiring as a player? The game has moved on – well, so they tell me – and life has certainly moved on, not always in the direction that I anticipated. I'm now a doting 64-year-old grandfather, a divorced singleton who lives on his own in a Cardiff flat, right opposite where I grew up in Ellen Street, which is no more. I need to watch my weight and diet and slap bang in the middle of the Covid lockdowns had a stroke on one of my daily ten-mile walks. I feel the aches and pains of past battles every morning when I wake up. The right side of my body feels permanently numb – not painful, just odd and vaguely unresponsive – and sometimes I'm randomly crippled with gout, as well as the enduring agony of defeat and disappointment. On other days, though, when the creaking joints are quiet, I feel like a champion again in the gym and it's the glory days that come to mind, and all the friends I made along the way.

But why now? Well, if I'm being honest, it's for selfish reasons, mainly – it's a chance for me to make sense of it all, apologise where I need to say sorry and explain in a bit more detail why I did what I did. When I look back, the sad fact is, I didn't grow up until I was nearly 40. It took me until then to become a fully formed, functioning adult, which is a bit painful because I now have to account for some of my less-than-praiseworthy actions before I reached that point.

This book is also a chance to vent and let off some steam. In that respect, I should probably have put pen to paper long before now, because it can't be good for you to stomp around with so much anger and regret buried deep inside for so many years.

But it's a big step laying your life down in black and white. I was surprised how nervous and guarded I was at first when I started to speak to my collaborator Brendan Gallagher on our regular Sunday morning calls during Covid. Initially it was like going to confession, which is never something I've enjoyed, despite my strict Catholic upbringing. I was also wary of committing anything to paper until my ex-wife Kate and our two incredible daughters, Samara and Natasha, were OK with that process. As it happens, they've been very supportive and in fact encouraged it. It's also important to me that my daughters know what an extraordinary woman their grandmother Kathleen was – and indeed their mother Kate, who more than made up for my failings as a parent.

Another important moment along the way was the death of my great rugby mentor, and friend, Ray Prosser in November 2020. Pross was a second father to me and without his guidance and support, I'd probably have either ended up inside for a very long stretch indeed or six feet under before my time. In turn, I was something of an adopted son for him – a wayward young man who he tried to get back on track when I came out of prison.

His death moved me greatly and unleashed a flood of fond memories, but what hurt me was the pretty disappointing turnout at his funeral in Pontypool. Yes, I know it was Covid and everybody had their problems and worries, but that man breathed life into the club and the valley for decades and shaped hundreds of lives, not just mine. He put Pontypool back on the map and gave the local fans something to be proud of. We won't see his like again, and yet there were just a handful of us there to mark his departure. His story – or at least the part I'm acquainted with – needs to be better documented, and that provided the final bit of impetus I needed to really roll up my sleeves and get on with this book. Very quickly, my long chats with Brendan became a kind of therapy and were hugely enjoyable. I looked forward to them and couldn't wait for the next session.

I must warn you: there are passages that might offend. I apologise for that. I freely admit I am – well, was – a Jekyll and Hyde character and, especially as a youngster, the devil used to get into me. I can't walk away from that. I marched around Cardiff looking for scraps and fights, an angry and often dysfunctional young man who was much too quick to resort to fists and violence. It was the world I inhabited and that's how things were sorted. I came to know very bad people who did bad things, and although in my calm moments I could step back and know it was all wrong and feel remorse, I knew no different at the time and often felt powerless to change things.

I endured a tough and at times abusive childhood that scarred me. Please don't skip those passages because they're uncomfortable to read: they're integral to what followed. I loved my dad dearly as a son and he was an incredible sporting mentor – in many ways he stands alongside Pross as the best coach I ever worked with – but behind his publican's good cheer there was a dark side that impacted drastically on me. I was his 'product' in more than just a sporting sense, I regret to say. The apple didn't fall far from the tree. He was a popular man, and there might be those still alive who remember him fondly, so I realise some of what I write might upset them... but then again, I wonder if perhaps they also had some insight into his split personality, even back then?

At one stage I had an ego the size of Cardiff Arms Park, or the Principality Stadium, as we must now call it. I thought I was the best scrum half in the world while playing Union, with only Terry Holmes even remotely in the same league. Terry was class through and through. I know for a certain fact that I was streets ahead of Robert Jones and, to this day, I'm consumed with jealousy at the number of Wales caps he won compared to my solitary appearance against Australia. It continues to eat me up – I refuse to be mollified; there's never a day when it doesn't hurt. I'm not going to turn all diplomatic and philosophical, pretending otherwise in an attempt to make people think more kindly of me.

Becoming the starting Wales and Lions scrum half was my life mission – it was my dad's as well, come to think of it, as he looked to me to fulfil his ambitions – and my inability to process my failure to complete this mission played a big part in my descending into depression and cocaine addiction after retiring. It just meant way too much, and I'll never ever get over not having the Wales career I dreamt of; the career that should have been mine. The road not taken haunts me to this day. I thought it would get better with time, but it gets worse.

But that's down to me and my make-up. On my more mellow, contemplative days, I know it wasn't Robert Jones' fault that he always got picked over me. Of course it wasn't, and I shouldn't make it personal. He didn't pick the Wales teams or write the press articles slagging me off, and of

Introduction: Stolen Dreams

course it was never ever a simple case of who was the better player. He just got on with doing his thing and taking every opportunity that came his way. I can see all that now, in my calmer moments.

My own behaviour had put the Welsh selectors on red alert. They looked for reasons not to pick me, and at times I obliged and gave them one. They issued such a long ban for a single infamous punch – at a time when many club matches in Wales resembled a Wild West barroom brawl – that it would suggest I'd actually killed somebody on the pitch. The South Wales Police – not the most reputable organisation during the 1980s, as my good friend and old school rugby teammate John Actie will testify – were on my case and the police had a strong connection with the WRU. My card was marked. My non-selection and banishing to rugby's equivalent of Siberia was a complicated business.

I'm not the only rugby player in history with an oversized ego, by the way, but most are much cuter at disguising its less attractive sides. I'd go so far as to suggest that a huge ego is almost essential to succeed. It didn't really matter whether I was the best scrum half in the world or not; the only way I'd perform at my best was if I believed I was. That self-confidence is everything at elite level. Your confidence needs to be bulletproof.

I'm an open book: you don't have to read between the lines. I blurt out what I'm thinking; there's no filter. For example, I've said many times that on the occasions I sat on the bench for Wales in 1985, I was hoping Wales lost and that the individual playing scrum half had an awful game. That might sound shocking but it's the reality, and I can assure you most players on bench duties back then thought the same. They perhaps wanted the team to win, just, but their rival for selection to have a stinker. To pretend otherwise is dishonest. Bear in mind that in my time, most players expected to play the full 80 minutes – to be on the bench was to be a spare part. And in my own mind, I was never a spare part: I was always the main man. Which is probably another definition of self-confidence.

Throughout my life, there was also a madness and a manic energy – a rage, almost – within me, which was definitely not normal and which I struggle to explain. It saw me wade into a flooding River Taff to save a mother and her baby one winter's evening; it saw me survive, keep my sanity and even prosper in prison; and it saw me come back from a badly broken neck and near paralysis to resume my playing career when the medics had long written me off. Nothing was ever going to stop me. But that rage can have a dark side, which at times I struggled to control. It's part of my nature and that's also meant I've often failed to understand or particularly sympathise with players who don't have some degree of rage within. Individuals who wouldn't, or couldn't, go the extra mile.

I was never a huge boozer as a player – I'd get pissed and a bit punchy after just three or four pints, and don't let me anywhere near cider, or 'electric lemonade', as I know it – so I was usually a pretty cautious drinker and, although I smoked a little weed, I wasn't really into the drugs either in my playing days. Not by the standards of Cardiff on a big night in the mid 1980s, anyway, when there was a real scene... I got my highs from sport and being a strange creature of the night around the clubs, music spots, dens and pubs of Cardiff. I was damned near nocturnal for most of my playing career, rising close to noon for breakfast and taking it from there. Not a lifestyle I'd recommend now,

Introduction: Stolen Dreams

but I felt like I was living the dream, king of everything I surveyed, and I wanted nothing else.

After I stopped playing there was a huge void in my life and the buzz had gone. I got into cocaine – which is pure evil, let me tell you, and which fed my anger and paranoia and sent me on a spiral of depression that I've been fighting ever since... Mental health issues in sport are nothing new, let me assure you. I know hordes of my rugby mates and other sporting contemporaries who are suffering as well – mainly in silence, despite the subject no longer being taboo. It may or may not be related to head injuries and the concussion issues the game is dealing with now, but regardless of that, it's very easy to quickly become depressed when you stop playing any all-consuming sport. Many remain silent, but I'm more than happy to talk about it because it's not going away and it needs to be addressed head-on.

So, strap yourself in. Feel free to be as disgusted or sympathetic as you want. I won't spare the bad side and, in many ways, you can consider this a textbook in getting things wrong and not fulfilling your potential. Although I'm hoping you'll also glimpse aspects of a kinder and more nuanced person, and a sportsperson who didn't enjoy a normal sprinkling of luck. I love my sport and always gave it everything for every team I ever represented. I enjoyed some magical rugby moments with Pooler, loved my sevens and grew to enjoy my days in Rugby League with Hull Kingston Rovers, despite picking up way too many crippling injuries.

I love my family, although I'm painfully aware I've often failed as a husband, father and son. I've made amazing friends along the way – many away from rugby – including later in life, which has surprised and delighted me. People have stepped forward and offered help and friendship when

I least expected it and I am, I believe, extremely loyal to those who are loyal to me. I still get a buzz from meeting both Pooler and Rovers fans, and was always happier having my couple of pints in the supporters' bar at Pooler and Hull than in the players' tap room. I am blessed.

I seem to have an automatic affinity with those who are fighting the odds or who have been dealt a tough hand. One of my very best friends is Wobbley – the nickname he insists allcomers use – who's a desperately disabled Hull KR supporter, but an absolute warrior in his own right and an inspiration to me for many years in his perseverance, straight talking, good humour and friendship. If I'm having a bad, cranky day, it only takes five minutes on the phone with Wobbley to put a smile on my face.

I'm hoping this book can also capture, in a small way, the excitement and buzz around Cardiff in the 1970s and 1980s in particular. Everybody champions their home city and I'm no different – I bloody love Cardiff, warts and all: it's in my blood. In many ways, it was a harsh environment. Life could be extremely tough and wild, very alpha male and macho, and it still had that legacy of being a big port at the centre of things, even if the golden days had gone. Growing up in Cardiff, we also had the 1970s Welsh rugby teams to follow and hero-worship. The game's position in society was huge – overwhelming, as I was to discover. If you achieved any status as a rugby player, you were likely to appear on the back pages of all the papers four or five times a week, and sometimes you'd be on the front as well. Heady stuff. You were waved into the VIP areas of all the nightclubs, you filled big stadiums, and got recognised everywhere you went. A paper or a pub's profitability depended in part on the rugby players and their exploits. We basically lived the

Introduction: Stolen Dreams

life of a rock star or Premiership footballer – except most of the time we scarcely had a pot to piss in, unless you had a 'proper' job as well. We had to duck and dive, negotiate a few bungs and sometimes just plain beg for a few quid from family and friends to keep afloat. It was surreal, and not right.

Occasionally, I still wake up howling and raging, bitter and twisted, and wanting to relive my life and do things differently... In my dreams, I'm often getting called up for the 1983 Lions, when Terry Holmes got injured, or starring for Wales at the 1987 World Cup and somehow helping us to a miracle win over New Zealand in that semi-final. Sometimes I'm there in 1988, helping turn the Triple Crown into a Grand Slam, and my crowning glory comes in 1989 with the Lions in Australia. They were my dreams as a youngster and remain my dreams in approaching old age.

Just recently, around the time of the 40th anniversary of my only cap, I had the weirdest dream of all. Rob Ackerman, back for a few weeks from Australia, had sent a nice text remembering the anniversary and saying how proud he was to have been alongside me for my one cap, and that I should have had so many more. We met for a quiet glass at Valentino's (my Italian of choice in town for nearly 40 years) to kick back – two old greybeards chewing the cud – and that night it all went off in my subconscious.

Normally when I dream, I'm 25 and in my prime, but this time I was in my sixties, overweight, with a dodgy knee and going bald. I was heading to the Principality to watch Wales against New Zealand, got delayed by some family matter, and arrived ten minutes before kick-off. There was a panic. Both the Wales scrum halves had suddenly gone down sick in the changing room, literally five minutes earlier, and no replacements could be found. Assistant coach Rob Howley was going to start, but they needed a replacement. A call went out, but all the recent Wales scrum halves either weren't there or were lashed up in hospitality. None of those I used to compete with for Wales caps seemed to be around. "I'll do it," I said, and unbelievably Warren Gatland agreed. It was payback time, and I was thrilled and terrified. With most dreams, just a little bit of you knows it's a dream, but this was playing out for real. It was actually happening. Suddenly I'm out there, warming up, the crowd singing. I'm sobbing my eyes out come the anthem, and next thing I know, I'm there facing down the Haka. About five minutes in, Rob Howley does an ankle and I'm running on, feeling a million dollars – a man reborn. And that, alas, is where I woke up, absolutely gutted it was a dream and not reality.

Sometimes I wonder where other parts of my life have gone so wrong. Lifelong friends and muckers such as Lyndon Faulkner, Paul 'Pablo' Rees, Peter Lewis, Eddie Butler, Peter 'Pedro' Souto and Terry Borley – I've known Terry almost since the day I was born, and to this day we go down the gym together – have gone on to be very successful and wealthy businessmen, or in Peter's case, a top surgeon and then an NHS administrator. Eddie Butler, whose death is still very raw, became the respected voice of rugby, succeeding Bill McLaren. Enviable success stories as human beings. As are many of my contemporaries, to be honest. And I'd be lying if I didn't admit to wondering what made them so accomplished after their rugby careers. As opposed to me.

Sad, I know, but don't you try to relive parts of your life in your dreams? And does that reliving process ever end, I wonder? I don't know, is the candid answer, but I'm hoping this book will help. The final reckoning, if you like, after which I can perhaps find some peace of mind.

CHAPTER 1

Irish Town

WHO DO YOU think you are? That question's spawned a popular TV series that's been going nearly 20 years, and as I review my life and career – picking through the wreckage, some might say – it's a question I've started asking myself. Where did I come from? What moulded me? Why did I behave like I did? Nature or nurture? It feels important.

There are two strong strands in my DNA. There's the Irish immigrant side through my mother Kathleen, who was a true daughter of Irish Town in Cardiff – or 'Little Ireland', as it was also called for decades before they tore it down in the second half of the 1960s. Some call it Newtown, but Irish Town was a very specific part of Newtown. I'm proud to say that until the age of 5, I lived in the very heart of Irish Town – Ellen Street – and as we all get older, that's a badge of honour to wear around Cardiff. The number of former residents of Irish Town who are still alive and kicking diminishes with every passing year. I also, as it happened, married into another great Cardiff-Irish clan, the Cashins. My ex-wife Kate's uncle, Fergus Cashin, was a legendary Fleet Street figure, a news editor and brilliant entertainment correspondent with the *Daily Mail* for 30 years or more, and a trusted drinking friend of the likes of Richard Harris and Richard Burton. He was particularly close to Burton and

Elizabeth Taylor, and rarely moved from their Dorchester suite when they were in town. He wrote biographies of Burton and Mae West, and also went down in Fleet Street lore as the man who predicted a West End show was sure to 'run and run' three days before it closed down. Everybody thought he was Irish, but he was in fact Cardiff with a strong green tinge. Fergus' brother Donal – my father-in-law – was another larger-than-life character, in many ways even more outrageous than Fergus and just as talented. One time he told his wife Jean – my mother-in-law – he was just nipping out to watch David play rugby, and headed straight for Heathrow and then Hong Kong, where I was indeed playing in the Cathay Pacific Sevens. The first Jean knew about it was a telegram home, followed by a postcard.

And then there's the west Walian – Swansea, to be precise – strand, the Bishops, who had a strong roguish element with a tendency, it would seem, towards violence. Mercurial and moody, and also very political.

My dad's father Joe – my middle name is Joseph, as I was his only grandchild born before he died – was a well-known WRU referee, and also a boxing referee who took control of many of the fights at the 1958 Empire Games in Cardiff. He was a fiery left-wing union man who worked very closely with former Prime Minister Jim Callaghan, who was MP for Cardiff South for years. Joe was Callaghan's political agent and essential go-to man. As a Hampshire native and former tax inspector, Callaghan wasn't the obvious MP for a rough-and-tumble constituency based on Cardiff Docks, and Grandfather Joe was the man who effectively delivered the vote and did the deals. He was also a political ally of Aneurin Bevan and by all accounts some operator. Joe was dead by the time Callaghan became Prime Minister, but he often used to call in for a cuppa and catch up with his widow Rowena, my grandmother, causing a bit of a stir in her road with his police outriders and security men.

My great-uncle Gerald Bishop, Joe's brother, is the great enigma of the Bishop side of the family. A huge, athletic, handsome, violent man, he was a gangster-type figure in the Swansea docks and the Greenhill – Irish – part of town. Talking to people down that way, the one constant was that "you didn't mess with Gerald Bishop". A very accomplished boxer, he was certainly employed on occasion as a sparring partner for World Heavyweight Champion Ingemar Johansson – although the family lore that he once decked the Swede in training cannot be confirmed. There's no question that Uncle Gerald was my dad's hero and role model.

I'm intrigued by my Bishop genes and we're only gradually learning more about them. My great-grandfather, Robert Bishop, was an English farm worker from Claydon in Oxfordshire who moved to Pembrokeshire, and his second wife was an Irish woman, Theresa Green from Waterford. An interesting mix, for sure, but it's the Cardiff-Irish side of the family I most identify with. My mum was Kathleen Frost, whose Healan ancestors apparently travelled over from County Cork in the nineteenth century in the wake of the potato famine. Like many of the Irish immigrants and labourers, they provided an important part of the workforce for the docks, with Cardiff fast becoming the busiest port in the Empire as it shipped the finest coal in the world from the Valleys. The men worked transporting the coal, while the women often worked loading and unloading the potato and fish ships. Irish Town was a self-contained area of six streets and exactly 200 houses, hemmed in by the railway to the north and the docks and wharfs to the south and east. The much bigger Butetown, which housed immigrant workers from all corners of the world, was to the west.

It was my mum's manor. She literally knew everybody there and she continued to think of it as home even after we left and started moving around Cardiff. She was a brilliant storyteller: very humorous, could paint the picture vividly and recall the names of everybody she encountered, and used to regale us with tales of Irish Town and her friends. The six streets of Irish Town were North Williams Street, Pendoylan Street, Pendoylan Place, Roland Street, Rosemary Street and Ellen Street. To be a true resident of Irish Town, that's where you had to live – although obviously many other Irish immigrant families lived in Cardiff, some very close by in Newtown. With the world's busiest port on the doorstep, there was a 24-7 work environment there for many decades, and there was a lot of 'hot-bedding', with more than one family living in the two-up, two-down houses. Life was bloody tough. But, by all accounts, there was a camaraderie and neighbourly spirit of helping out and sharing whatever you had. I remember my mum telling me one time there was a woman in Ellen Street who had 36 grandchildren, and 33 of them lived within the confines of Irish Town. Nobody locked their front doors; they were always left open... People moved freely from house to house and popped in anytime. If you were from Irish Town, you were trusted by all fellow inhabitants.

My mum – always known as 'Mamma' in the family – was one of thirteen children, although five died in infancy, and like most in Irish Town was a devout Catholic. The Catholic Church held massive sway and the old St Paul's church, under the flyover, was the heart of the community along with the Vulcan pub (now to be found, rebuilt brick by brick, at St Fagans National Museum of History, just outside Cardiff). Mamma brought me, my brothers and sister up as Catholics and we did the whole shooting match. Baptism, Confirmation, Holy Communion, Confession, serving at Mass. She was a 100% unconditional believer – that faith got her through some pretty dreadful times and made an impression on me. I might have strayed a bit from godliness and virtue, but old habits die hard and I've always got down on my knees said a prayer or two last thing at night and at times of stress, when my life was hurtling out of control. No matter how late, how drunk or occasionally off my head. I'm not a regular churchgoer but it's very difficult to 'unbecome' a Catholic. It's in the system whether you like it or not, and I'm still very at home and at ease on those occasions I do attend – funerals, weddings and the occasional Christmas service – and I retain my faith in my own way.

So that's where Mamma's tribe came from, and I couldn't be prouder. The big hero of Irish Town – the individual who epitomised the best of them all and whose life story and legend was handed down and discussed endlessly by Irish Town families – was Peerless Jim Driscoll. He was one of the greatest boxers of the early twentieth century and lived his entire life in Ellen Street, even after he'd made a few bob and could have moved away and lived anywhere he wanted. I read somewhere that he lived at number 6 and then number 12, and years later we lived at number 11, which in my mind always forged a connection. Neighbours geographically, if not chronologically.

I'll talk more about him later on because I based my campaign to overcome a broken neck and play rugby again from Jim Driscoll's old gym at the Royal Oak pub, and used to look at his memorabilia and cuttings most days. For now, though, it was just his example that was inspiring. A kid from Ellen Street became the British and Empire featherweight champion and drew a fight in the USA with Abe Attell for the world title. And if you draw a fight in the USA against an American fighter, that basically means you won comfortably. Certainly, that's how even the newspapers in the States called it: a win for the Welshman. He was a great early technician, incredibly fit – he ran seven miles every morning – and he proved that you could achieve anything if you wanted it badly enough. He gave most of his 'fortune' away to charity – he was a huge supporter of Nazareth House, which in those days was a house of refuge for the orphans and the elderly – and what was left he gambled away. He was a flawed hero, but a hero nonetheless, which has always appealed to me. More than 100,000 people lined the streets of Cardiff for his funeral in 1925.

The authorities started moving everybody out of Irish Town at the end of 1965 with a series of compulsory purchases, with a view to demolition and redevelopment. Breaking up such a close-knit community was painful for everybody involved, with the families placed all around Cardiff. Some kept in close touch and the spirit lived on; others, though, fell off the radar. It was at this time that we became almost an itinerant family.

We moved around a lot. There was a spell at Braunton Crescent in Llanrumney, then a long period at 43 Dunster Road, outside of which was a triangle of ground which we called The Patch. That's where I honed my emerging rugby skills day and night, and we had pick-up matches of every sport – rugby, cricket, football, baseball. It seemed huge at the time, a proper sporting arena, but of course when you go back as an adult, it's diminished considerably in size

– probably the equivalent of two tennis courts put side by side. Dad would watch me the entire time from behind the curtains of their bedroom – nothing escaped his attention, as you'll discover shortly. If he saw me kicking with my natural right foot, he'd call me in early. If he saw me practising with my left, I'd get another half hour running free. You soon pick up on these things when you're 7 or 8.

After that, it was accommodation over Rumney Rugby Club, till Dad got sacked as the steward there, and then a spell in Pentwyn, which was rough, before Dad finally got a job as publican at the Tudor Pub just over the bridge from the National Stadium, which is where I spent most of my teenage years. It was an odd, unsettling lifestyle, and never really stopped. At the start of my year in prison we were still at the Tudor, but when I returned a year later, the family had moved again to Llanedern, where Dad was running The Retreat. Not long after that, there was some unpleasantness about the beer being watered down and, before we knew it, we'd moved to the Admiral Napier, near Sophia Gardens, where we were when I won my solitary cap in 1984.

Having to leave Irish Town was a blow. Make no mistake, the houses where the old inhabitants ended up might have been a marginal improvement on those in the famous six streets of Irish Town, but that's missing the point. It was the community, shared experience and friendship which made Irish Town tick, and to have that ripped from you late in life was devastating.

My grandfather – Mamma's father, Grancha Billy Frost – died not long after we left Irish Town. I was playing for Cardiff U11s v. Carmarthen U11s. Ray Williams, who was to feature quite prominently in my life, had organised a curtain-raiser ahead of a Wales game, and I was feeling very pleased with myself as I trooped off, having scored all 16 points, when I was taken to one side and told of Grancha's death. It was my first experience of death, other than vague memories of going to my infant sister Wendy's funeral after her premature death when I was four, and not really understanding what was going on as the family gathered around her shoebox of a coffin.

Cast adrift from her beloved Irish Town and on her own, Nanna Frost started to really struggle. She tried to commit suicide by cutting her wrist and tried twice more to kill herself when she was in a nursing home before, remarkably, she was considered well enough to go home and fend for herself. I remember the day she died in 1976 vividly because, just a few minutes before that devastating news came, we'd been listening to reports of Mervyn Davies suffering a brain haemorrhage playing for Swansea against Pontypool. Suddenly the world seemed a very unsafe place.

I'll talk at length about Dad soon, but Mamma comes first. Let's be honest, I was her golden boy and the bond was incredibly tight, even if we argued on occasion. Mamma and Dad had been trying for a family for six years after getting married, and had virtually given up when I came along one thundery Halloween night in 1960 – their little miracle. Mind you, having broken their duck, my parents then produced another five children in the next six years – Michael, Terry, Sean and Cecelia, and Wendy, who was the victim of a cot death. For seven or eight years, Mamma was rarely without child, and it must have been exhausting.

I was a trial, as well as a joy. As she used to tell me, "David, I cried to have you; God knows I cried when I was having you; and you've been making me cry ever since, you little bastard." I should add that Mamma swore fluently and completely without offence or insult, a habit I developed very early in life. You shouldn't be alarmed when I slip into what seems like bad language – it's just my way of punctuating my thoughts and adding emphasis.

Mamma was a proper Irish matriarch, but she was a wise owl as well. Whereas just about any conversation with Dad other than about sport would end up with a blazing row and a fight, Mamma was calm, a good listener and that devout Catholicism gave her a fatalism and resignation my dad didn't have. I'm pretty sure Dad was jealous of the close relationship mother and first-born son shared.

There was a very natural, deep connection between the two of us. I could talk to Mamma about anything: from Kate, my girlfriend and then wife – "She's much too good for you, David. You'll break her heart one day." – to life in prison, worries about my fitness, worries about being a good dad to my two beautiful daughters, and everything. No subject was off limits. I could tell her my inner secrets and, talking to mates over the years, I now realise that wasn't the norm. I was blessed.

She wasn't bothered about the rugby. She only came to watch me once – when, bizarrely, she suddenly decided to attend a charity match of little consequence; for Crawshays, of all teams. Her concern was totally about me and my health and happiness. She prayed for me before every game and, after my broken neck and whenever possible, I called round for her to splash some holy water on me. When I was on the road, she kept me supplied with bottles of the stuff, blessed at Lourdes. If anybody from the parish went down to Lourdes, she put in a bulk order for the real stuff – blessed at the main grotto itself – and seemed to have access to industrial quantities. I've still got some unopened bottles somewhere.

I stopped using it when I stopped playing. Perhaps that's where I went wrong?

She, along with Kate, got me through my broken neck. When that potentially life-changing injury occurred, my old man died a little inside, because his dreams were disappearing as well as my own, but Mamma was the strong one and kept my spirits up. Dad didn't really encourage my comeback – well, not initially, although he did come round eventually – but Mamma knew I needed to play again; not to play would have been a living death. It was non-negotiable. She was with me every minute. Her faith became my rock. What a woman.

Given the difficulties she had with my dad, which we'll come to later, it was remarkable that Mamma had any emotional energy left to comfort me but, then again, she was an incredible woman. My fondest memories of her would be watching a film together on a Sunday afternoon, or perhaps a Saturday afternoon when I played for the school in the morning, and it was too wet outside to be messing about with the lads. Dad would be out at a rugby match, playing or watching, down at Cardiff International Athletics Club RFC (CIACs) or Glamorgan Wanderers, and the house would be quiet and peaceful.

We both loved all the old black and white films. *Angels with Dirty Faces* with Jimmy Cagney was my all-time favourite, and everything stopped when that was on, which seemed to be quite frequently. I watch it regularly to this day, and it always makes me cry. It's all about two tough Irish-American kids getting into crime and robbing a train. The cops come. One of the two lads – Rocky Sullivan – is caught and embarks on a sordid life of crime while the other, Jerry Connolly – played by Pat O'Brien – runs for it, escapes and eventually gets the calling and becomes a Roman Catholic priest. There are lots of twists and turns when Rocky comes out of prison, but the film ends with Jerry accompanying Rocky to the electric chair after he's sentenced to death for killing two people who threatened the priest's life. Jerry begs his friend to repent, and perhaps be spared, but the execution goes ahead. After Rocky's death, Jerry finds the Dead End Kids, a bunch of local young hoodlums and street basketball players who worshipped Rocky and his criminal notoriety. He asks them to join in prayer "for the boy who couldn't run as fast as I could". That's when I usually tear up.

I have no idea why such a film appealed to both me and Mamma, but the idea that there are *Sliding Doors* moments in life – different paths, roads not taken, turning points – has always played a huge part in my psyche. The film has stayed with me in a big way, and in fact at one stage I was going to title this book *Angel with a Dirty Face*. That's me. Light and shade, good and bad, Jekyll and Hyde, Rocky and Jerry all rolled into one.

Mamma was a miraculous cook, conjuring up feasts with the limited produce we could afford. There wasn't much to go round, and as kids we were never allowed to go for sleepovers because we were in no position to invite school friends back and feed them. We couldn't repay the hospitality and Mamma's pride wouldn't allow us to be seen as spongers, takers not givers. No, she just wouldn't allow that. It was only when I was a little older that she sadly told me why she'd banned sleepovers. But somehow, we made do, and occasionally there were real treats – she was always plotting and planning and conjuring something up. Cannily, she had two part-time jobs, involving serving in a butcher's and a baker's, and at closing time was often given some of the unsold meat and bread that had just gone past its sell-by date to bring home.

The other big plus back then was that offal such as liver and kidneys was considered barely edible. It was either dirt cheap or sometimes the butcher would just load Mamma up with it all once a week because he couldn't give it away. These days it's considered a delicacy by some, and liver's very healthy indeed. We all loved it, which was fortunate. Liver, bacon, mashed potato, gravy and peas was the greatest treat of the week, and often saved for the Saturday night, after we'd all been to confession. It was a sort of bribe to get us there. No confession, no liver and bacon. She also did an incredible curry from off-cuts.

Mamma's job at the bakery was a boon, with plenty of slightly stale bread coming our way, which wasn't a problem at all. Firstly, it could be added to Mamma's soups, which again is very fashionable these days. *Panzanella*, they call it down my favourite Cardiff Italian, Valentinos. And then there was breakfast. We didn't have – couldn't afford – cereals or eggs and bacon for breakfast, but instead we had hot bread and milk hash, which was bloody lovely. Mamma would break up the stale bread, put it in a saucepan, pour the milk in, simmer it, add sugar to taste, and serve, I suppose it was our version of porridge – in fact, Mamma called it Irish Porridge. I swear by it to this day, although I sometimes add honey instead of sugar. We could never have afforded proper porridge back then.

Her speciality was a glorious Irish stew, which both my wife and daughters have learnt to cook, to keep the tradition going. As I don't intend to write a cookery book, I've included the recipe for those who are interested as Appendix 1 at the back of this book. I've never tasted better.

Mamma left us much too early in 1997, when she was just 62. A few weeks earlier, I'd dropped by for her for 62nd birthday – I'd put £62 in an envelope with a note saying I looked forward to the day when I'd be putting £100 in an envelope. And then, on the day she actually died, I'd called in to say cheerio for a couple of weeks, as I was going on a supporters' trip for the 1997 Lions. She reminded me to bring back a bottle of vodka and 200 fags, which was her standing order whenever I went abroad.

I had to nip out to get something and I asked her to fix me a sandwich while I was gone. A few minutes later my sister Cecelia phoned to say she'd collapsed and was very ill and the ambulance was on the way... I sprinted back and she was being stretchered into the ambulance, oxygen masks and tubes everywhere, and taken to hospital. She might technically have been alive, but I looked into her eyes and could see she was gone.

I quickly became very emotional: "Mamma, don't leave me now, not now after everything!" I cried. We'd been through so much together.

It was all too much. I ran off into the street, unable to cope with what was happening. Drama queen that I was, I made it about me, which I greatly regret. Sometime later, it was Kate who phoned and told me Mamma really was gone. I was distraught: nothing had prepared me for this, and it was a long while before I calmed down and took it fully on board.

We laid her out for a week. Strangely – did she have a premonition? – we'd been talking about funerals just a few weeks earlier and she was quite explicit that she didn't want to be "locked up in a fridge" before her funeral, and she didn't want to be cremated.

"We Catholics need to be buried in the ground, not burned like bloody witches. Make sure you do that for me, David. Make sure that I'm laid out properly and that we provide hospitality for anybody who turns up to pay their respects."

That's exactly what we did. There was a steady stream and on the night before the funeral, we took the body down to St Peter's Church to be laid out, and there was a big crowd outside – about 300 to 400 people. I assumed another funeral was breaking up, but no: it was the old Irish Town community, gathered to pay their respects collectively to one of their own. I was choked up just seeing it, and was very emotional again the following day at the funeral, when I couldn't find the words when it came to my eulogy. Nor could I read her favourite poem, 'Footsteps' – my daughter Natasha had to take over. You know the one, about there only being one set of footsteps on the sand because somebody you love has been carrying you. That was my mother.

CHAPTER 2
Rugby for Beginners

MOST OF US have a few treasured memories of our early playing days squirrelled away, but I'm lucky enough to also possess a unique memento of what I looked like and how I shaped up as an 11-year-old tyro. Through sheer good fortune and the blatant opportunism of my father, two other lads and I were the guinea pigs – the models, if you like – for Ray Williams' definitive coaching book *Rugby for Beginners*, which came out in 1973 after we had worked on it over the previous 18 months. Amongst other things, it's a reminder of how small and slight I was. Throughout my early years, I always imagined myself to be in a David v. Goliath fight, a mindset I maintained for the rest of my life, even when I filled out.

Mr Williams was a cutting-edge coach and administrator ahead of his time and a product of Loughborough University. Based in England, he'd played most of his rugby for London Welsh, Northampton, Moseley and the East Midlands. He'd returned to Wales as the WRU's first Coaching Organiser in 1967, the world's first professional full-time Rugby Union coach and an important architect of Wales 1970s Rugby Union dominance. He set up coaching classes all over the country, with his summer camps up at Aberystwyth quickly becoming world renowned, with PE teachers from all over

Britain and beyond attending. He firmly believed that if you got the basics right, if you honed children from an early age, rugby could be a simple game.

So, to assist in that process, he set out to write a coaching book for complete beginners – i.e. the basic core skills that you need to nail down and perfect from the youngest age. The book is generally reckoned to have signalled the start of mini rugby, so simple were its aims, but much of it still applies at senior level. I look around today and see way too many professional players who haven't mastered the basic skills illustrated in *Rugby for Beginners*. There's no excuse, and it annoys me a little.

Mr Williams needed three willing volunteers and as ever Dad – David Bishop senior – had his ear to the ground and, in that commanding Sergeant Major way of his which encouraged no argument, he informed Ray that I would be one of the lads and we would pick two others. All organised by Dad – I think Ray was frightened to contradict him. The book project sounded like fun, with time off school and photo sessions over at the Arms Park on the hallowed National Stadium pitch, so when Dad asked who we should go with, I picked Douglas Actie, my half back partner at St Cadoc's Primary School in Cardiff and Kevin Trevett, my opposition scrum half at St Alban's and a very good player. Our paths continued to cross – myself and Kevin played together for Cardiff Schools and Youth and were members of the Wales Youth squad at the same time, although Kevin got capped the year after me. Kevin, who was also a considerable baseball player like myself, went on to play for Cardiff proper and occasionally Pontypool, but alas died in his early thirties, when he was involved in a car crash, God rest his soul. He was a brilliant sporting all-rounder – and that included his ability to beat the bookies: he was a proper student of the turf. I was proud to be one of his coffin bearers.

Douglas was another very useful player, who I enjoyed many a schoolboy success with in the St Cadoc and Cardiff Schools teams. He was tall for his age and a good athlete, just like his cousin John Actie, who I also knew very well. John was much bigger and stronger and a bloody good rugby prospect himself, also playing for St Cadoc's, although, alas, he became better known for being wrongly implicated in the murder of Lynette White – a disgraceful episode which has recently been fully revealed in documentaries and an outstanding book by Ceri Jackson, who also produced an award-winning podcast series on the miscarriage of justice. John's a lifelong friend who has overcome and prevailed.

We had a hell of a good side at St Cadoc's. For two years in a row, we got to the final of the U11 sevens at the Snelling Cup – we contested the final as a curtain raiser to the main final in front of 20,000-odd fans at the National Stadium. On both occasions we met Fairwater; the first time they beat us but the second time we won easily. One of my most treasured pictures is of us celebrating that win, lifting our skipper Paul Trebilcock high on our shoulders. From memory Joseph Stitfall, whose uncle was a star with Cardiff City, Timothy Cross and Robert Rice were also on the team. Where are you all now, lads? Fancy a beer? We won the Clare Cup that year – a season-long fifteens competition for Cardiff schools – and the entire schools scene was incredibly well organised, way ahead of its time. Welsh rugby was on a massive high, remember, so there was a tidal wave of energy and volunteers. We had a Cardiff representative side at every age group that played against all the other Welsh Districts, and we won the U11 competition – the D C Thomas Cup – and then a few years later we won the U15 title, the Dewar Shield. Playing competitive rugby, often on the big club grounds in Wales and sometimes even on the Arms Park itself, was absolutely bog standard for my generation. It's what we did.

Just as an aside, but also vaguely related, I also enjoyed the extraordinary, surreal experience in my mid and late teens, when my dad ran the Tudor pub, of often exercising our dogs on the Arms Park, the National Stadium, which was just over the river from us. We treated it like a local recreation ground. No, really... After chucking-out time and tidying up, we would walk over as nonchalant as you like about midnight with two or three dogs and, believe it or not, there were always a couple of gates you could just push open. Dad always knew which ones. Suddenly we would be stepping over the dog track and on to the hallowed turf, letting the dogs run free and do their business down at the River Taff end – the Canton end, as some called it. In fact, it was the end at which I scored my try for Wales against Australia. My father, amongst many things, was an extraordinarily anarchic figure but also a rugby romantic. Sometimes he would put his arm around me and just say, "How do you fancy playing for Wales here one day, son?" It felt then that the Arms Park would become my regular playground, but that wasn't to happen.

After letting ourselves out, we'd walk round the back of the old Thomson House, where the *South Wales Echo* and *Western Mail* presses were thundering away, and there was a little back door where you could poke your head around and get a morning edition as it came hot off the presses. If I was involved in a midweek game and Dad was tied up at the pub with a lock-in – the local police were thirsty drinkers when they came off shift – my youngest brother Sean would be sent over there about 1 a.m. to get the papers so Dad could read the report before he went to bed. Pre-internet days, remember.

Back to the coaching book. Mr Williams prepared the text and at regular intervals needed us three to demonstrate the skills he was discussing. He photographed us over a long period – certainly at the start I was still at St Cadoc's, wearing my red-and-white-hooped St Cadoc's jersey. Yet by the end I'd obviously transferred to St Illtyd's and was donning their distinctive green jersey. I don't remember any kind of reward other than the thrill of running around on Cardiff Arms Park and the occasional ice cream on hot days.

Leafing through *Rugby for Beginners* now, well over 50 years later, I'm amazed and rather proud of the skills I displayed, which I can mostly credit to my father. The body shapes I was making then in the early 1970s – when completing a touch kick, when sweeping low to begin a spin pass or extending my arms to add pace and power to a pass – are exactly the body shapes when I was playing 10, 15, 20 years later. The muscle memory was hard-wired into my body from an early age, the neural pathways established. Even the facial expressions are the same. I notice, by the way, that I managed to miss the day when Mr Williams did tackling technique.

So, a big hat tip on this occasion to my father's relentless perfectionism – he was well ahead of his time. I may have cursed him and his apparent OCD fanaticism in getting the basics right, but even by the age of 11 I could pass fluently off both hands, kick with both feet, drop kick without a moment's hesitation, launch long touch-finders, kick for goal, thread a grubber through a gap, blast a skimmer into the ground that would bounce up as if by command on the third bounce every time as desired, and a dozen other skills. When I look at myself in *Rugby for Beginners*, I see a proper rugby player in the making, somebody who could and should have taken on the world. It didn't quite happen like that, as we will see, but my God I got off to a flying start, no complaints there. I enjoyed the best grounding anybody could have experienced.

The unseen influence in the book was Gareth Edwards. He, Sid Going and John Hipwell were my dad's heroes and he coached me to mimic their skills, but in particular Edwards. Even by the early 1970s, I'd seen Gareth play occasionally live, or TV coverage of the Wales games. I wanted to master everything he could do, including those reverse-spin passes he sent out, and his wide range of grubbers and kicks along the ground. I vividly recall that he often used the fired grubber along the ground to find touch – he could complete the kick much quicker than having to set up for a big kick out of hand, and that counted for a lot back then, with back rows living offside and getting away with murder.

Anyway, there it all is in *Rugby for Beginners*, I'm in about 30 of the pictures, looking like a well-scrubbed choirboy with my immaculate kit, washed and ironed by Mamma the night before. I used to have a copy or two around the house but have lent them out over the years, never to be seen again, so I had to track down another copy to look at for this book and lots of it still makes sense. The basic skills don't change, even if the laws and tactics do. In fact, improved technology i.e. much easier-to-handle rugby balls, rather than soggy bits of leather, surely make the basics simpler. There's no excuse for not having all the tools in your kitbag. Learn them, make them part of your rugby life – have them so mastered that you don't even have to consciously think about them.

CHAPTER 3

Misspent Youth

THERE WAS NO question in my mind – nor Dad's, for that matter – that I was going to be the next Gareth Edwards. However, at this early stage there was one massive problem: I had no top-end speed or acceleration, no gas. I could sidestep and jink, I could hand off, I had all the kicking and passing skills, but I was slower than a tax rebate. And, for a long while, puberty seemed to pass me by. I didn't get that growth spurt and sudden appearance of muscles that normally kick in during your early or mid teens. It really affected my game and, to my huge disappointment, I missed out on a Wales U15 cap, which had been a big early ambition. I'm pretty sure my lack of pace and inability to make a break and threaten around the fringes was held against me. In fact, during that U15 year, I often found myself playing full back for Cardiff Schools. The coach, Martin Truran, moved me from scrum half to full back and, wrongly or rightly, I transferred the blame for not getting that schools cap to him.

Jumping ahead a little, a few years later I was invited back to present the Dewar Shield – Wales' top U15 competition – and to say a few words. With all the lads lined up waiting for a pearl of wisdom and me feeling a bit nervous, a bit of anger reappeared almost from nowhere and I suddenly found myself imploring the lads not to listen to their teachers. It went down well with them, but nobody else except Dad – who greeted my advice with a loud "Hear, hear" from the back of the room before marching out of the clubhouse. Mamma was embarrassed and wanted to know why I'd said such a thing in front of Mr Truran, but even then I couldn't help myself. I tell it as it is. It's a dreadful habit, on occasion.

To be fair, you can only do so much without pace and, although I'm jumping ahead again here, the strangest thing happened when I went on a lads' holiday to Spain for two weeks when I was 17. I don't know if it was the sun, sangria, chasing girls or something they put in their meat over there, but I flew out a coltish youth and arrived back home as a man. At the first Cardiff training session on returning in August I felt turbo charged: I was three or four yards quicker than just a month before, I had bulging muscles in my legs where before there had been none, and I ripped it up in training. I was in a group with Brynmor Williams and we were normally level pegging – if anything, he had the advantage over me, and he was no speedster. But when I came back, I was caning him in the sprints. He wasn't happy.

Other than puberty apparently arriving overnight, I can offer no explanation, and even puberty rarely endows you with sprinting pace – normally it's more about strength and endurance. Bloody odd, but I wasn't complaining.

So that was my early rugby. Sport generally – boxing, baseball, judo – also featured large in my life, but I'll deal with that elsewhere. The odd thing, though, is that somewhere in the 24 hours allotted to us each day, I managed to fit in an entirely separate life. No wonder I struggle to make sense of my childhood and what came after.

Again, it was down to my father. As well as on occasion being a tyrant and a vicious bully (I'll stop sidestepping the issue and go into the details soon), he was also wildly eccentric and mercurial, which made life difficult for my mother and myself. Yet he was also incredibly supportive and encouraging with any sporting pursuit.

Most people have me marked down as a city kid, an urchin from backstreet Cardiff, sports-mad and up to no good most of the time, and there's a good deal of truth in that. But there was another side to the Bishop household growing up, especially after our move out to Rumney, which is close to some seriously nice open countryside. Dad didn't believe in bikes – he would never buy me one – and I just walked endless miles, never tiring or thinking it was odd.

If it wasn't a school day, we – the gang, perhaps half a dozen of us – were off after breakfast and didn't come home until teatime, dirty, tired and hungry. We got up to all sorts – it would never be allowed today, and even 50-plus years ago it was pretty radical. Dad gave me an air rifle for Christmas at the age of 7, and the gang would hit the woods and fields, shooting anything we saw: mainly squirrels and rabbits, starlings and magpies. I have no idea if it was legal or not. We got caught by a farmer trooping home with half a dozen rabbits from his land one time and thought we were for the high jump, but it transpired he was sick to death of them as they were making nuisances of themselves, and he was soon paying us 20p a rabbit. It was like Custer's Last Stand for a few months as we blazed away, shooting anything that looked remotely like a rabbit so we could add a bit to our pocket money.

Then Dad got into proper game shooting. When he was earning decent money, laying the roads as a tarmac specialist, he shelled out £500 for a beautiful double-barrelled shotgun and he took me along to all the shoots he somehow got himself invited on. There was a bit of the social snob about him. Back home, I would lovingly clean and oil his gun and one day, aged 11, the temptation became too much and I borrowed it and went roaming in the woods with the lads – Terry Borley, Andrew Lee, John Actie, my brother Terry, John Churchill and a few others. I'd seen how he used and handled the gun. I was completely confident I could handle it. He would leave boxes of cartridges lying around the house like bags of sugar. I broke the shotgun down into three – lock, stock and barrel – put it in my bag and loaded up a very cool 24-shell ammo belt and wore it under my anorak, Mexican bandito style. Myself and John Actie lagged behind a bit until we came across some prey – starlings and squirrels up in the trees – and the lads started firing off. I assembled the shotgun in seconds flat, like *The Day of the Jackal*, loaded up and aimed at a couple of starlings high in a tree. I squeezed the trigger. BOOM! It was like Big Bertha going off. The recoil nearly knocked me off my feet and the lads dived for cover in fear of their lives as half a dozen birds and squirrels fell from the tree stone dead. Bloody hell!

So there I was at the age of 11, walking the countryside with a loaded double-barrelled shotgun. Pretty reprehensible, really. Today I'd get five years for possession and/or marched to a place of safety. I worked my way through four or five boxes of cartridges in a couple of months before it was the official shooting season and Dad needed it again. He was pretty nonplussed that he only had a couple of boxes left and gave Mamma a hard time over it, but she never let on. She of course knew what I'd been up to – she even insisted that I clean the gun properly every time I used it, to cover my trail – but somehow she convinced Dad that he must have used more than he thought or had lost some in the fields.

Mamma put up with so much. When we were at Rumney Rugby Club, it was like the bloody Durrells in Corfu. We had dogs – spaniels and Alsatians, mainly – we kept hawks, owls, ferrets, and Dad owned some greyhounds. Don't ask me where the money came from.

And there's more. For the best part of four years, I even had my own incredible horse, named Shaft. He was a complete mongrel in terms of breeding but was the quickest thing I've ever seen on four legs. Completely wild, four white socks (which to my eyes were the equivalent of go-faster stripes on a car) and we got on just fine. Kindred spirits.

There's no question that I had a natural affinity with horses – perhaps it was the Irish genes? We had lots of travellers locally and I liked hanging out with them and their horses. If one ran away, it was often me who managed to chase it, calm it down and bring it home. I learnt very early on to ride bareback and much preferred that to saddling up. I was very small and jockey-like in my early teens – agile and just good on a horse. Dad noticed that and, one day in 1973, randomly announced that he'd bought a horse for me for 200 guineas.

Bloody hell, Shaft could shift. I rode him bareback from dawn to dusk, hands on the reins and grasping the back of his mane at the same time, and, although a 'natural', I suffered some spectacular falls as I learned the tricks of the trade. I could have broken my neck three or four times riding Shaft before I suffered that fate playing for Pooler at Aberavon. One time I was left hanging on for dear life around his neck, like a Hollywood Wild West stunt rider, before finally losing my grip, slipping under his hoofs and getting the trampling of my life. Nothing in rugby compared with the shoeing I got that day.

We stabled him down at Hanfords' farm, long gone now, and it cost my old man £4.50 a week. Again, I have no idea how we could afford that. It was where all the rich Cardiff families stabled their kids' horses. I loved mucking out when we weren't riding, but couldn't be bothered with saddling up when it was time to ride. That's another reason I rode bareback – I was way too impatient just to get out there on the hacking paths.

I would disappear for the entire day, and sometimes most of the evening as well. I understand now that it was a release from the looming presence of my father, who dominated and tried to control every facet of my life. He might have bought me the horse, but he had no interest whatsoever in horses or horse-riding. In fact, having engineered the situation, he then wanted me to stop riding because it was interfering with my boxing and rugby.

Horse-riding was my time, though, and I utilised it fully to let off steam. When I got a bit older, especially before I started playing rugby for Cardiff Youth, I would play for Old Illtydians in the morning, head for the stable and spend the rest of the day riding around the area like some juvenile John Wayne, calling in on the rugby clubs to watch the afternoon games. I would end up at Rumney watching the game sitting bareback on Shaft, with the best view in the house. It caused a stir, but I enjoyed the attention.

It all seems inexplicable looking back, a rogue chapter in an odd life, and it came to a sad end of which I'm not proud. When Dad lost his job at Rumney Rugby Club, the money suddenly dried up and he stopped paying the £4.50 a week. I was working as an apprentice welder earning £15 a week, of which £7 went to Mamma for lodging and £3.50 a week on my bus pass, which didn't leave a lot for normal living, let alone stabling a hungry horse. Mamma started borrowing from a money lender to meet the costs – and those of our extended animal kingdom – and that didn't end well when Dad found out. I copped a right hiding for supposedly allowing that situation with Shaft to develop – as if he hadn't created the situation, and I had any way of paying for the horse. And then one day somebody from the stables appeared at the house to say what a deplorable condition Shaft was in. Something had to be done. We had to sell, for the knockdown price of £60. It broke my heart: the horsey phase of my life was over, although I have occasionally jumped back on. My daughter Sam treated me to a day's galloping on the beaches in Australia a few years ago. Incredible, pure happiness. Perhaps I should have stuck with the nags.

As a teenager, life quickly became very complicated. Ever since returning from that Spanish trip, my hormones were running wild. I was getting into all sorts of fights in town and getting arrested, bailed, warned or fined on a regular basis. I could get in a fight just getting the bus from Rumney to the city centre – over nothing, really. There was a violent, wild streak inside me which I didn't know how to control. The ugly side of my personality was to the fore, with all sorts of bad stuff going on in the background as part of my ongoing fight with Dad. There was an unpleasant side to me that I can neither deny nor fully explain. I was living very close to the edge. Riding for a fall some, might say.

My rugby had been progressing through all of this, though. After playing for all the Cardiff age group sides from U11 to U15, it had been assumed that I'd go straight into the Cardiff Youth (U19) set-up with all my contemporaries, but Dad had other ideas. Youth rugby basically covers the 16–18 age group and with stacks of talent around, gametime might be very limited in the first year, just when I needed loads of rugby. At scrum half, not full back.

If I couldn't go to Cardiff, I wanted to be the cool kid on the block and go the multiracial, laid-back, fun-loving CIACs team, where Dad was a former skipper and where I already had some mates. But he wasn't having that either: he wanted me to play with the well-connected boys of Old Illtydians, with some of the guys who regularly gave me detentions at my secondary school. I hated the thought of that, but he played his trump card. If I didn't play for them, he'd kick me out the house/pub and I'd have to work for a living. Dad didn't take prisoners when he was trying to get his own way.

I succumbed, and I'm glad I did. Dad was right. Away from the school, the Old Illtydians were a great crowd, a rich mix of maverick characters and talented individuals from all walks of life, who I soon grew to like and then love. They're a club I've constantly returned to over the years. I enjoyed a fantastic first year with them and they'd lined me up to be their Youth captain for the following season, when Dad executed the next move in his master plan. Now was the time to join Cardiff after all. A year older and stronger, with more game experience than others my age had had at Cardiff, and with every prospect of getting a start right from the off. He was a control freak, but he wasn't wrong – it was exactly the right move at the right time.

Cardiff Youth were very strong, as you'd expect, and I scarcely ever remember us losing a game. Myself, Mike Powell, Pedro Souto, Tim Crothers, Phil Ford and Kevin Trevett all won Wales Youth caps while Owen Goulding, Bob Lakin and the Millar brothers, Steve and David, were also top players.

Misspent Youth

I didn't make life easy for myself, mind. I was still very immature and a home bird. I was awkward and didn't enjoy travelling and mixing much, and I hated being dragged out of my comfort zone. With Wales Youth at the time, before the end-of-season Internationals, they always took the preliminary squad to Aberystwyth for a big training week and trial matches – it was essentially where they picked the team. But I didn't fancy that one bit and made my excuses – a bad bout of flu, I seem to remember. Ridiculous, really.

Miraculously, the selectors didn't seem to hold it against me, and the proud day came in 1979 when I ran out for Wales Youth against France Youth at a very muddy Eugene Cross Park, home of Ebbw Vale. As ever, they had a huge pack – with Laurent Rodriguez and Jean Condom to the fore – and they threatened to overwhelm us for much of the game, given the conditions. But we were only trailing 7-3 with 15 minutes to go when we got a second wind, especially up front. We absolutely battered them for the rest of the game and went close three or four times, but we just couldn't get over the line and lost 7-3. I couldn't accept we hadn't found a way of winning, and was cranky for two or three days afterwards. I was also puzzled that some of my teammates didn't seem as devastated by the defeat as myself. To me, it seemed like the end of the world.

Wales had one or two interesting characters in that team. Malcolm Dacey played centre – although he was to switch to fly half for most of his senior career – while my half back partner was Gary Pearce, who I got on very well with. Gary, like me, loved his sevens, and we played alongside and against each other many times over the years that followed, and he was also to turn professional in League like me. Up front, Tim Fauvel was capped by the senior Wales team in 1988, but the real star for me was our brilliant openside flanker Ashley Jones, whose younger brother Lyn was capped by Wales. Ashley was class – a peg or two up from Lyn, even – but unfortunately ran into injury problems early in his career. Both brothers were to be hit by prostate cancer later in life with both, touch wood, coming through.

After that narrow defeat, it was England away in Hull a couple of weeks later and I was looking forward to recording a win in Welsh colours. But in between times I'd managed to get sent off playing for Cardiff Youth against Pontypridd and, at the last minute, I was withdrawn from the Wales Youth team. My name's still there in the match programme, but I didn't play. Ray Giles was drafted in at the last minute instead and Wales won 12-11, with Gary Pearce and centre Peter Hopkins scoring tries.

As for the sending-off that saw me sidelined, I'd made the mistake of answering a last-minute SOS to play for Cardiff Youth when many of the lads were down with flu. It all ended in tears for me. The opposition's flanker was a gobby cheap-shot merchant who'd been putting it about all afternoon, punching and kicking, and eventually I lost my rag. I went flying at him, all guns blazing. My intention was to hit him with the hardest tackle of his life, but I was pretty reckless as to which part of my body made contact first and, as it happened, it was my head on his head. A butt, the referee called it. I didn't start off with the intention of butting the bastard, but I accept that's how it all ended. I was sent off and, somehow, the real villain of the day remained on the park, as is often the case. In rugby the retaliator, acting on instinct, almost always gets caught and punished, whereas the person whose calculated act started the chain of events often slopes off unrecognised or unpunished. This needs to change.

Players in the last year of Youth occasionally found themselves playing with Cardiff Rags, who were stronger than many senior club First XVs at the time. It was common to find yourself playing with four or five Welsh Internationals who might be coming back from injury or looking for an extra game, or who were just unable to get into the First XV. It was high-quality stuff and, of all those I played with, the one I remember best is an Englishman and one of the best backs I ever played with or against, in either Union or League. I'm talking about Huw Davies – not a name that causes much of a stir these days but, bloody hell, could he play. He was from the Midlands and was a student at UWIST (now Cardiff University). Smallish but muscular, very quick off the mark, tough as old leather and had all the skills. Huw was another brilliant sevens player and, though he won 21 England caps, he never nailed down that ten spot and got messed around as the ubiquitous utility back. I kid you not: if I was picking my all-time XV of those I've played with or against, Huw would be right up there as a contender at fly half. England had no idea what a talent they had. Thank God!

Another time, towards the end of my final Youth year, Cardiff seniors went on a pre-season tour – well, a jolly, really – to the Lake Garda area in Italy. It was a Rags/First XV combo, and I was the youngest member and the butt of everybody's jokes. I didn't get a game – was clearly never going to get a game – and served effectively as the gofer and tour bitch for the senior players. I had to tidy up after everybody, carry the kit, take it to the laundry, clean the boots, order and carry the drinks at the bar, all that nonsense. And on top of that, I had to carry around the hideous massive club teddy bear, which I didn't realise at the time was virtually a club relic and artefact.

THE BISH

It was plain daft. No self-respecting hard case from Cardiff like me was ever going to put up with shit like that, and a few days into the trip, tying the bastard bear to a few rocks just to make sure, I threw the awful creature into Italy's deepest lake, where it met a soggy demise. There, that's my belated confession to the Cardiff committee. It was me. Good riddance. I just couldn't be doing with this subservient earning your stripes, rites of passage stuff. Bollocks. Plain embarrassing. Judge me on what I do on the pitch and how I act as a mate off it.

At one stage, being the baby of the group, the older guys – after a good session in the bar – decided it was time to throw the kid into Lake Garda, where a thunderstorm was threatening and the waves were whipping up a bit. What fun they were all having. Now, I've always been a very competent swimmer, but I kicked up like merry hell and fought the four or five guys off, screaming that I couldn't swim and to stop fucking around. Eventually they got bored with the idea and left me alone. The next morning, when they were nursing their hangovers, I made a point of going over to the hotel diving board and doing a couple of double somersaults with twist and a perfect clean entry into the swimming pool. Sod the bastards, I'll go for a swim and a dive if and when I want to, not for their pleasure and amusement. Another time Barry Nelmes – who was actually the Cardiff captain that year – and a few others thought it would be a great laugh if they hid my passport and I spent three or four days stressing about that. Pathetic. Piss off, the lot of you.

I was disillusioned. This wasn't the Cardiff club and the players I idolised. To my mind, I was an equal member of the playing party. I hadn't even wanted to go on the bloody tour – I'd have been happy to stay at home, but the club

Misspent Youth

committee insisted. I was out of my comfort zone, behaved badly and came back an even angrier young man.

My card was marked after that. I copped a two-week internal ban for disruptive behaviour on tour, and my days at Cardiff were numbered. My behaviour was getting worse in town and the run-ins with the police were mounting. There was little doubt that I was heading for a spell inside sooner rather than later. I did make one First Team appearance, off the bench at Penarth in September 1979 when Brynmor Williams did a hamstring, and we won 12-0. For some reason, I was really nervous and a bit self-doubting, but before the game Dad gave me a good dressing down and virtually pinned me up against a wall and made me repeat after him that I was as good as the next man. It wasn't playing against Penarth I was worried about, it was playing with Cardiff! It was the pep talk I needed: never again did I feel inferior to anybody on a rugby pitch.

My Cardiff career came to an end soon after that, following a trip to London to play Harlequins, when I was on the bench – and unused – again. Cardiff never stinted on these trips, and there was an overnighter at a hotel afterwards, during which Spikey Watkins got a bit worked up and managed to inflict serious damage on his room. Now, I was present – no question – but not participating, so to speak. Not that it did me any good. For some reason it was decided that us younger players would say we'd been involved as well – collective responsibility, I suppose – in the hope that Spikey would be treated more leniently. That backfired, particularly for me, with memories of my disruptive behaviour in Italy fresh in the committee's mind, and the axe fell. I was unceremoniously kicked out of Cardiff RFC, my hometown club and the only team I wanted to play for.

CHAPTER 4

Mother and Baby Doing Fine

MY LIFE WAS always a rollercoaster as a teenager. Never was that truer than on Tuesday 13 March 1979, just three days after I'd won my Wales Youth cap against France at Ebbw Vale.

I was still mourning that defeat, but at that time was still enjoying my time with Cardiff Youth as I chased down that Wales Youth cap and tried to make a name for myself at the club. I was still going to be the next Gareth Edwards, no question. I was on course; nothing was going to stop me. Dad was running the Tudor pub at the time, so I was just over the River Taff and round the corner from the Arms Park, and their training ground down at Sophia Gardens was very handy as well. Rugby and boxing were my main outlets. I was making some good friends, including Phil Ford, our wing at Cardiff Youth, who went on to enjoy a stellar career in Rugby League after he joined Warrington in 1981. Great player Fordie: a bit special.

It was a wintry March evening, and it had been raining non-stop for what seemed like a month or more. Grangetown had been flooded out and the river just outside the pub was in spate, much higher than normal. I was on the phone downstairs, talking to my girlfriend Kate and just getting

Mother and Baby Doing Fine

ready for training at Cardiff when Phil, on his way to training, came running into the pub and shouted up the stairs.

"Bish, there's a woman and her baby in the river outside – they look like they're drowning. They *are* bloody drowning, man. We've got to do something!"

Phil wasn't a swimmer and wasn't at all good around water, but he knew I was and presumably thought I had more chance of pulling off some kind of rescue – although frankly, God knows what exactly I could do.

Still, there was no time to think about anything. I sprinted out of the pub over to the river, the adrenalin pumping. I was an instinctive rugby player, well-coached but with my own mind and ability to read a situation, and I went straight into that instinctive mode as I rushed towards the bank. There was no textbook here. I would play it by ear and just do what I could. What choice was there?

There, on the bank above the river, was a group of guys shouting at a woman who was in the water, desperately clinging on to a branch with one arm and on to a pram containing her baby with the other hand. She was waist-deep in very fast-flowing water and hanging on for dear life, trying to keep out of the deeper water. It was an alarming and worsening situation, with probably just seconds to play with before it got completely out of hand. Do the wrong thing here and she and her little one were doomed. I didn't fancy their chances in the river at all. I didn't fancy my chances much, either. The men shouting were bloody useless. Worse than useless, to tell the truth: they'd done nothing, and in fact I was sensing some aggression towards the woman from them, a bad vibe. Something very bad had just happened here and they were making no effort to intervene. I later learned that one of them was her ex-partner and there'd been an incident between them that had seen her and her baby fall into the raging river. This was a heavy domestic situation as well as a crisis.

She was losing her grip on the pram so, uttering a quick prayer to myself, I stepped into the icy water – about waist high – and braced myself against its force, which was unbelievable. Then I leant into the pram and crudely ripped the baby out of her bedding and almost in the same movement threw her up to Phil, who was standing on the bank. It was last-ditch, Hail Mary stuff. Thankfully, Phil had good hands that day and caught her, and I can still recall the look of astonishment, shock and relief on his face... One down, one to go.

Now for mum. She was being dragged further into the deeper water; she was weakening and didn't have long before she'd be washed away, so I carefully stepped a bit deeper into the river and the freezing water took my breath away. She was beginning to tire badly and lost her grip on the tree branch she'd been clinging to, and of course was in panic at what was happening, and where her baby had just gone. It was all very confusing for her. In her panic, she lunged for me and started to drag us both even deeper into the river. I had to do something instantly, otherwise we were both in trouble. Firstly, I had to get physical and fight her off, free myself from her death grip, so to speak. I can't remember if I actually clocked her one, but I was very forceful. This was life and death for her, and possibly me as well. We were losing the battle; she was being swept away from me – as a last resort, I stretched out and dragged her towards me by her long blonde hair, which was the only part of her I could reach. It sounds bloody crude – it was, but I make no apologies. I pulled her towards the shore by her

Mother and Baby Doing Fine

hair, which must have been very painful, before I finally got a grip on her with my arms, and bodily threw her onto the bank, where a crowd was gathering. It had been a close-run thing, no question.

This all happened in less time than it's taken to tell here but, even so, as I dragged myself out of the river, police and medics were by now in attendance, as well as a load of bystanders just looking on. But such was my tunnel vision that the moment I dragged myself out of the river, I went back into rugby mode. I now risked being late for training and copping a bollocking from Roger Beard, the coach, who was taking that night's session and who I really rated. I didn't want to let him down. I sprinted back into the pub. Mamma briefly went mad as the muddy River Taff leaked from my clothes and shoes onto the carpets and furniture, but as I sprinted up the stairs, I shouted back to her what had happened. It had all occurred so quickly that not everybody in the pub had even been aware of what was happening. I was shaking, a combination of cold and adrenalin probably, but quickly stripped off, towelled down, threw some clean clothes on and was back down inside two minutes to head for training with Fordie.

An hour later, we were mid-session down at Sophia Gardens, at the back, where the cricket ground is, when we saw a police patrol car approaching with its blue lights on.

"What have you been up to now, Bish?" asked Roger, with a worried look on his face.

"God knows, Roger – there's nothing left to nick me for."

Two officers approached Roger and he called me over. They were very friendly and shook my hand. Mother and child were OK: they'd been checked over in hospital and now the police needed to take statements from myself and

Phil. We stood aside to do that and then, soon after they left, the photographer from the *Western Mail* and *Echo* turned up unannounced. Word had spread quickly, and the following morning it was big news. I'd scarcely had a chance to absorb it all, and at that time I had other stuff on my mind, such as a big court case for assault hanging over me.

We'll deal with the court case later, but about a year after the River Taff rescue, after the assault charge had come to trial and I'd been found guilty and sentenced to three years in prison, I was getting used to life in Aylesbury nick when I was asked to go to the Governor's office at 11 a.m. the following morning. I'd been trying to keep my nose clean so this had me worried, and I couldn't sleep all night. It turned out he'd received a letter and package from the Royal Humane Society, awarding me a certificate in recognition of my bravery and the saving of life. Usually this would involve a trip up to Buckingham Palace to collect it, or perhaps a ceremony at Cardiff Castle or something grand, but obviously there was no chance of that. He handed over the medal, shook my hand, said, "Well done," and then ordered me to be taken back to my cell. That was it.

I reject any notion of being a so-called hero and was quite glad that, because of my incarceration in Aylesbury, there was the minimum of fuss. I'd just acted on the spur of the moment. I didn't feel I'd done that much compared with the many examples of proper heroism and bravery you read about from ordinary people – those in the Armed Forces or blue light services who just consider it their duty and routine. I didn't dive headlong into the river and swim against the raging torrent to pull off the rescue, as some reports suggested. There was no Superman stuff – it was all about staying calm and just doing what needed to be done as quickly and efficiently as possible. In sporting terms, it was a tricky play that needed to be perfectly executed first time. There would be no second chance. The only moment that still brings me out in a cold sweat is grabbing the women by her hair. Another couple of seconds and she'd have been gone, and then I don't know what I'd have done. I might have dived in after her, I just don't know. Luckily, it was a choice I didn't have to make.

This is not false modesty on my part, I've just never considered it a big deal in the great scheme of things. I'm not even sure where my certificate and citation is, to be honest – possibly at my sister's – but I know it made my mum very proud, and that does bring a warm glow, because I tested her patience and love to breaking point over many years. As for the woman and child, I've never heard from them since. You might think that odd, but it isn't really. The police immediately put a ban on the media identifying her or the child because she was fleeing a dangerous ongoing domestic situation and felt her life was in danger, and I certainly never learnt her name.

CHAPTER 5

Love at First Fight

BOXING AND RUGBY are my two great sporting passions. In the end, I had to make a choice between them and rugby got the nod. But it was a close-run thing. I enjoy all sports and was pretty good at most – particularly baseball, which I looked on mainly as relaxation and fun with mates. Winning was nice, but not essential. With boxing and rugby, though, it's different. I'm obsessed with both. They consume me.

It was my former rugby teammate at St Cadoc's, Paul Trebilcock, who lit the fuse. He and his family were into boxing. In fact, Paul was a British Schools and Youth champion, and he kept suggesting I give it a try down at the Splott YMCA club. His dad even agreed to call by and pick me up one evening. I had no excuses, but my dad took this badly. He preferred me doing judo, which he considered much safer, and wasn't at all keen on boxing, where the potential for injury is much higher. Considering the brawler he was, I find this all rather ironic, but his resistance didn't last long. I refused to back down and one night, after Mr Trebilcock again turned up with Paul to give me a lift, he crumbled totally. My control-freak dad liked to be in charge of everything, and saw this as undermining his authority. If his son was hell-bent on boxing then he, David Bishop senior, had to be in charge and running the show. So he gave my boxing the green light, and of course then displayed the zealotry of the newly converted and instantly became a boxing fanatic, following me all around south Wales and organising coaches to take regulars from the pub to support me for my big fights. They were great nights at working men's clubs and sports centres all over south Wales. Smoke-filled rooms, the smell of beer and liniment, lots of side betting going on, a noisy, raucous crowd. It was everything you'd imagine it to be. I loved it all.

It was surprising, actually, that I hadn't got into boxing at St Illtyd's, because the school was steeped in boxing tradition. One of its most famous old boys was British and Commonwealth Heavyweight Champion Jack Petersen, who occasionally looked in on the Splott club and attended fight nights. As I took my first steps in boxing with my adopted club, I realised some of my fellow pupils at St Illtyd's were also into it and attending club nights. Given the harsh school environment, it was hardly surprising.

I will never forget the first night Mr T took me down the gym: it was love at first fight. We were met by Roy Agland and Paddy Wheeler. Roy was an ex-pro, former Wales Middleweight Champion and a legendary figure in the Welsh boxing world. Along with Ray Prosser, he was the best sports coach I ever encountered. No coaching certificates, but millions of miles on the clock. They had forgotten more about their chosen sports than most people would ever know. Roy's sidekick and foil, Paddy, was terrific as well. The moment I stepped through the door to the gym, it felt like home. I loved the whirring noise of those crazy skipping-rope routines and that satisfying noise – the expulsion of air – that a punchbag makes when you hit it just right. Others were working hard on the speed balls, throwing medicine balls around and sparring in the ring. There was sweat and effort everywhere and I couldn't have been more entranced. This was my world.

Roy was from a tough background and had been there and done it all. He was British Amateur Middleweight Champion in 1948, but damaged his wrist and had to miss the 1948 Olympics in London. He turned pro in the Fifties and was a Welsh champion, but coaching was his real genius. During the 1970s, when I was lucky enough to be taken under his wing, he was at his peak and, by 1980, was the deputy to GB coach Kevin Hickey at the 1980 Olympics. I couldn't have been in better hands. There was nothing Roy didn't know about the boxing game and he was also a shrewd psychologist and worked out pretty soon that I was a sportsman who, generally speaking, needed the carrot rather than the stick. Start shouting and ordering me to do something and it would ignite my ego and I would do the exact opposite just to annoy somebody and win that mental battle. Cajole, encourage and convince me something is worth doing in a particular way and I am much more likely to fall into line, at least in the short term.

You may have heard that old boxing cliché: if you are up against a fighter, box him; if you are up against a boxer, fight him. Roy tried those words of advice with me a few times, and it didn't work. My attitude – my ego – worked the other way. If I was up against a fighter, I would want to outfight him. If I was up against a boxer, I would want to outbox him. After a few bouts, Roy didn't go down that route any more. He sussed his man out very quickly.

That first night, we went through a few routines on the punchbags and he taught me a few simple combos on the pads before he put some gloves on me and I did a 90-second round against him. I was exhausted by the end, and when I then did another 90 seconds, my arms felt like lead and I felt dizzy from the effort. I rated myself as fit, but boxing's a different level of fitness to any other sport – it's off the scale if you want to box well. It's boxing fitness – or striving to reach it – that got me through my broken neck and, much later in life, my stroke at the start of Covid. At various stages of my life when I'd been overdoing things, I've taken myself in hand and used old boxing routines to get back in shape. My admiration for our top boxers is total.

For the next four or five years, I was in the Splott gym every night after school before heading for home for supper. It appealed to my addictive personality, and it was a safe, controlled environment: there were no arguments and shouting matches or tension in the air like there were at home with Dad. It was my happy place, to use a modern expression. I quickly learned to skip properly and was soon doing all those flash cross-hand routines and skipping backwards (which is another tough skill to master), and until recently, when the joints finally rebelled, I would get a rope out and get to work if I was feeling fat and sluggish and needed to sharpen up. It's not just an endurance exercise – once you crack the technique, it's all about balance, footwork and rhythm. And you need to get up on your toes to skip properly – it's much softer on your knees than running. I would advise any sportsman or woman to take the time to master skipping.

Boxing was a great release and, with Roy in my corner teaching me tactics, I soon showed real ability. I boxed 58 bouts, losing just five, I think it was. I won two Welsh Boys titles, at 36 kg and 48 kg, and represented Wales Youth against England a couple of times. I also qualified for a

British final, but sadly had to withdraw, with broken ribs that I'd sustained during my semi-final win.

That semi-final – or eliminator, as we called them – was held in Coventry. I was trailing badly after two rounds, but rallied to knock the English boxer out in the third with a big left hook. I was in another world: the red mist had descended and I stood over my beaten opponent giving him a barrage of verbals, like Muhammad Ali did at times, and I refused to move away when the referee demanded I go back to my corner. In my moment of glory, I nearly got disqualified, but for once the sporting gods were kind and I escaped with a finger wagging. That fight was one of those occasions when I had to change my tactics. The English kid was a real scrapper, a fighter, and Roy still insisted that I needed to outbox him. It wasn't working, I was trailing badly at the end of the second round and was pretty beaten up, so I changed tack and came out swinging in the final round – with huge success. When in doubt, fight it out. It was really frustrating to miss out on a shot at a British title through injury, though. I only really started feeling my ribs a few days later, when I hurt them badly again playing rugby, and that was me out of action for a few weeks. It was even more frustrating a few months later when I beat the guy who took the British title in a fight in Wales.

Roy was adamant I had the talent to go all the way, although we'll never know on that one – I'd have been a nightmare to coach and manage, that's for sure. When I attended Paddy Wheeler's funeral, Roy still insisted I was a better boxer than a rugby player, which was one of the nicer compliments I've received. As a boxer, I was basically a ducker and a diver, an elusive little bastard with a solid left jab and a really explosive left hook, which was my big weapon. Because I

Love at First Fight

could potentially deck anybody in an instant, I was always a danger, even against classier and older opponents. As well as the physical release and the sheer pleasure of landing a sweet punch, which is never to be underestimated, I loved the chess element of boxing: moving your opponent around, dummying a punch here and there and then setting him up for the big knockout blow. You needed to be quick on your feet and have 360-degree vision to avoid the incoming blows – good training for my time at scrum half, when most teams seemed intent on putting me in hospital.

I don't honestly know if I'd have made it to the big time. Roy and Paddy thought so, but I'm under no illusion about how hard the fight game is and the spartan lifestyle required to succeed. Could I have handled that? Perhaps, but possibly not. The money would have been a big motivator but there's no hiding place in a boxing ring if you've been burning the candle at both ends. I loved the scene, though, and the raw honesty of a fight, that's for sure. They were great days. I would have a coachload of supporters cheering me on for my big fights. Paul Lewis, later to become one of Wales' most decorated amateur boxers, was my great rival. He ended up winning 14 Welsh finals at all ages and levels, reached the ABA finals five years on the trot and went toe-to-toe with the likes of Terry Marsh and Nigel Benn as an amateur. He was a class operator.

Paul was a Newport lad and he was also well supported by a travelling band of fans. He became a good friend and has always kept in touch during my various scrapes and personal problems. When you've been in the ring five times with the same bloke as teenagers, there's a bond forever. You get to understand the true measure of a man, and Paul's one of the best.

My memory isn't what it was, and it's nearly 50 years ago, but I've checked with Paul and we're both agreed he was leading the series 3-2 when I stepped back from competitive boxing. They were invariably close and pretty classy affairs. My best win was for a Welsh title up in Cwmbran for which, as ever, Dad had organised a 52-seater coach of supporters. That evening was memorable for all sorts of reasons.

Firstly, it was my best-ever performance against my most respected Welsh opponent. Secondly, a load of the De La Salle brothers – the Catholic teaching order who ran St Illtyd's, my secondary school – had travelled up on Dad's coach to support me, and they only went and got into a ruck in the crowd with some of the other more excitable supporters who were present. The Reverend Brothers had travelled in civvies and Dad had been plying them with whiskey tots, so they were in lively form, to say the least. And finally, so exuberant was my dad on the coach back home that he paraded down the aisle and did a full moon – revealing a couple of interesting tattoos on both cheeks.

My other win over Paul was in a Welsh semi-final, but they were always great scraps. After that semi-final win over Paul, the final was down in Swansea, and I was lined up against their local hotshot. First, though, I had a big game that afternoon for Cardiff Youth against Neath at Sophia Gardens in the Dewar Shield, and only after that was over could I concentrate on the fight as Dad drove us down the M4. My great-uncle Gerald, the Swansea 'gangster', was very excited about the fight and recklessly had a £100 winner-takes-all bet with one of his cronies – a decent sum in those days, the equivalent of about £2,000 now... He, of course, was completely potless at the time, so no pressure then... As it happened, I won comfortably but wasn't too impressed when my reward from Uncle Gerald was 50p as he flashed a big wad of notes around in the changing room. 'Tight-arse' barely does it justice.

Another highlight was an unexpected fight at a big black-tie charity fundraiser the Chepstow Round Table were organising. My brothers Sean and Terry were involved in bouts and I went along as a spectator, but as we gathered came the news of a big crash on the motorway, and a few of the bigger-name boxers were struggling to make it in time. The organisers asked if I'd be prepared to step in and fight – Brian Elias, I think it was, the reigning ABA Youth Champion, one year and one weight division above me. He hadn't been defeated in four or five years – if ever, actually. I could never resist that kind of challenge and, though he battered me good and proper most of the opening round, I then got a great left away and made off with one of my best-ever wins.

The following year, 1977 by my reckoning, came my third and final defeat against Paul in the Wales Youth 55 kg category at the old Ocean Club in Cardiff. What a venue that was! This was a crunch moment. It was a split decision, but that flattered me. I knew I'd been well beaten on the night. I was 17, playing most weeks for Cardiff Youth, gunning for a Wales Youth cap, and being talked of as a big rugby prospect. For the first time, I'd been missing training sessions down the gym due to rugby commitments or having to take it easy because I was sore with rugby knocks. Mixing the two was proving problematic. Don't get me wrong, what with rugby and boxing I was still incredibly fit – I doubt if there was a fitter 17-year-old in Wales – but in muscling up for rugby and trying to put some poundage on my skinny frame, I'd lost some of the stamina and endurance I needed to take my boxing to the next level.

After that last losing fight against Paul at the Ocean Club, Roy was very animated in the changing room, which was unusual for him. He knew he was slowly losing me, and made one last impassioned pitch.

"Bish, listen: you've got to make a decision. You've got fire in your belly like I've rarely seen before and a left hook that sends people to sleep. You could make real name for yourself as a boxer, Bish, I'm telling you. But it has to be either boxing or rugby. You won't be able to do both, I'm telling you. I'm sorry, lad – rugby and boxing don't mix if you want to be a champion in either sport."

My head was spinning, and I still couldn't catch my breath from the fight which had ended just minutes before. I pushed through a door in the changing room and found myself outside, and lay down on the grass – in fact, I pretty much collapsed, I was so tired. I was still fighting for breath, but gradually I got it under control. Roy was right: it was decision time and, when push came to shove, playing rugby for Wales was always going to be the ultimate for me. Rugby it was. I went back inside to tell Roy my decision. I quit there and then. I never fought competitively again, although throughout my life I've never been happier than working out with the crew in a boxing gym. The smells and noise there are heaven to me. Did I make the right decision? I sometimes wonder, given that ultimately my rugby career ended in disappointment and underachievement.

Many decades later, in 2010, an old boxing and rugby mate phoned. It was Stephen Franks, another Old Illtydian who boxed at Splott with me and was also a Welsh champion – my God, we had a strong team in those days, winning the Driscoll Shield, the main team competition in Wales, more than once. Stephen was also my Old Illtydians rugby captain when I was player-coach there after I came back from Rugby League. He was slow as a carthorse but even stronger than those beasts of burden, and tough as old boots. One of the best men imaginable and, despite his pen-pushing day job as an architect, a proper hard case. Potter, as everybody calls him, had decided at the age of 45 that he wanted to win the British unlicensed heavyweight boxing title – which is not messing around, let me tell you. Anyway, he couldn't find anybody brave enough, stupid enough or good enough locally to work him hard sparring, and one day he rang to ask if I fancied helping out. I was overweight, demotivated, a bit depressed and generally a mess, but he needed my help and I didn't think twice. It would be a little project, something to get my teeth into. He was, of course, in great shape already and I clearly wasn't, but he knew I had the ring craft to stretch him and a left hook that needed guarding against and would sharpen his reflexes. We worked our socks off. I got fit and trim again and started to feel good about myself, and began to work him harder and harder. Blow me, Potter only went and won the British title! Proud of you, mate. Happy days – in fact all my boxing experiences were good and, as the saying goes, it's cheaper than therapy!

CHAPTER 6

Violence as a Way of Life

I'VE SKIRTED AROUND the subject enough: it's time to stop avoiding the issue and address a pretty dark side of my life. Then we can move on. There's no getting around the fact that I grew up in a world in which excessive physical violence and mental abuse was frequent and almost normalised. I knew no different. Resorting to fisticuffs or dishing out beatings was how arguments were sorted out. It was how you dealt with bullies or people throwing their weight around. It was how you dealt with your frustrations. That's not to make excuses for my sometimes appalling behaviour over the years that followed, but I have no doubt that my background explains some of my demons and hang ups.

For all the love Mamma provided, life was just so bloody stressful. That's what I remember most about my early years. I used to regularly wet the bed until the age of 14, and then occasionally till I was even older from sheer fear and anxiety as to where and when my next beating might arrive. I felt terrorised. Always on edge, a cornered animal, and it took decades to shed those memories and step out of that nightmare. I would agonise about the next beating, anticipating it, dreading it. I would resolve to stand up for myself and to defend myself but, ultimately, I was just a pint-sized kid. What chance did I have?

When I was young, there were two major strands of recurring violence to deal with. The biggest and most important came directly from my dad, David Bishop senior, and the second came courtesy of the Reverend Brothers at St Illtyd's, the Catholic secondary school I attended in Rumney. They backed Dad up with a devotion to savage corporal punishment that verged on the fanatic, having been given specific instructions by my father that they were to beat me whenever they saw fit. Not that they needed much encouragement. More of that later.

My father could be an extremely violent, mercurial, erratic man, who I both loved dearly and lived in fear of until I finally stood up to him and won a savage domestic power struggle. When I mention that I both loved and loathed my father, most people look at me in disbelief, although a few have occasionally nodded knowingly. If you know, you know. I remain conflicted in my feelings for him to this day, because he helped shape my sporting life like nobody else and in many ways was an extraordinary mentor who would leave no stone unturned to further my career and my prospects as a sportsman. In his mellow moments, later in life when we'd largely resolved our difficulties, he could be great company and a good friend. But, my God, back in the day he could also be a complete nightmare to live with, an absolute brute whose moods and violence would hang heavily over the house.

How can I describe David Bishop senior? He lived every second of my sporting career. He really cared. He was the sort of dad who, when I broke the javelin record at school sports day, rushed out and bought me my own javelin. How many dads buy their sons a javelin, for Christ's sake? When those flash lightweight Georgie Best football boots came out at some ridiculous price, he bought me a pair. They were like slippers and absolutely useless for playing rugby, but I had a pair, nonetheless. When I was boxing, instead of the £3 boxing boots in Woolworths, he promised me state-of-the-art £15 Adidas boots if I won a certain fight. And he was good to his promise, although he also used such gifts and treats to exert his control. If I did something wrong or displeased him, he'd then take the flash boots away in an instant. It was almost like training a dog or a wild animal. Reward, withdraw, reward, withdraw again until you get the desired result. I could handle that, to a certain extent, but there was always that extra sinister strand to my dad. He could be a right nasty bastard, make no mistake.

My dad was the aggressive alpha male personified, and those habits and latent violence were accentuated in drink. He was rarely an obvious roaring drunk – in fact, he had periods when he abstained totally, thank God, and a temporary peace descended on our lives. But some days he was just different, and I learnt to appreciate when he had a few drinks on board. You daren't say a word out of place or look at him the wrong way. When he was in that mood, you could do nothing right – just prepare yourself for the probable thumping that beckoned. My mum used to try and head him off at the pass by slipping his sleeping pills into his tea – he was a fanatical tea drinker as well – in the hope that he'd nod off and wake up in a better mood. Sometimes it worked and we could all relax just a little; on other occasions, alas, it didn't. Mamma used to tell me quite frankly when we had our chats that many of her friends were dealing with similarly violent husbands. I don't think our situation was unique by any means in certain parts of Cardiff in the late Sixties and Seventies.

Some of my earliest memories, unfortunately, were lying petrified in bed listening to Dad raging and shouting as he battered my mother in their bedroom next door. It was terrifying to hear her scream in pain and fear, but I was paralysed with terror. I should have been in there defending her, but what could I do? I was just a snotty-nosed kid in shorts. And very soon he turned his attention to me, the precious firstborn, of whom he had such high hopes, but of whom he expected unrealistic standards of obedience, discipline and achievement in all fields. Given his mentality, I was always going to be in the firing line.

Dad was a Sergeant Major in the Welch Regiment when Mamma met him, and a fine figure of a man he was in his uniform on parade. Off the back of that background, though, he assumed total obedience and instant compliance when he spoke. Mentally, he was still marching squaddies around the parade ground or working them in the gym, but he made no compromises for me as a 6- or 7-year-old growing up. He viewed me as some sort of wild horse that had to be broken in. A battle of wills that, of course, he had to win.

A chilling early example comes to mind. When I was just 6 or 7, I was out on the patch one evening practising my rugby skills with my mates when a massive young thug arrived on the scene and started throwing his weight around and picking fights with everybody. He was probably 10 or 11 – which is a big age difference when you're that young – and at least twice my size. Eventually, he turned his attention to me, the smallest. I squared up briefly, but he was a scary individual and eventually I thought, 'Sod it, I'm going indoors' – it was late anyway.

Dad, as usual, had been watching all this from behind the curtain up in their bedroom. He could never relax and flick the off button. His need to control was total. Normally, he was there checking that I was passing off both hands and kicking off both feet, but this time he'd been watching me back down from the big bastard. I walked through the front door all hot and sweaty and there he was he was waiting for me, red of face and bristling with anger. I didn't realise at the time, but he almost certainly had a few drinks on board.

"What's that all about with the big kid, the bully?" he asked aggressively.

"I dunno, Dad. He just turned up. He's huge. Why can't he play with boys his age? Hopefully we won't see him again."

"Too bloody right, we won't be seeing him again," shouted Dad as he reached for the plastic baseball bat he'd bought me for Christmas. "You're going right back out there now and teach that big bastard a lesson. And if you don't, I can assure you the beating you get from me now will be much worse than anything he can dish out."

Oh, Christ. I was gobsmacked, but the batterings and whippings with his leather belt at home had already started and I would do anything to avoid them. So I grabbed the baseball bat, marched out there and, with the red mist descending, beat the shit out of the big lad, hitting him across the head and shoulders, arms and arse. He was shattered and we never saw him on the patch again – God knows what happened to him. In a way it was a valuable life lesson for both of us, but what a world to be growing up in.

Meanwhile it was almost impossible to avoid the violence back home. Being late back in, being cheeky, bad reports from school that disappointed Dad in some way, or perhaps he was just in a mood after a bad day or a few too many whiskeys. It didn't take much to earn a hiding or a belting, and Mamma was pretty much powerless to intervene, even though she tried. In many ways, she was a strong woman, coming from that hard background in Irish Town. She could be fiery in her own right, but there was no way she could stop my father in full flight. And she would never abandon us kids to his mercies… so she chose to stick it out. The fate of many women during this period, I suspect. It was incredibly courageous of her.

And then, of course, there was school. Now, getting a caning off the Brothers at any Catholic school was nothing particularly new during this era and, indeed, I remember Mamma telling me about the canings she and her friends used to get off the Sisters at their convent school. It's difficult to understand and accept now, but corporal punishment was absolutely routine in Catholic schools and indeed many state schools as well. However, the way they went about it at St Illtyd's was particularly cruel.

If you arrived a minute late, or did something that wasn't appreciated, you had to stand outside the classroom for the rest of the lesson. And that's when the torture started. There was a Brother Bernard, who used to patrol the corridors outside the classrooms, looking for pupils who'd been sent out of their lesson, at which point he'd escort us to Brother Terence's room. Brother Terence would then basically assault us with a cane, which he'd produce from up the sleeve of his cassock. Always armed for combat. He'd produce his thick bamboo cane with a flourish and flick it around, making a horrible swishing noise which brings me out in a sweat to think about to this day.

Brother Bernard sometimes left it to the last five minutes or so, and you were just thinking you might have miraculously got away with it when his head would pop around the corner and he'd smile with pleasure at another victim for Brother Terence – who we called Titch and who was no size at all, despite possessing the strength of three men when dispensing punishment.

Titch could be a right sadist. Once I got hauled up for two strokes on the palm because it was the second time I'd been caught doing something wrong that week. Now, it takes some ticker to stand there without flinching and, as the first stroke came down, no matter how hard I concentrated and vowed not to move and to soak up the pain, I involuntarily twitched. He only caught me a glancing blow across the hand. He was enraged, and completely lost it.

"Right, it's three strokes for you now, Bishop. That will teach you."

Then he put every last ounce of effort into the second stroke, and I flinched just a little again. He still caught me a very painful blow across my fingers – he hadn't missed the bullseye by much – but he wasn't satisfied with that.

"Right, four strokes, Bishop." At which point Titch went berserk and started hitting me with the cane across my head, my neck and on my buttocks and legs. People have been sent to prison for much less – it was ABH by a schoolmaster against a minor, nothing less.

I copped the last of that barbaric regime at St Illtyd's. A while later, when I'd made a name for myself as a rugby player, it had changed drastically. St Illtyd's had become co-ed and the Brothers were being edged out. Soon after that, there was a school reunion at the Old Illtydians Rugby Club and Titch was there. We got talking. He knew everything about my career and ups and downs. He'd kept a cuttings book of my successes – can you believe that? –

and we exchanged pleasantries as if absolutely nothing had happened. We actually enjoyed a good laugh together, if I'm honest, but it was totally surreal – probably something to do with the close-knit school and Catholic community. All I can say is that I've been trampled by New Zealand Māoris, flattened by flying Fijians and survived some torrid League games in Papua New Guinea, but nobody ever beat me and inflicted as much pain as Brother Terence.

One of the problems was that, as I mentioned, Dad had given the Brothers the green light to do their worst. There was an incident at school which had ended with my brother Michael, who had just started, being taunted for looking like a gypsy by a few classmates. My mum got to hear of it and was outraged and sent my father up to the school to sort it out. But that was a very bad move indeed. I saw him arrive, and sometime later I got called out of class. Michael was already outside the headmaster's office and, as we went in, my father was there enjoying a large whiskey with headmaster Brother Alex. It was barely 11 a.m. Kindred souls in a number of ways, it would seem.

My dad, a stickler for a smart military appearance from his days on the parade ground, told Michael that if he didn't have his tie tied properly and had his shirt hanging out, then of course he would be called a gypsy. Instead, he needed to stand tall, always appear smart and polish his shoes so he could see his reflection in them. And then Dad turned to the headmaster, and I'll never forget his words.

"Brother Alex, you have my personal permission to beat my children anytime you see fit."

You have my personal permission to beat my children anytime you see fit. Unbelievable. My heart sank. It was bad enough at home, but now it was open season there as well, so it seemed. At school, as well as the canings, there was no such thing as a simple telling off or even a few strong words, let alone somebody taking the trouble to explain things. Oh no, they went straight for the violent approach. You'd get rulers across your knuckles, a slap round the back of the head, or your ears and cheeks yanked painfully. It was a pretty constant campaign of terror if you were identified as one of those who were badly in need of correction.

With the benefit of hindsight, it's quite clear to me that Dad had significant behavioural and mental health issues. I saw it when he was playing for Glamorgan Wanderers and CIACs. He was an absolutely filthy player and totally cynical with it. Shameless. Back home, he was always reaching for something to hit me with – normally belts or sticks, but anything would do – and he was more than handy with his fists. He had no off button, no restraint mechanism or internal alarm to tell him he was getting out of order. I can see now he was excessive in almost everything, and his violent traits were part of that. He was excessive in his support for my sporting career, with his constant presence, 24-7 dedication and manoeuvring on my behalf. It was all OTT – excessive and obsessive.

Anyway, he was clearly battling demons. One time, when I was 15, he broke my ribs and punctured one of my lungs with a punch when he attacked me at the Tudor pub in Cardiff, where he was landlord at the time.

As the son of a publican, I had the run of the pub despite being underage, and one evening myself and Phil Ford got on the beers and acted up a little. We weren't legless but had clearly been drinking. I could see Dad was ticking. He chose his moment, when the pub cleared after last orders, and eventually cornered me in the pub kitchen and absolutely piled into me. He hit me with a mighty body blow – one of the best punches anybody ever landed on me – that busted my ribs and caused all sorts of internal damage. I went down like a sack of spuds.

"Get up, you little bastard, get up. Call yourself a man! Get up. You're no son of mine. Pathetic."

My mother came storming in. "Get off him, you bastard. You've gone too far this time," she screamed. "Get off him this moment. Stop hitting your son."

Dad suddenly seemed to come round – he used to go into a daze when he was dishing out the treatment – and realised I was badly hurt and that he needed to get me to hospital. We went down to Cardiff General and there was a Chinese doctor there who was suspicious right from the off. It possibly wasn't the first domestic assault he'd seen. Cardiff could be a rough city. Dad and myself had arrived at the hospital with two of his police cronies and drinking partners from the pub – let's call them Ken and Bob, although those weren't their names. Ken was a CID Inspector.

The Chinese doctor started questioning me as well as examining me.

"I fell awkwardly in the bath. I drank too many beers and wasn't feeling myself," I said, thinking that I had to say something to save my dad's arse. Dad, though, was having none of it. Sometimes he really didn't have the sense he was born with.

"No, he didn't, I gave him a clip for being drunk and out of order. He deserved it. He's my son: I'll deal with it as I see fit. I'd do it again."

"Really?" said the doctor, "You shouldn't be doing that. It's against the law, Mr Bishop. You do know that, don't you? You could end up in serious trouble."

"Don't you go telling me what to fucking well do. I'm his father. I know what's best for him."

At that point I remember Ken stepping in and telling Dad to shut the fuck up and to leave it to him.

The doctor lost his rag and said he wanted to call the police; this was a police matter.

"We are police," said Doug, trying to calm things down.

"No, I want independent police here, uniformed officers. This boy here has been brutally assaulted by his father," said the doctor, who was standing his ground bravely. Fair play to him.

After a while, a couple of beat coppers were summoned and arrived at the hospital, although of course they knew Bob and Ken. There was a brief conference between them all as they came in, before they walked over to question me.

"Hi, David. So what happened?"

"I got a bit pissed and fell in the bath, sir. It was totally my own fault."

"OK. If that's your final word, get better soon, lad, and be more careful. You're too young to be drinking, really. I'm told you're a very promising sportsman: we don't want you laid up too long, do we?"

The doctor was pulling his hair out. He finally got me alone for two minutes and spelt out that I had a couple of broken ribs, a punctured lung and internal bruising, including the spleen. "This is serious, David – if your father's done this to you now, what else is he going to do to you?"

I kept going. I had no other option. This had gone too deep. "I'm fine, honestly Doc. I fell in the bath: you've got to believe me. I just want to go home."

He gave up and put a tube in me, pumped my lung back up and a couple of days later I was discharged.

Violence as a Way of Life

The physical abuse and intimidation continued on and off through most of my early and mid teens, but as I got stronger, things reached a tipping point in terms of what I'd put up with. I was getting into rucks and fights in town and finding myself in a lot of trouble with the police, frankly, and my father no longer put the fear of God into me. I had other stuff going on. The big showdown was just a matter of time, and it finally played out over two separate but related incidents.

I was in trouble again at home over something and Dad had imposed a strict curfew of midnight when I went into town. Now, at this stage I was already developing my night-owl tendencies and midnight felt like teatime to me, but I'd been trying to comply. Then one night I was out with Michael, and it was getting towards the witching hour. We were only ten minutes from home at the Tudor, but Michael was getting twitchy and left ahead of me. He actually got in before midnight, but Dad was working up a head of steam and ploughed into him.

"Where's David? What's he up to? You've been with him. Why can't he get in on time? I don't ask much."

About ten minutes later, i.e. about five minutes past midnight, I come through the front door and he hits me with an absolute piledriver, catching me completely off-guard and taking the wind out of me. He drags me into the kitchen and sits me down at the table so we're opposite each other. He stares at me with pure hatred. He's not in the mood to listen to any excuse or even apology I could give for being a few minutes late.

Then he turns around to Mamma and orders: "Get me some tea, Kathleen. I want a mug of tea." Mamma was little more than a slave on occasion.

He keeps eyeing me up, like an opponent in the ring, and eventually Mamma comes in and puts a big mug of steaming hot tea on the table by him.

"You fancy yourself as a bit of a hard man up in town, don't you? Look at him, Kathleen – the boy thinks he's a man."

As he said that, he grabbed the scalding hot tea and threw it all over me. I can hear the screams of horror from Mamma to this day. I jumped up, ready for a fight.

"At last, at last! Look, he's not a coward after all," he sneered at me. He was actually pleased with his handiwork.

I snapped and hit him with an absolute piledriver of my own to the jaw, one of the best punches I've ever landed. He went out like a light, literally, just as it happens in the movies. Within a few seconds, he was snoring away.

Mamma was horrified. "David! Run, son – get out of here as soon as you can, before he comes round. He'll kill you. Run. Run!"

She was right. I grabbed a few things and ran off to my nan – Nancha Frost – where I lived for the next six months, partly in fear for my safety but mostly in fear of what I might yet do to my father when I saw him again. The tables were about to turn.

My nan ran a small guest house and eventually she started dropping strong hints that it was time to go back home. She couldn't afford to be missing out on letting my room for much longer, and sadly she was in poor health. She'd probably had enough of me as well. I was staying out all night or bringing girls back to my room. Dad was also relaying messages begging me to come home. Chapter two of the big showdown was about to start.

I went back full of good intentions. Dad had admitted he'd been out of order, and I wanted everything to calm down for my sake and mostly Mamma's, but deep down I knew there'd be a moment of reckoning. He'd insist on having the final word: the alpha male in him would demand that. I was very wary from the off, even though we rubbed along fairly well for quite a long while – mainly by avoiding each other. We still bonded whenever I was playing rugby, when he was a constant support and a proud father. Like I say, it was a very strange relationship. On occasion, he was exactly the kind of dad you wanted fighting your corner. But, oh my God, the dark side.

The moment of ultimate reckoning duly arrived. I was idly practising in the skittle alley at closing time when he stormed in, clearly pissed on the Brains SA, which he'd developed a liking for. "Everybody out," he ordered. It was a quiet night so there were only a couple of people who needed to move on. I knew what was coming, that's why I'd stayed away from where he was in the main bar. I knew this wasn't going to be pretty.

I thought it would be a fist fight, but instead he grabbed a pool cue and started coming at me. "Still think you're a man, you little shit? Let's see you have a pop at your old father now. Come on, this is your shot at the title, son. That was a lucky punch last time." Always the boxing talk with him.

There was a battle of wills going on and he badly needed to reassert his supremacy. This was his last chance to tame me. Deep down, I was still trying to avoid a scene and stayed passive, but suddenly he took a big swing at me with the cue, like he was splitting logs with an axe. I turned and ducked in self-defence, and he hit me square across the back. My God, it hurt, because those snooker cues are weighted at the end. If that had hit me across the head, it could have been curtains.

I was staggering around and next thing I knew, he'd got me round the neck and was throttling me. He was fighting dirty. I was really in trouble: he'd got me wrapped up and I couldn't breathe. I was fighting for my life, but he'd got me locked in a stranglehold and was still a strong bastard who knew how to fight. I couldn't breathe: my eyes felt like they were popping. I was gone. This was it. I'd made the mistake of letting him start the fight, and he was dictating it. Stupid me.

Then, thank God, the cavalry arrived. At that precise moment Miriam Karea, one of our barmaids, came in – a formidable and brave lady of Middle Eastern heritage.

"You bastard, Bishop – put your son down. What the fuck are you doing? Are you mad?"

My dad just dropped me on the spot there. Miriam had shocked him back to his senses.

Then Mamma came in and Miriam said she was reporting Dad to the police.

Mamma shrieked she was leaving him. Dad told her to get upstairs before she got a backhander as well.

By now I'd come round a bit, and I charged him. I picked Dad up by the throat, slammed him into the wall next to the phone. I felt supercharged with anger, energy and strength. The adrenalin was pumping. The tables had turned, I got him in a headlock, and I was much stronger than he ever was. I wasn't going to ease off until this was sorted.

Mamma was screaming at me to put him down. I chose this moment to lay down the new ground rules that would be followed in the Bishop household going forward.

"If you ever lay a hand on my mother again, I will fucking kill you. Do you understand? I said, do you understand? Do you hear me?"

Violence as a Way of Life

As drunk as he was, I could see the pure naked terror in his eyes. I continued – I hadn't finished yet, not by a long chalk.

"If you ever hit my brothers and sister, I will fucking kill you and not think twice about it. Do you fucking understand, or do you want some more? 'Cos I've got all night, and we don't leave here until this is sorted. Do you hear me?

"And if you ever lay your hands on me again, you are dead. Do you hear me? I won't think twice."

I loosened my grip a little and all he could utter was, "Yes, yes, yes" and "Sorry, sorry, sorry".

My poor mother was standing right next to me now and, after looking at me in horror for a few seconds, turned her gaze to Dad and looked him straight in the face. She had something to say as well, something to get off her chest. The whole scene had traumatised her.

"This is all down to you, you bastard. You've tried to beat the devil out of David and all you've done is beat it into him. He's becoming you, but he's better than you at everything, and you can't accept it, can you?"

We stood there, speechless. It had been a truly ugly scene, which had been building for years.

His time as top dog was over. I dropped him to the floor like a sack of spuds and we left him there to sleep it off, sober up and lick his wounds. We begged Miriam not to report anything to the police. It had been sorted. I knew instinctively the worst was over.

From that moment on, in many ways, Dad was a much-diminished man, a bully without a victim to taunt – although I only learnt recently that he still occasionally had a go at my brothers when I wasn't around. But the positive is that, in quick order, I got much more of the devoted sports-loving father, the ultimate camp follower who couldn't do enough for me. Somehow, we renewed and revived our father-son relationship, and I give him much credit for that, but on a very different footing. He would never lay a hand on me again. He knew exactly what the consequences would be. He didn't doubt for a second that I'd carry my threat through.

Not long after that, I went to prison following two convictions for violence and, once I'd settled down in prison and fought the usual turf wars you have to win to survive there, life almost settled down in comparison with my teenage years of constantly fighting Dad. Yet still I loved him, and my mother still stayed with him because she loved him and there was a young family to bring up. Fact is always stranger than fiction: people often stick together for as long as possible, and sometimes it comes good again and works out, but all I can say is if there are any victims of domestic abuse out there, either current or historic, you have my sympathy and understanding. It's a horrible place to be and the damage can be long-term. I wouldn't necessarily advise the drastic measures I ended up taking, but sometimes it's unbearable and you get pushed to the very limit. I've been there. It's a nightmare.

CHAPTER 7
Prisoner A79816

FOR JUST OVER a year of my life – from March 1980 to March 1981 – I was Prisoner A79816, which was abbreviated to 816. I mentioned earlier being convicted for assault and being sentenced to three years for GBH, and all the screws from the Governor downwards, bar one – my Physical Training Instructor, David Daisey – simply called me '816' when they shouted instructions and orders. Part of the depersonalising process, I suppose. The screws weren't meant to get to know you as an individual and a human being – that could apparently be dangerous – while I suppose the theory is that the prisoner should try and forge a new persona, ditch the past and concentrate on being a new, better version of himself. Of course, amongst the lads, I was still 'the Bish' or, less to my liking, 'Taff'.

Aylesbury was a high-security specialist young offenders' prison that catered mainly for the 18–21-year-old bracket, which meant you had the complete cross section of offenders there. Murderers, sex offenders of every description, psychopaths, armed robbers, petty thieves, fraudsters, arsonists – we had 'Tom the Bomb' with us, who'd achieved notoriety by blowing up abortion clinics – IRA types, violent kids like me who kept getting into fights, and a small but not insignificant number of individuals who were innocent of what they'd been convicted of. Leading that list was Michael Hickey, who was wrongly convicted of the murder of Carl Bridgewater in 1978. Everybody in the prison knew he was innocent of the charge he was convicted for, including all the screws, but when the Establishment have cocked up bigtime in this country, they're very slow to admit their mistake and he didn't get out until 1997. An utter disgrace.

I was due to be there for three years and mentally I clocked on for three years, but all the time I was also working away to get parole at the first opportunity, which came after a year. I vowed to keep my nose clean and avoid trouble – which wasn't easy in such a volatile environment – and I behaved myself and attempted to earn brownie points wherever possible. I'd got myself into this mess and I needed to get out as soon as possible. One more day on top of my allotted three years inside would have killed me, or rather I'd have ended it all myself. I'm not made for incarceration.

I say I spent a year at Aylesbury... Actually, the first six weeks of my sentence were served at Cardiff while they decided what to do with me after Judge John Rutter – 'Rutter the Nutter', as he was nicknamed by the screws, who were used to his harsh sentences – sent me down. My brief Bernard de Maid had warned me I'd be going down. I'd 'got away with' two previous warnings and fines, and another time the guy I got into a fight with, Shaun McCoy – later to become a friend – failed to turn up to court to give evidence and the case was dropped. This time there'd been two separate fights with students on the same night. I was out of control. I deserved to spend some time inside but Bernard had been confident that, at the age of 19 – in fact 18, when the offences occurred – they'd send me to a borstal, not jail. That's what we were pinning our hopes on, but how wrong he was.

Almost the first thing they did was to shave my head with the obligatory prison crew cut, and I spent most of my time in Cardiff jail in solitary, with very little of what they call 'association' – exercise and general mingling. It was a harsh introduction to prison life. I was now a fully-fledged prisoner, not just on remand pending a hearing, and I had just one visit per week at that stage. On his first visit, when he came with my Uncle Michael, the sheer awfulness of what was happening really hit Dad and he sat there sobbing for the full hour, his hand resting on mine, scarcely able to utter a word. He clearly felt for me, my fear and shame, but I know he was also humiliated on behalf of the family. I also wonder, thinking back, if he was reflecting on his part in creating this violent jailbird son. His 'never take a backward step' attitude and the batterings and violence of those early teenage years had played a part, for sure. I sensed a great deal of remorse. "You're beating the vice into him, not out of him," to borrow from Mamma again.

Being Dad, he showed his support in his own way. Below my cell in Cardiff, with its barred window, and just over the wall out of sight was a public pavement which I couldn't actually see, and he would take to walking along it at all times of day whistling the family whistle, which he had taught us when we were young. Don't ask – I have no idea what it was all about, probably some Army thing, but there was this distinctive whistle like a bird tweeting, which we could all do. And then he discovered that if he stood the other side of the road by the fire station, he had direct line of sight to my window and he would stand there every night with his binoculars, waving and gesturing so he could be "close to me" and show his solidarity. A psychiatrist would have had a field day trying to get into my father's mind.

The Bish

I began to appreciate the realities of being a prisoner. I had a long-standing appointment at the Heath Hospital for a procedure on my nose, which I'd broken playing baseball the previous summer. To my surprise, the prison authorities allowed me to go, but of course I was handcuffed to a screw the entire time and another uniformed officer accompanied us. For some reason, that was when the disgrace of it all really came home. Banged up in my cell on my own, well, it was just me dealing with my issues and the consequences of my actions. But out in public, in a hospital, where I could easily bump into friends or acquaintances, it was just plain humiliating. I kept wanting to stop and tell people that actually I was a fairly decent bloke, and I wasn't really a criminal. But I was. I experienced that again when I was finally driven to Aylesbury in a minibus, and we stopped off at the services for a coffee and a leak. People either avoided any eye contact at all or stared at me in amazement when I was led around the canteen in handcuffs by the uniformed screws. How I wanted it all to be over.

Aylesbury was different gravy from the moment I arrived. This was proper bird. I had to go through four different sets of doors, all slamming shut behind me, before the handcuffs were taken off and I was handed over. It was *Porridge* without the humour. After a quick registration, it was solitary confinement for a week – induction week, they call it. No contact with anybody other than screws, when I was processed and given a quick medical. There was some psychological profiling going on, with various questionnaires and tests. The main object seemed to be deciding what I might be good at in terms of prison work, and I must have done quite well – whatever that means in prison terms – because I was sent to work in the braille room, which was considered the best job outside of cheffing in the kitchen, and paid the princely sum of £4.10 a week to spend in the canteen tuck shop every Monday. Skinflint that I am, by the way, I still managed to save most of mine. I spent 80p a week on two stamps – for letters to Mamma and Kate – and a few bob on a bottle of pop or a packet of crisps. And that was it.

The braille room was an amazing place and I'm quite proud of my time there. You sit in front of these specially adapted typewriters and type out books and magazine articles in braille on to special paper which is then bound and distributed to the blind who have learned to read braille. So, as a prisoner, you end up both learning to type and getting a feel for braille as well. It was an eye-opener for me, and a strong message that there are people out there dealing with problems far more severe than your own. In one way, it was considered a cushy number, about a dozen of us working quietly away in a comfortable environment, but it was quite challenging to pick up the typing skills and to then concentrate and make a good job of it. The whole process did me a power of good.

After a week, I got moved to C Wing, where life began to get interesting. The prison was massive and made up of six wings. A, B, C and D were what I would call regular wings and were where the regime was probably the harshest. Less free time, more bang-up, fewer privileges, more visible discipline. On those wings you only got three association periods a week – time when you could mingle on the wing. Then there were F and G Wings. G was for the lifers – 'all-dayers', as they were called – and F was for the new boys and those doing shorter sentences. It might seem counter-intuitive, but it was slightly more relaxed in F and G wings, which were like a separate prison within a prison, really.

There, we enjoyed association periods every day. Just to make life bearable in the case of the lifers and not to leave too much of an imprint on the shorter-term cases, I'm guessing – I don't really know, as it was never explained to me.

On C Wing I had the very good fortune to immediately pal up with a top Cardiff lad of Asian extraction, Jamshed – alas, now dead – who was a clever guy and benevolent ringleader who took me under his wing. Our shared Cardiff background gave us much in common. I was there for two months or so and he undoubtedly saved my chances of getting parole one night when the entire wing staged a sit-down protest strike in the mess hall after our evening meal. Now, this was a real dilemma for me as the new kid on the block. If I didn't go with the flow and support their action, if I headed for my cell and bang-up, I'd get labelled a scab and my life would be made hell. If I supported them, I could probably kiss goodbye to any chance of parole, at least first-time round. I'd be looking at a minimum of two years inside. Early parole would be off the menu.

Jamshed was aware of all this and cleverly got up and in a very loud voice, so everybody could hear, said, "Bish, fuck off back to your cell. You're not part of this, you bastard – it's not your fight."

I tried to sound outraged but didn't make a good job of it. "No way, Jamshed, fuck off. I'm with you guys all the way, you know that."

"Don't be a fucking idiot all your life, Bish." And with that, he grabbed me by my shirt and, with help from a couple of his mates, dragged me back to my cell – or 'cage', as we called it – making a lot of noise about it to make sure the screws could see what was going on and that I wasn't part of the protest. Then Jamshed and his buddies rejoined the sit-in. People use that expression, 'honour amongst thieves', which I didn't really understand until that point. That was a moment of real class and courage from Jamshed, and I loved him for it.

Before I was moved to F Wing after two months, I had one other dodgy moment on C Wing, which came with one of the other inmates, who was spoiling for a fight with me for some reason – perhaps he'd heard I was a boxer. I'd gone in with the sworn intention of never starting any trouble in prison, and in fact I was true to that promise, but what you have to realise is that, in prison, despite the brave smiles, gallows humour and what you think is camaraderie, everybody's having a really bad day most of the time, even if they try and make light of it. Massive emotion and anger are always very close to the surface and can erupt spontaneously almost from nowhere. When that happens, you have to stand your ground.

Anyway, one day this guy – I don't even remember his name – came for me inexpertly and I decked him with a decent left – a 'chin check', as they call it in prison – and that should have been that. Except I'd cut him as well, there was bit of blood, and the fight had caused a bit of a commotion. Normally you went down the Recess – the toilets – to sort out a dispute and minders would keep an eye out for the screws, but this had bubbled up from nowhere. Luckily, my great ally in the prison, PTI David Daisey, had been close on hand and immediately stepped in before we got hauled in front of the prison officer in charge of the wing. "It was a bit of friendly horseplay that got out of hand, right, lads," he whispered to us urgently under his breath as he marched us off. "It was an accident, it wasn't a fight: don't change your story." Both of us religiously stuck to this fabrication and despite the prison officer clearly being sceptical, he decided not to log it, and I preserved my clean record. I still had a chance of parole, but I was riding my luck a bit.

That summer I got moved to F Wing, and there was one more big hurdle to clear before I could relax a little and concentrate on just getting through my stretch. F Wing seemed to be run – from the prisoners' point of view – by a big Londoner who fancied himself as some kind of Godfather figure. He clearly ruled the roost with his bullying ways and demanded total subservience, and he seemed to have a problem with me arriving. Perhaps word of the fight in C Wing had reached him and he sensed a rival, which I wasn't in any way. I craved the quiet life. Anyway, the moment of truth came when he sent one of his runners – he had four or five wing men – to my cell, demanding tobacco or the money to buy tobacco. I told him to fuck off and to tell his London guvnor to buy his own smokes, at which point the runner, a big Rasta guy, ushered me into the Recess. Another runner was posted by the entrance to the Recess to look out for screws. This was being done in an organised way and was getting very serious. Suddenly Cedric, the Rasta guy, went for me. I knew what was coming and was ready. He lunged at me, with little shaving blades taped to his fingers to maximise the damage. I couldn't mess around: time was of the essence, and I sent him to sleep with one punch. There he was sprawled on the floor snoring away. His mate looked terrified and backed off, as did the prisoner who'd been standing guard at the entrance. This wasn't in the script. When push came to shove, they were powerless and clueless. This time there was no comeback from officialdom: it had all been done quietly in the Recess, there was no hue and cry, and the screws knew nothing about it. When Cedric came round, he was a humbled man, and the incident had actually worked in my favour. The word got out: Don't mess with the mad Taff. Let him be.

There was one other key moment that cemented my reputation amongst the lads and granted me immunity from random attacks, violence and general nastiness. We had two PTIs at the prison. The junior one, the previously mentioned David Daisey, was an outstanding human being who retained his authority while at the same time working with you as an individual to get through your stretch and a return to normality. The other, his boss, was a complete bastard. Let's call him Mr East. He was an ex-Army Sergeant Major and amateur boxer who used to get his kicks from goading prisoners in the gym, getting them worked up playing murder ball, and then inviting one or two of the likelier lads to put some gloves on and get in the ring with him. The chance to deck a screw proved irresistible, but of course he would absolutely rip them to pieces and cause a lot of damage. He was a real sadist, who couldn't inflict enough pain. I later learned that a few months before I arrived, he'd made short work of John Actie, who was briefly at Aylesbury before being moved north somewhere. Now, John was as fit and strong as most top rugby players... but had no experience boxing.

Eventually East's attention turned to me. I was barely half his size. He didn't know I could box – Daisey accidentally-on-purpose seemed to have omitted that piece of information – and I hammed it up a bit, making a meal of putting my gloves on and not going straight into a stance which might alert him to the fact that I knew what I was about. I could see he could box a bit – fair play, he was no idiot in the ring – but I had the advantage that he thought I was just a cocky

Taff and not a two-time Welsh Junior Champion who would have boxed in a British final but for injury. This needed to be quick and decisive, though. No messing about. Suddenly I clicked into gear, hit him with two rapid combos and a vicious right hook and he went down like a felled oak. He literally didn't know what had hit him.

Daisey came up to me in a panic. "Bish, you fucking idiot, he'll make you pay for this. What have you done?"

I begged to differ. Firstly, a few screws other than Daisey had strolled into the gym and had seen everything. They'd seen their colleague invite me into the ring, where he intended to beat the crap out of me just for the sheer pleasure of it. They'd probably seen him do the same half a dozen times. There was no question that he'd brought this on himself, and I got the feeling one or two of the screws had rather enjoyed it.

And secondly, I was fast becoming an expert in dealing with bullies. If you call their bluff, if you confront them and rout them, it's like pricking a balloon. The air instantly goes out of their life. They've got nothing left. Their defeat and humiliation is total. I had no bother from Mr East for the rest of my stay.

So I'd been through the rites of passage many prisoners have to deal with; now to the business of dealing with incarceration, I found it difficult at first: I seemed so adrift with just one visit a month for my dad or family. Mamma found it too upsetting and only came up a couple of times, although she wrote to me just about every day of the 12 months. It was just the days and months stretching ahead that did my head in. Remember, I was still not allowing myself the luxury of believing I'd get parole first time round, but the thought of that wasted time was killing me. I had

Wales caps to win and a Lions tour in 1983 that I wanted to get selected for. Then one of the lifers took me aside and gave me a pep talk. "David, believe me: you're not here for life; you're not even here for three years if you keep your nose clean. Take it from me. If anybody's going to get parole first time out, it'll be you. So do the maths. You could be out in just eight months, next March – that's just eight more visits. Draw yourself a calendar on a piece of paper and put it up on your cell wall."

And that's what I did. I didn't do a daily calendar, that would still have been too depressing – I just divided the page up into eight months and eight visits: August, September, October, November, December, January, February and March. I'd count it down that way and feel better for it. Just eight boxes to tick off felt better than 32 boxes, one per week, or 224, one for each day.

Life began to look up, but bear in mind always that prison is no fun at the best of times. It's all relative. Part of you is always on red alert. I remember one sunny lunchtime daydreaming, looking out of the window wistfully down in the mess hall, and a screw I didn't know casually said, "Dreaming of getting out, 816?"

"Chance would be a fine thing!" I jokingly replied, thinking we were just passing the time of day, a private jokey moment. Five minutes later my cell was being searched – a 'rub down', as it was called – and I was being strip-searched. The process was repeated the following day as well. That's jail for you.

Racism was/is an ever-present thing in prison, way more than in society generally, and I had to be careful there. Coming from Cardiff, I had no racial hang-ups whatsoever: race was and is totally irrelevant to me and I found myself hanging out with the black guys even more than the white. I loved their music, and I was never happier than when they had control of the record player, which they were allowed one night a week. All that was very natural to me, but to start with, before people got to know me, it caused a bit of suspicion on both sides.

My friendship with David Daisey, the PTI, was the key to everything for me. Daisey was enthusiastic and not at all cynical: he loved sport and wanted to make a difference. Very English, to my view, but then again, I've always got on well with the English, which some in Wales have never really understood. He was a bit unconventional for the Prison Service, who probably frowned on some of his fraternisations with the prisoners, but he was undaunted. He would do it his way, and I salute him for that.

He sought me out the moment I arrived, probably because he sensed an able sportsman to work. Being Welsh, he automatically assumed I'd be a rugby player, and he'd always wanted to get a rugby team going at the prison even though he knew nothing about rugby. Initially I tried to fob him off. I told him I hated rugby, in fact I hated sport, and that I just wanted to get through my stretch and piss off home. As with the Army, Dad had told me never to volunteer for anything in prison.

A couple of days later, he approached me again with some newspaper clippings, which he proceeded to flick through. David Joseph Bishop, Wales Youth cap at scrum half last year against France, promising Wales prospect who'd moved from Cardiff to Ebbw Vale, twice Junior Welsh Boxing Champion, outstanding young baseball prospect.

"OK, it's a fair cop. I can play a bit, but I don't want any trouble. I don't want to put my head above the parapet."

"David, there'll be no trouble. You're going to help me form a rugby team here and train the lads up, and I intend to get us some fixtures. It'll be something to keep you motivated, and you need to stay in shape anyway because you'll need to make up for lost time when you get out of here."

He was right, of course, and from that moment I threw myself into the rugby project. Daisey negotiated two long training sessions a week and, importantly, those wanting to play didn't lose their payment for the work they'd miss. We had fantastic facilities at the prison – better than any rugby club in Wales at the time – so the one thing we could do was get fit. We had a football pitch that we could convert to rugby, which was inside a 400m athletic track, and we had a seriously equipped gym with space for judo mats and everything. We had basketball courts, the lot. I'd emerge from this prison as the fittest rugby player in Wales!

And so it began. There were some serious athletes among the inmates: some of the black lads were like lightning and there was some real muscle around. A few had definitely played before – there was one English guy, as cockney as you like, who was very useful indeed, and in fact I bumped into him soon after we both got out, playing for a prestigious English team at the Aberaeron Sevens. He went at it just like me.

About 25 to 30 of the lads were up for the challenge, the majority complete beginners, and I loved the coaching role I now undertook. It was straight out of Ray Williams' *Rugby for Beginners* – I had the perfect template already in my mind. I could remember just about every routine, and later on Dad found a copy to help Daisey.

We'd work away at the basic skills, enjoying the fresh air and sun, and gradually we would progress to touch rugby games, full-contact touch rugby, sevens, scrums, line-outs and finally as many a-side as we could muster from the numbers. It was mostly 12 a side, full on contact. It was brilliant to see the guys progressing, it worked off a bit of steam and, wonder of wonders, Daisey had organised the schedule so we had an hour to kick back in the gym after training, when we could enjoy a drink of cordial or fruit juice and put the world to rights.

Increasingly, there was an element of *The Mean Machine* about the project – you know, the Burt Reynolds film that had come out in 1974, about the inmates of an American prison, training up a team of their own to play the guards in an American football game.

We were getting good and needed a game. Daisey said he had a few games lined up locally for later in the season but there was nothing on the horizon for a while, until he was contacted by the HM Prison Service XV, who needed a warm-up game for their big matches against the Police, Fire Service and others. It seemed a bit ambitious to me – they would be a pretty decent standard – but we took the challenge on nonetheless.

We had a few things in our favour. Rather like the boxing PTI Mr East, they would expect us to be rubbish and would be off their guard to start with. In addition, the circumstances of playing us behind a prison wall could be pretty off-putting and also there was the strong possibility of it disintegrating into more of a fight than a rugby match, which would suit us more than them.

All of that came into play to a lesser or greater degree. Come the big day, the Prison Service XV was shocked by how good we were, went behind early on, then started to get on top and then got diverted by an outbreak of fights and niggles. Miraculously, we scored a try to win it three minutes from time, 21-18 if memory serves. It was one of the best rugby memories of my life. I was manager, selector, coach, skipper, rub-a-dub man, commentator, scrum half and star man all rolled into one, which appealed to me greatly.

It was an amazing moment; one we enjoyed on our own in the gym, where some better-quality-than-normal food and fruit juices had been laid out. The Prison Service XV guys didn't join us, which was pretty disappointing – they headed for a pub in town to lick their wounds. None of us, of course, have a picture or mementoes of the day, and I often wonder if any of the prison officers took some pictures.

I had hoped this would be the start of something big, something really special – a couple of other prisons had been in touch, seeking a game for their combined Screws/Inmates XVs – but soon afterwards there was a nationwide prison warders strike, and it just wasn't possible security-wise to stage any more games.

Daisey had also been contacted by the Buckinghamshire RFU about the possibility of me being granted day releases, accompanied by Daisey, to play for them in the RFU County Championship, but that proved impossible. With the prisons operating on a bare minimum of staff, Daisey couldn't be spared for the day. He was gutted. I think he secretly hoped I'd inspire a David v. Goliath run by Bucks, or that I'd get spotted by the England selectors and become an honorary Englishman. I wouldn't, incidentally, have made any effort to escape, as one player from Littlehey open prison did when their team played an away match. I knew which side my bread was buttered on. Do my time and get out: I didn't seek any complications.

I was sad that there were no more matches, although we continued to train after the strike. The bonding experience between us had been incredible and that was brought home to me a few years later when I bumped into one of the lads in civvy street. He'd just been released from a prison up in the Midlands – Leicester, I think. Incarcerated there had been Butler, our big, athletic second row at Aylesbury – one of those raw talents who was starting from scratch but could have been quite a player. He was doing 'all day and night', which meant he was a lifer, with no prospect of parole either, and apparently his cell up in Leicester was festooned with pictures of me and clippings from my matches and the news stories that surrounded my career. He'd followed me closely from our period at Aylesbury and spoke constantly about what a great time it was.

Around this time, the 12-month Parole Board began to dominate my thoughts. How to put my best case forward? There was a London lad, a Jewish guy, who was very bright or had a very good lawyer (or both), and just before he got let out, he slipped me his notes on how to fill out all the parole forms – a sort of template for the correct answers the screws expected. That helped. Then, unbeknown to me, my dad was working overtime on my behalf. Everything to excess with Dad. Firstly, he'd been tapping up Rugby League clubs all over England and had got four – Warrington was one of them – to write letters of support, saying they'd be willing to offer me a contract on my release. i.e. there'd be a job waiting for me, which was one of the most important boxes the parole board like to tick. And then he'd been buttering up Daisey. Now, there was no need to get Daisey on my side as he was already firmly in my corner, but in the January Daisey, having discovered a passion for rugby, went down to Cardiff, where my dad had got him a ticket for the England game and put him up at the pub for the weekend.

On the Monday morning, when I saw him next, his eyes were bloodshot and he still stank of Brains SA.

Daisey was always going to sing my praises for my work with the rugby team and general demeanour and, with his help regarding that incident on C Wing, I'd managed to keep my disciplinary record clean. I'd put in – and enjoyed – some long shifts at the Braille Centre, and while in prison I'd also received that Royal Humane Society award, which brought me to the particular attention of the Governor. I'd been noted and, importantly, hadn't done anything to queer my pitch. Another little incident from my past was also revisited to paint me in a good light. Just before I'd gone to prison, I was down in my dad's pub, the Tudor, one night when it all kicked off outside with a big fight. I rushed out with my dad and Keith Burford, a Cardiff CID officer who used to drink down the pub. It was beginning to settle down when, out of the corner of my eye, I noticed a young kid with a huge 12-inch knife coming out of the shadows and heading for Keith. I was quick out of the blocks and intercepted him, knocking him to the ground and taking his knife from him. Dad was about to give me a bollocking for getting involved when I didn't need to when he and Keith saw the knife. Keith had spoken on my behalf at my trial and, while I was inside, he'd recommended me for a Police Commendation for bravery. All of which played out quite well when the details were read out for the Parole Board.

I began to believe I was in with a shot and, for that reason, I turned down home leave as we got towards the end of the 12 months, when the Parole Board was imminent. A few months out from your possible release, the system was to let a prisoner out for first a weekend at home and then four or five days, to reacquaint themselves with the real world, so it wasn't a huge shock. It's a very humane and sensitive idea, but I knew for sure that if I went home for a weekend, I would get the sniff of freedom and not return. And in the long run, that would be the end of my career. They'd catch up with me and I'd have to serve the full three years plus a few extras.

Come the big day, I said my piece to the Board as they read my application. Dad produced the letters of prospective employment from the Rugby League clubs. Daisey sang my praises and there was very little on the debit side other than that I'd already enjoyed the luxury of serving two three-year sentences concurrently rather than consecutively, which was considered over-generous in some quarters. Getting out after just a year for what might easily have been a six-year stretch might be frowned on a little, but eventually they gave me the thumbs up. I was out.

Prison had been a frightening time, made bearable by some unexpectedly good friends amongst the inmates, the help and encouragement of Daisey and the love and support at all times of my family and girlfriend Kate, who wrote nearly as many letters to me as Mamma. It had been an eye-opener for someone who was still young for his years in many ways. Yes, there was a hardcore group of psychopaths and perverts – just plain wrong 'uns – housed in the prison, and you had to remember that at all times, but in truth I'd judge a good number of inmates to be pretty regular blokes who'd taken a very bad wrong turn or endured a moment of madness. Prisons are full of people – human flesh and blood – who lost the plot horrendously for just 30 seconds or so in their otherwise unexceptional lives, especially with crimes of violence and passion. 30 seconds before the incident they were 'normal' and 30 seconds after the incident they were back to 'normal', and would never be abnormal again. I met a few of those, most notably a guy from Brecon who was as nice as pie and as sensible and philosophical as anybody I've met, who nonetheless one night strangled his fiancée to death after learning she'd cheated on him. I left a wiser man, determined to never ever spend another minute of my precious life banged up. I needed to live a slightly quieter, less dramatic existence. My entire life had become a bloody soap opera, and I needed to dial things down a bit. Little did I know.

CHAPTER 8

Joining Pooler

FINALLY OUT OF prison, I needed to quickly pick up the threads of my rugby career, which had been beginning to gather pace before my 'time out' at HMP Aylesbury.

It had been a hectic, tumultuous period. The river rescue in the Taff, my court case and then a year in prison – we need to pick up the rugby side of things from when Cardiff and I parted ways in the autumn of 1979, five months before I'd been tried and sentenced.

Being kicked out of Cardiff was difficult. I'd represented Cardiff at rugby, baseball, boxing and judo, and was proud of the city. I was a Cardiff boy – I loved my grubby, beery, lively, edgy city, and I wanted to be the successor to Gareth Edwards and Terry Holmes, both Cardiff RFC legends. Cardiff was my club. Yes, I was a problematic bolshie teenager with a bad attitude – a fair few such individuals have made brilliant rugby players over the decades by the way – but I was shocked when the word came down from on high after that trip to Quins and the hotel incident for which we the younger players were told to take the blame. I was expecting a two-week ban, tops – instead I was shown the door.

Dad was furious. His cunning plan had been for me to become such a key player for Cardiff when Terry Holmes

Joining Pooler

was absent – with Wales, injured or resting – that I would in no time be challenging him for his Wales position. I wasn't quite so confident that was the ideal route. I knew just how good Terry was – remember, this was when he was absolutely flying, before he got his bad injuries – and once I'd calmed down, I was bit more upbeat about being kicked out of Cardiff. It could be worse. Objectively there was a strong argument for being away from Cardiff, starting and starring for a senior club every week, and now I'd been pushed out, this was my opportunity. It's an ill wind that blows nobody any good, and all that.

I trod water for a few weeks, not quite knowing how to go about things, while also waiting for the date of my court case to be determined. I was in limbo in more than one sense. Rugby-wise, I ticked over with a few games for the Old Illtydians, the school's old boys club, but that was it. Should I be doing the rounds touting my wares, or was I already considered promising enough to sit back and wait for clubs to contact me? Already my sightly illogical but hard-wired bias against west Wales was such that the big clubs down there held no interest for me, so that narrowed the field. Dad heard that his old club, Glamorgan Wanderers, were interested and pushed me strongly in that direction – but then, out of the blue, Ebbw Vale got in touch. Pablo Rees had moved up there at the start of the season and had been singing my praises. Could I play that Wednesday, away against South Wales Police at Waterton Cross, their once swish home ground which now lies derelict?

Yes, I certainly could. It went well and we won, handily – the side scoring five tries, with myself involved in most of them. Afterwards Arthur Lewis, their coach, asked me if I wanted to join. Why not? Steve Lewis, who once got an

England trial, was their scrum half of choice, but I reckoned I could win that battle easily enough, and with Vale celebrating their centenary year, they had a massive fixture list for the season so there'd be plenty of rugby for everyone. There was also an end-of-season tour of the USA to further entice me... At just turned 19, I was going to get a stack of starts, and that was not to be sniffed at. Being old for my year, most of my Youth rugby contemporaries were still playing a final year of Youth or Second Team rugby while – over the next four or five months before I went to jail – I was going up against the likes of Llanelli, Cardiff, Neath, Pontypridd and others. Heady stuff for somebody who, up to that point, had enjoyed 20 minutes off the bench against Penarth.

And there was more. I travelled up to training and games in a car with the likes of Michel Van der Loos – the very useful Dutch International who also had to leave Cardiff – Pablo and a few others, such as prop Gerry Wallace, wing Neil Collins and lock Anthony Ellison, who'd also joined from Cardiff. I never had to drive, yet it seems I qualified for £30 travel expenses paid out in a brown envelope after the game every week. More than handy pocket money back in 1980, when a pint was about 40p. This was all a bit of an eye-opener for me. People valued my services and Ebbw Vale, who were by no means a rich club, took good care to feed all the lads after training and matches every week. They made you feel wanted and the atmosphere was great, win, lose or draw. I can't speak highly enough of the club.

Arthur Lewis was a good, encouraging coach and although generally outgunned by the bigger teams, Ebbw Vale had some more than useful players – we gave the big boys a good run for their money, and we enjoyed our rugby. Skipper Phil Gardner, lock David Fryer and flanker Clive 'Budgie' Burgess were seasoned campaigners, and Budgie was a fantastically hard and ballsy flanker who took me under his wing and became my minder in the games we played.

Against Llanelli soon after I joined, I was sprinting across the field to a ruck when Wales flanker Paul Ringer clipped me with a nasty little cheap shot from behind, just to let me know who was boss. Absolutely bog-standard fare for Welsh club rugby at the time I should add, despite the holier-than-thou mob who try and tell you otherwise. Or that only Pontypool got up to that kind of skullduggery. Give me strength.

Budgie saw it and pulled me aside. "Leave him to me, Bish, don't go getting in trouble." Now, he and Paul were bosom pals and drinking partners from Paul's days at Ebbw Vale – old-school warriors hewn from the same rock – but Budgie wasn't having his young pup at scrum half treated like that. There would be retribution, rest assured. A couple of minutes later, Paul was trapped at the bottom of a ruck, preventing release. It was the moment Budgie had been waiting for. He kicked Ringer in the ribs. Not an absolutely full-on kick, but hard enough to make you wince – a warning shot, if you like. Budgie was shaping up for seconds when Ringer screamed out.

"Budgie, you bastard, leave it out! I'm playing against France next week."

"Well, lay off the fucking kid then, Ringo."

"OK, right – whatever you say."

And that was that, sorted in an instant. I enjoyed an armchair ride for the rest of the game, got some decent write-ups and larged it with a pint with Paul and Budgie in the clubhouse afterwards, when we joked about the whole thing. That's how it rolled back in those days.

I played for Ebbw Vale most weeks until I was sent to prison in March 1980, when they explained diplomatically in the programme that I'd be unavailable for a while, as if the fans hadn't read the paper and known what had gone down. I'd enjoyed every moment, and they kept in touch when I was up at Aylesbury. They were a rugby lifeline during a difficult time, and I still considered them my club. Pablo and others sent me postcards on a daily basis from their tour to California, featuring scantily clad beach babes and detailing their various triumphs on tour, so to speak. It was, I suppose, their way of saying they cared and were thinking of me.

When I finally got out, the first thing Dad and I did was get on the train west to watch them against Swansea. A week later, I was scoring a hat-trick for Ebbw Vale Athletic against Cardiff Rags on the top cricket ground pitch at Ebbw Vale. The Rags included Terry Holmes, Gareth Davies and Pat Daniel that day and it was a hell of a win for us, which got as much publicity as a First XV game.

Coming off, Terry Holmes commented to Dad, "The boy looks sharp today, Mr Bishop."

"So he bloody well should, Terry. He's had a year off getting fit inside. There shouldn't be a spare ounce on him," was Dad's reply.

I saw out the final weeks of the 1980/81 season with Ebbw Vale, but was undecided during the summer of 1981 as to what to do next. I was in a hurry, looking to make up for lost time, and knew a big, painful decision was looming. I needed to be with one of the big four clubs to make the so-called Big Five selectors, responsible for picking the Wales side, sit up and pay attention. Frankly, that meant Newport, because I refused to countenance playing for Llanelli or Swansea even

Joining Pooler

if they were interested in me, and Cardiff were obviously out of the question. My hurt pride wouldn't allow me to go back even if asked. Ebbw Vale sensed all this. They made me vice-captain, raised my money – sorry, expenses – to £40 a week and we had this sort of informal arrangement that I'd at least stay until I'd got a Wales B cap.

What I did know was that I was as fit as is humanly possible, playing out of my skin and getting close to Terry Holmes, in my own mind if nobody else's. Whatever the state of flux as my next move worked itself out, I had to maintain standards and I trained like a bastard that summer and played every sevens tournament going. I think Vale won at least three, and reached another final. We had some useful sevens players, like Pablo, Wayne Bow, David Hussey, Richard Owen and Des Parry. I sensed a big move around the corner but wanted to leave Ebbw Vale with only good memories. Blaenavon, Blaenau Gwent, Monmouth, Aberaeron and then the Snelling Sevens. It was like being on tour as we bounced from tournament to tournament, one enjoyable weekend to another... All this was on top of my prison fitness, when I was able to train hard most days. I was fit to bust. It was during this period, incidentally, that I first met a leggy young flanker called Mark Brown, who played on loan for us from Cwmbran. Bloody hell, could 'Shaft' play sevens? Could he ever. There was nobody he couldn't chase down and tackle – including Test wings, who he could catch without breaking sweat even when they had a 5-metre head start.

I started the new fifteens season playing really well – partly a farewell gift to Ebbw Vale, partly putting myself in the window to advertise my wares. And then a bloke called Tony Faulkner phoned me at the pub one Tuesday night. Now, in many ways, I was still an incredibly naive kid. I knew very little about the history of Welsh rugby and the big names of the Seventies and their club allegiances, and what they were doing now. All I wanted was to be Gareth Edwards, with perhaps a nod to Barry John and Phil Bennett as well. I wasn't bothered with the forwards and their lives on and off the field.

So when the phone rang, and Mamma said it was a Tony Faulkner asking for me, I was nonplussed.

"Hello, who are you? Where are you from?"

"It's Tony Faulkner from Newport, David."

"Tony Faulkner? Never heard of you, mate. Do I know you? I've heard of Charlie Faulkner, the old Pontypool prop."

"That's me, you daft bastard: I'm Charlie Faulkner. This is Charlie Faulkner speaking."

"So who's Tony Faulkner?"

"It's a long story, Bish, and I haven't got time. Do you fucking well want to play for Newport or not? Yes or no?"

The penny dropped and Charlie quickly sold me the idea of a move to Rodney Parade. Pablo had gone to Newport from Ebbw Vale over the summer – there must have been another exotic tour in the offing – and as my unofficial agent, had again been singing my praises, just as he'd done with Ebbw Vale. Charlie rang again on the Thursday, and I gave him my solemn word, although no registration forms were signed or anything. I'd play for Vale on the Saturday and see him at Newport for training the following week. Job done.

Come the Saturday, Ebbw Vale were decimated by injury and unavailability and we got hammered 49-0 by a full-strength Pooler team, who were at full bore. Strangely, I enjoyed probably the best match of my senior career so far, both in attack and defence. If it's possible to be Man of

Joining Pooler

the Match in a team that gets stuffed 49-0, I was that man. Everybody was saying so, even Pooler fans in the clubhouse bars afterwards. It was all slightly surreal.

I was chuffed with myself but also nervous as I sipped a pint up in the players' bar at Pooler, a cosy little inner sanctum tucked away up in the roof, or so it seemed, and only accessible by about three flights of stairs. How to break the news to Ebbw Vale? This was awkward, but then the coach Arthur Lewis and a few Ebbw Vale committee men wandered over. Arthur was well-connected. He had friends everywhere. He knew. It was the moment of truth.

"We hear you're off to Newport, Bish," Arthur said, without any rancour or anger. "I don't suppose there's anything we can do or say to change your mind? You've been great for us, and I think we've brought the best out of you as well."

I started to well up. It doesn't take much to get me started, even today.

"Sorry, guys. Ebbw Vale have been fantastic. You've supported me so much and I've enjoyed every moment here, but guys, I need to move. You know how it is."

They nodded in resignation. Scores, possibly even hundreds of promising players in Gwent have made the same journey to Newport and other bigger clubs. It was a time-honoured tradition, a well-worn path. The so-called Big Five rarely bothered with the north Gwent clubs – they assumed that if you were any good, you'd already have migrated to Newport or, if you were a forward, Pontypool or occasionally Cardiff. It was a process of natural selection that made their job easier. The big clubs would sort the wheat from the chaff for their regions... but they were very wrong. Clive Burgess, for example, should have had 30 or 40 caps, to name just one who stayed loyal to a smaller club. He was class all the way, but nothing would budge the Welsh selectors on this one.

Having dealt with that excruciating moment, I skipped down the stairs two at a time to the big supporters' bar down on the ground floor. A weight had been lifted. Time to go home. Walking into the bar, I saw Dad chucking a whiskey down his throat, surrounded by a bunch of Pooler bigwigs and players.

A big, thick-set bloke, mid-fifties and still wearing his donkey jacket, stuck a huge paw out to shake hands – rather formally, as if it was his privilege rather than mine.

"David, Ray Prosser. Very well played today... I've been talking to your father. I hear you're joining those black and amber bastards. Why would anybody fucking well do that? No good ever came out of moving to bloody Rodney Parade. What have you got to say, son? Explain yourself."

A bloke I recognised as Bobby Windsor joined in and didn't spare his old mate Charlie Faulkner from the mickey taking. "Going to play with Charlie and his lot? What the fuck are you thinking about? That's unbelievable, Bish. Get a grip, man, you can do much better than that."

I looked to my dad, wanting and needing a bit of support, not to mention a quick getaway. It had been painful enough making the decision to leave Ebbw Vale, but now it was done, I was happy to be heading to Newport. Decision made, job done. But Dad was seemingly in no hurry, and it suddenly dawned on me that he might have been plotting something with Pross, and that this was a pre-arranged ambush.

"Dad, let's go, I'm going out tonight with Kate, remember? Let's fuck off and get out of this madhouse."

Pross then puts his hand on my shoulder in a very fatherly way. The charm offensive was now fully underway.

"David, why don't you come and play for us? You should be here with us at Pooler... We're playing Australia in a few weeks' time; do you want to play? If you come and train with us, I guarantee you a start against Australia. Join us, be my scrum half and this fucking team will fly, and that will be down to you son."

Talk was cheap: where were the guarantees? How on earth could anybody guarantee me a start against the Aussies and that I'd immediately become an integral part of that team? I started to protest along those lines and then looked over at Pross and Bobby, and also assistant coach Ivor Taylor, who'd now joined the conversation, and suddenly realised what a huge gaffe I'd just made. Pross was Pooler and Pooler was Pross. If he was offering me a place at the club, it *was* guaranteed. If he said I'd start against Australia, bar injury, I *would* start. He was the main man, the Godfather, the boss supremo and everything in between. This was his kingdom and his power there was absolute. What he said was gospel.

Pross sensed I was beginning to bite, but decided to absent himself from the next part of this dramatic scene. He exited stage left, muttering something about needing to find a decent cup of tea – he didn't drink much alcohol at this point, as I recall – and instead we were joined by a large, roly-poly end-of-the-pier sort of individual: Peter Lawlor. He was the club chairman and sponsor, who essentially bankrolled the club at the time. Peter, as ever, was wearing his distinctive garish tweed jacket and very expensive sheepskin coat, both of which were well-known at the rugby clubs of south Wales.

Peter turned and addressed me directly.

"David, welcome to Pontypool. I understand you might be interested in joining us. Do you drive? Yes? Good. I'll give you a car for your use and free petrol if you're to join the club. Obviously, you'll need transport."

"Well, that's very generous, Mr Lawlor, but I'm getting £40 a week expenses at Ebbw Vale and Newport have promised to look after me very well. They reckon they can afford to give me..."

I wasn't allowed to finish my sentence. Peter was warming to his task.

"I'll also give you £200 a week to cover all the many expenses which you'll naturally incur playing with Pooler. Clearly, we wouldn't expect you to be out of pocket."

I was all ears now. £200 a week. Bloody hell, this conversation had taken a dramatic turn.

"Plus £10 a point and £5 a try. Hopefully there'll be lots of points and tries."

"Well, yes, of course, Mr Lawlor – I'd be trying very hard, obviously."

"Yes, of course, And by the way, have you got a mortgage, David? No, that's a shame, you should get yourself on the property ladder as soon as possible. But never mind. Instead, I'll offer you and yours three weeks' holiday a year in one of my houses in Spain. Flights included, naturally."

Naturally! Although, funnily enough, that was an offer I was never able to take up. My head was spinning... Pontypool were making it abundantly clear that they wanted me, and the extras were very enticing indeed, but they weren't the clincher. You'll have to believe me when I say that it was the guaranteed start against Australia and my dad's hero, John Hipwell. Barely six months earlier, I'd been leading a team of thieves, armed robbers, murderers and sex offenders against a Prison Service XV behind barbed wire on a converted football pitch at Aylesbury nick. And now here I was, with the

Joining Pooler

chance of playing against Australia at Pontypool Park. Put in a good performance there and Wales would begin to take notice, and I'd be on my way... The money and goodies were the cherries on the cake, although very welcome cherries. Thoughts of joining Newport just disappeared in an instant. Sorry, Charlie.

In retrospect, the meeting and dramatic turn of events in the Pontypool clubhouse after that game with Ebbw Vale weren't quite as spontaneous as I thought. Pross had a scouting network second to none, and virtually every player in Gwent had been tracked at some stage. A few years later, I was talking to Ivor casually and he mentioned that he'd travelled to watch me – and a few others – in those pre-season sevens tournaments with Ebbw Vale that late summer before I'd joined, and had reported back to Pross that he'd seen Wales' next scrum half. And the next openside flanker, for that matter, because Ivor gave Shaft a five-star rating too, and he also joined Pooler that autumn of 1981.

From that first meeting, there was an instant lifelong connection with Pross, which we can look at later. But it was far from an instant love affair between me and Pooler generally. In fact, if I'm brutally honest, the relationship could be a bit rocky, although the fans quickly adopted me.

Many at the club, including senior players and many long-serving committee men, were deeply suspicious of me. I was a flash Cardiff git, a thug who'd been inside. I knew nothing of life in the Gwent valleys and the tough mining communities up the road, nor what the club meant to everybody in the locality. I didn't have much respect for elders and betters, and reputation meant nothing to me. I wasn't concerned with the Pooler hierarchy. I was teacher's pet, brought in over the heads of many others by Pross. I habitually turned up later than I was supposed to for matches – although what they didn't know is that it was never by neglect, it was always by intent. I hated arriving early at grounds, sitting around and making nervous small talk in changing rooms, endlessly reading the programmes before a game. It made me feel anxious and nauseous. After the games I sometimes left early to head back into Cardiff and the bright lights, and that was wrong in the eyes of some as well. They perceived me as not being a dedicated trainer, which was completely untrue – my methods were just different. I kept fit for 12 months of the year. I topped up with big sessions in the boxing gym, I played sevens every spring and August, when many players were on the piss, and I played baseball at least twice a week in the summer as well. Very few at Pooler had got a handle on me at this early stage, although in the fullness of time I became firm lifelong friends with the likes of Eddie Butler, Peter Lewis, Lyndon Faulkner, 'Madman' Chris Huish, Mike Goldsworthy, Roger Bidgood and Mark Brown, in particular.

Everybody at the club, however, totally believed in Pross and his decisions, and that gave me more than a little breathing space. Ray Prosser had seen something in me, and they definitely respected that. I was the chosen one; they wouldn't rock the boat, but I'd have to work extra hard to win them over completely.

I didn't make it easy for myself in those first few weeks at Pooler, because I suddenly started playing like a drain. My early-season form deserted me just when I needed it most. There are valid reasons, which I'll list... but when you're the new boy on the block, nobody wants to hear excuses.

To begin with, I picked up the first major concussion of my career in the first ten minutes of my debut against

Joining Pooler

Aberavon at the Park, although of course we didn't call it concussion back then: it was just a head knock. Anyway, after this head knock, I couldn't remember anything from the game, and I didn't feel right for a few weeks – including in the match against Australia, to be honest. I was a second slower in everything I did, and nothing was coming easily and naturally. I felt sluggish, as if I was half drugged or going down with flu, and operating at 75%.

And then there was the change of circumstances. I was no longer a talented young maverick from whom everything good could be viewed as a bonus. I was a big new signing of whom much was expected, and I'm assuming – given how no secrets remain secret for long at rugby clubs – that most of the squad had a fair idea what I was being bunged in financial terms. Some would have been resentful, whereas those with good jobs probably didn't give a stuff. The old 'amateur' days were odd like that. There was, however, real pressure on me to perform, and promising Man of the Match displays in defeat and adversity simply weren't good enough any more. Now I was required to guide Pooler to victory twice a week.

And finally, I was confused. At my first training session, after a few warm-up stretches and laps of the Park, we broke off into forwards and backs and I went off to introduce myself to my new fly halves and three-quarters, to sort a few calls and signals out.

"Where the fuck are you going, Bish?" shouted Pross. "Get your arse over here… scrum halves train with the forwards at Pooler. Let those useless lily-livered bastards with two fucking numbers on their backs get on with it with Ivor. He'll sort them out. You can have five minutes with them at the end if you want to introduce yourself."

Given the obvious importance attached to the Pooler forwards, I was expecting to be operating behind a totally dominating mean-machine pack that blew everybody away, but the reality was far from that. To a certain extent, the entire Pooler pack thing was a bit of a myth by 1981 – a myth we took good care to perpetuate, mind. It was the great con trick of the mid Eighties in Wales, and only a few rumbled us. At their peak in the Seventies, with that front row in their roaring prime and Terry Cobner directing things from the back row, I can well believe they ate opposition packs for breakfast, but that was then. By 1981 and then onwards, it was different. We were rarely the biggest and strongest at set pieces – far from it – and we could struggle on occasion. What we did have was the aerobically fittest club pack in Wales, Britain and possibly beyond. The Pooler pack could keep going forever, and when opponents were wilting in the last 20, the Pooler eight would suddenly assume control and boss affairs. They would accelerate into the distance just when the opposition were hitting the wall. It's not much more complicated than that. Speed endurance was our pack's superpower, and that's why, at the death, you'd get hugely lopsided scorelines that suggested total domination, whereas in fact it had been pretty even for an hour. Unmatchable fitness was Ray Prosser's Holy Grail, and he was way ahead of the game in that respect.

For those first 55–60 minutes or so, we often struggled to dominate up front and it took a bit of getting used to for me, the interloper expecting a red-carpet ride at scrum half for the full 80 minutes. Pross always likened it to an arm wrestle – and arm wrestling was a big thing at Pooler amongst the boys, if I recall: it was considered a true test of strength and everybody used to challenge each other. When you arm wrestle, you'll be there face to face and for the first few minutes nothing really happens either way. Sometimes your opponent might even gain the advantage a little and you have to dig in. And then, just as suddenly and with no warning, they weaken, you get on top and in no time, you've completely recovered and are forcing their hand down to the table. The capitulation is often instant, the victory total. To this day, it's still the best analogy I know as to what happens, more often than not, on a rugby field. The trick is to never be the one who cracks physically: always be the person and the team that raises their game and intensity at that key moment late in the piece. Combating that was nigh on impossible, although of course having eight replacements these days has made 80-minute fitness almost optional for over half the team. That's probably the biggest single thing wrong with the modern-day game. Don't get me started.

So I was on a steep learning curve in those early weeks at Pooler, as well as struggling a bit from the concussion and, alas, I was a long way from my best come the big day against Australia. They paid Pooler the compliment of fielding one of their strongest teams outside the Tests, and sadly I was poor that day, as were the whole team, frankly. There was no platform up front. Terry Cobner had dropped out after breaking a cheekbone against Abertillery the previous week – a game I was playing in, come to think of it – and we missed his organisation and leadership. The pack didn't surge on the hour; in fact they were totally bossed from start to finish. I couldn't get anything going and was outplayed by my dad's hero John Hipwell, who might have been a veteran but moved around the field with an economy of effort, executing all the basics faultlessly in his own time. Watching him – and frankly I was reduced to being a spectator for long periods of the game – was like a walking, talking coaching manual. I'd never played with fly half Paul Crabtree before, which didn't help, and we were well shackled by a classy Wallabies back row of a young Simon Poidevin, Mark Loane and Greg Cornelsen. No second raters there. It was a huge wake-up call.

Looking back, for such an eagerly anticipated match, played in front of a record 20,000 crowd at the Park, our preparation was a bit shambolic. But the truth is, the Aussies were much too good. Sometimes you just have to suck it up. I was still only just turned 21 and my time would come. Soon after the match, I began to feel like myself again and play much better, and my optimism for the future returned. Little did I know that another life-defining moment was just around the corner. One way or another, 1981 threw the kitchen sink at me.

CHAPTER 9

Lucky to Escape with a Broken Neck

ON SATURDAY 28 November, a few weeks after the Australia game, we were down at Aberavon at the Talbot Athletic Ground, by the steelworks there, and it was going better personally. I was feeling more like myself. Aber could be a tough side at home, and we were just getting control midway through the second half when I went to tackle my opposite number (and old rival from Wales Youth days) Ray Giles as he made a break. I went in hard but a tad too high – overeager, nothing malicious or illegal – and slipped off him altogether and ended up on the ground rather stupidly in a sitting position and quite vulnerable. Ray was still in possession and had started squirming back towards me when he was hit hard by Shaft (Mark Brown) and another Pooler defender, and the three of them drove into me from behind, with my neck taking all the weight. Complete rugby accident. It'll happen 1,000 times and 999 times everybody gets up safely.

Not this time, though. I felt all my breath exit my body as I lay prone, face down in the mud. I tried to bounce back up as you always do, but nothing: the neural messages were blocked somewhere between my brain and my limbs.

Then I tried to just wriggle a toe or a finger. Nothing. Limp, lifeless.

I started to panic. 'No, no, no!' I cried to myself. 'This can't be happening.' Anything but this. I desperately wanted the last 10 seconds of my life back. Just 10 seconds ago I'd been a fit, healthy sportsman making – or rather missing – a routine tackle, and now this. I wanted that time back to do things differently. That's what I think people mean when they say their life races in front of them when something bad or life threatening's happening. Your first reaction is to try and reverse up mentally and do everything differently.

But it doesn't work like that. I lay there completely motionless for I don't know how long, before suddenly something like a massive electric shock followed by excruciating pins and needles spread throughout my body, from head to toe. My lifeless carcass jolted back to life agonisingly, my muscles started twitching crazily and I tried to get up again. There was still no joy on that front, but at least I could feel parts of my body trying to work and fire up. It was a start.

Our sponge man, Eddie Mogford, who'd seen every kind of injury over the years, came over looking more than a little worried, which didn't reassure me much. He already knew I never stayed down, no matter how hard the knock. Our captain for the day, Bobby Windsor, trotted over too. "You alright, Bish? C'mon – get up, man. We need you to help finish these bastards off." With that, he jogged back to the troops, seemingly unconcerned. He'd seen nothing to particularly alarm him. Tough man, Bobby.

I sort of hooked my arm into Eddie's arm and tried to drag myself up, and was almost upright when I felt extremely ill and faint and slumped back to the ground. Doc – our full back

Lucky to Escape with a Broken Neck

Peter Lewis, who was a junior surgeon at the Royal Gwent in Newport at the time – now sprinted over and thankfully took control. He carefully took my boots off and tried tickling my feet. No reaction. He could see it might be serious – I caught his slightly worried look to Eddie – and he ordered me to lie still and calm, and a stretcher was called for as he reassured me everything was going to be OK. People only say that when things are really not OK, don't they?

My entire body then went into an agonising spasm, wracked with nerve pain. I couldn't begin to straighten myself to lie on the stretcher. Eventually I was carted off curled up in the foetal position and taken directly to Neath General, where I was admitted to Casualty.

I was sedated a bit, I suppose, sent down for X-rays – just the standard X-rays, that's all local hospitals had back in the day – and eventually found myself stretched out on a bed on one of the wards with sandbags either side of my skull to stop me twisting and turning. I was feeling calmer, though, and such was my lack of comprehension as to what was going on that I was still wondering if I could make it back to Cardiff for the night out with Kate I had planned.

The men in white coats arrived. A serious neck-ligament pull or tear and probable spinal concussion to boot was their initial verdict. It would hurt like hell for a while and I'd have to be detained for a few days, but it wasn't too serious. I let out a sigh of relief and tried to get up, but still almost no reaction. No night out in Cardiff, but I'd be OK, and suddenly I was ravenous. I needed to eat, so sent the old man out for a Chinese takeaway. A couple of the Pooler lads and committee turned up and, as it didn't seem too serious, they headed home and presumably reassured anybody who asked that it wasn't as bad as at first suspected.

The next four or five days were a weird interim 'Phoney War' period. I didn't feel great but everybody said I was basically OK, and during the day I could get up and wander around the ward slowly, even if it did make me nauseous and dizzy with the pain. I had to wear a neck collar, though, and was still sandbagged when lying down. Dad and Kate came to see me, separately, every day. Dad wanted his son the rugby player back safe and sound; Kate just wanted her boyfriend back. Dad rattled on about rugby non-stop; Kate didn't mention rugby once.

Eventually it was decided I was OK to be moved by ambulance to the Cardiff Royal Infirmary, and although I was in a full plaster cast from the chest upwards for the journey – a bit like an item of body armour – I was apparently fine to walk into the ambulance before lying down, and to walk out of it at the other end. The journey was bloody uncomfortable, though, and I remember thinking this was much more painful than it should have been if, as I'd been told down at the hospital in Neath, I was to be discharged later that afternoon.

At the other end, it all started to go pear-shaped very quickly. Clearly at some stage very soon after my arrival, my X-rays from Neath followed and landed in front of the senior spinal specialist in Cardiff, Professor Brian McKibben, a brilliant man, who went ballistic at what he saw and came sprinting into the waiting area.

"Mr Bishop, stop right there! Whatever you do, don't move: you've got a broken neck, and we've got to be very careful. Do you understand, David? Don't move unless I say so."

Shit. Events had taken a massive turn for the worse. At least, that's what I thought at the time – I was in fact

Lucky to Escape with a Broken Neck

enjoying a huge stroke of luck, which possibly saved my life and definitely salvaged my sporting career.

Professor McKibben was issuing orders to all and sundry. I was oh-so-carefully laid on a trolley and immediately taken into an operating theatre, where it all started to kick off. My neck cast was carefully cut open and thrown in the bin and then, with no warning or fuss, somebody stabbed two bloody great needles into either side of my skull to administer a large quantity of local anaesthetic for what lay ahead. It was agony, and I yelled like a scalded 5-year-old. I'm useless with needles anyway – absolutely pathetic.

"Fucking hell, Doc! Are you trying to kill me, you bastard? This is agony." Not my finest or bravest moment.

"Be quiet, Mr Bishop, we're trying to do a complicated procedure. It will hurt a little bit but you rugby chaps can deal with pain, can't you?"

"Not this one, Doc. I'm a coward with needles."

About five minutes later I noticed the theatre seemed to be filling up with all sorts of nurses and assistant doctors, all rushing around busily preparing for some big procedure. One of them strapped my arms down to the operating table, then my torso was strapped down too, and people started to hover close by and put themselves in a position to help hold me in place as well. One of Professor McKibben's assistants started up what appeared to be a Black and Decker precision drill and started boring into my skull. I could smell and feel the bone splintering and see small shards of bone flying off to the side. It was still agony despite the anaesthetic, and I swore the house down again. I wasn't stoical and accepting, I was bloody terrified and in pain. And I was off my head with the drugs they were pumping into me. My language became very colourful.

"What the fuck are you guys doing, trying to kill me? You must be Scarlets supporters. You murdering Scarlets bastards. You've always hated me." Apparently I put on quite a show.

Finally they started to erect a steel-frame cage contraption, which they bolted into my skull using the holes they'd just drilled, and from which they could apply weights and traction on the neck. They cranked it up to something like 40 kg of pressure, from memory, with a thing that looked like one of those old car engine starters. It all seemed very basic and industrial. And scary. I thought my head was going explode and I was nearly blacking out with the pain. In fact, I prayed I *would* black out and be spared the worst of it.

Eventually I was back on the ward, on the bed with the contraption, feeling very alone. They'd let things settle for four or five days to see if the traction worked and the C3–C4 dislocation – for that was now my confirmed diagnosis – righted itself before deciding whether they needed to operate or not.

Dad had been badly spooked by the scene in the waiting area and the sudden drama over discovering I'd suffered a broken neck, not just damaged ligaments, and should never have been moving around. He was angry as hell, as only he could be, and went charging off to complain to the Welsh media, insisting he was going to sue all concerned for negligence. It was, he said, totally unacceptable and somebody had to pay the price for such gross incompetence. I could have died. As soon as I heard what he'd done, I was furious and told him to wind his neck in and immediately stop such ridiculous threats. Everybody was doing the best they could. Nobody was to blame. I'd been spared, luck was on my side for once, one of the top men in Britain was

Lucky to Escape with a Broken Neck

on my case and in the weeks and months ahead we'd need those medics on our side, not fearful of court cases. Having calmed down, Dad decided that my approach was the best.

The full enormity of everything did, however, start to dawn on me. This was serious. It was around this time that an official delegation composed of Pross and Pooler committee men in blazers and ties arrived. I caught Pross' eye as he came in and he couldn't hide his shock – he went white with horror. I could read his mind. I was a goner as a rugby player, and might never walk properly again. There was a lot of awkward looking at the floor, foot-shuffling and half-hearted banter. What can you say? And other than my very new developing friendship with Pross, I was scarcely even on nodding terms with most of them. I still didn't know many people at the club.

There was a much-needed moment of humour when, with a flourish, they produced my get well present: a basket of fruit, the sort you raffled off at 10p a ticket at the Labour Club or the Pooler clubhouse on a Saturday night, which is all bulked out with cardboard and crepe paper to make it look like you're getting basket brimful of goodies.

I looked at the basket and then them in amazement for a moment or two and decided to milk the moment.

"You bastards. I'm lying here with this bastard broken neck, my life in ruins, and you bring me a basket of fucking half-rotten fruit you wouldn't feed to the dog. Is that it? Guys, a couple of miserable rotting apples and bananas are not going to heal my fucking neck."

For a few seconds they looked down at the floor, appalled and embarrassed, until they saw my smile. Not even Pross had got a handle on my so-called sense of humour at this stage. The truth is, there was absolutely nothing they could have given me that day – other than a time machine to go back and not make that attempted tackle on Ray Giles – that would have made a blind bit of difference. There are some things money can't buy, and chief amongst them is your health and fitness.

It soon became clear that traction wasn't going to be enough and that I needed the full-on neck operation I'd been dreading. They'd take a big graft of bone from my hip and then fuse it into my neck to stabilise the C3–C4 joints. Even back in the early Eighties, it was a relatively straightforward procedure – tried and tested for a decade or more – but it was still a long operation and meant being knocked out for 7–8 hours; longer if there were complications. When you're under for that long, there's always the potential for things to go badly wrong. After drilling out a good-sized chunk of hip bone, they were going to put me on my front – I have no idea how they did that – and open me up down the back of my neck and go in that way. I have a ten-inch scar down the middle of my neck and into my back between the shoulder blades as a memento. At least I can't see it, which is a mercy.

Happily, nothing went wrong, Lady Luck hadn't completely deserted me. Mamma had apparently been praying around the clock and nipping into church three or four times a day to light candles and do her rosary, so perhaps the big man also lent a hand... I'd been spared the horrors of paralysis and immobility for life, but I had experienced a small but terrifying taste of what it might be like, and it was the stuff of nightmares – for me, anyway. Initially, as I lay there recovering, I had to be fed, which is a strange thing for a grown adult. For a while, I had to be turned every four hours, religiously, to prevent bedsores and infection, and it was a trial. I don't think I'm talking out of turn when I say that for such jobs there tends to be an A team and a B team at most hospitals. The A team are on during the day and everything seems a bit cheerier and more efficient. The B team work in the depths of night – they're probably knackered with sleep deprivation themselves – and aren't so well drilled or attentive. I used to dread the nights for that turning process alone.

If you wanted to watch TV, you had to wear these glasses with specially angled lenses, which mean you can watch the screen when lying down: clever stuff. I didn't know they even existed. One of the doctors told me that during World War Two, they developed a system where they used a specially adapted projector to beam films onto the ceiling of hospital wards so that injured soldiers, on their backs, could watch. You just don't think of these things.

Then there was the humiliating moment when I had to go to the loo for the first time. I don't mean having a pee – that's easy enough with a bottle once you get the knack. No, I mean the full Monty. I'd been constipated for the first week or so, from when I first went into hospital in Neath and then up to Cardiff. There came the moment when I could wait no longer, but of course I couldn't get out of bed, so my newly qualified nurse – a lovely girl by the name of Laura, if I remember correctly – had to oversee all that and dispose of the waste matter. Too much information, I know. It was humiliating to start with, but the only thing you can do is try to have a bit of a laugh, and it also helped that Laura was so professional. The job nurses do is amazing, and I couldn't have been prouder years later when one of my daughters, Natasha, chose nursing as her profession.

She would have hated to nurse me! I was an awful patient – angry, demanding and impatient. In my mind, I was through the worst. My neck was back in one piece, and it only needed a good, concentrated period of rehab and everything would be absolutely fine. It would be just like getting back from a knee or ankle injury. Hospitals were for sick people, and I wasn't sick. I was David Bishop, future Wales and Lions scrum half. I was on the mend and going places. I needed to get out ASAP.

I had no idea how much my body had deconditioned in just a few weeks, and with the stresses and strains my neck had been though, and all the nerve damage. In truth, I needed to take it very slowly, but of course I knew better. I kept nagging away, made myself a pain in the arse and about five days before Christmas, they caved in and agreed I could be discharged on Christmas Eve. They started the discharging protocol. They had to bring me slowly off the traction and then sit me up in bed for a few hours at a time as I got my balance back. Then I'd sit in a chair by the bed for a couple of hours each day. And, finally, I was allowed to walk to the lavatory, although accompanied by a nurse. On the way back, I instinctively headed one of the Christmas balloons that was tied up outside the loo, football style, and got shouted at by the nurse, but I didn't care. I was on the way back. Nothing would stop me.

I'd spent the previous Christmas incarcerated at Her Majesty's pleasure, and wasn't going to spend another in what I viewed as a prison by a different name. It was way too early, but I'd made myself so unpleasant that they were glad to get rid of me, and I can only apologise very belatedly to all the staff. They were only doing their job. I felt there was an urgent need to return to normality and if I put the brakes on and took the cautious approach, I'd never get back to full health. Hospital wasn't for me. In the short term, it was a bad mistake, but in the long term I believe my eventual recovery was totally down to this self-generated urgency and momentum. I needed to blast out of the blocks and get up and running.

I got back home to Dad's pub and thought I'd sit around with my mates, but I felt awful and was helped up to my bedroom, where I grovelled on my bed, feeling like death warmed up. That night I tried to brazen it out and went to Midnight Mass with my dad at St Philip Evans Church, where Father Maguire was a family friend – I just wanted to feel things were normal – but again I felt bloody terrible and my body started to close down. I had to get back home and take to my bed with those horrible sandbag pillows pushed up against my temples to stop my head moving. I also had to wear what they call a Williams surgical collar, an elaborate neck-brace arrangement attached to what looked like a piece of medieval body armour, which I had to put on like an undergarment. Trying to sleep was a torment; amongst other things, it all felt very claustrophobic.

I should never have discharged myself, but when my dad phoned the hospital the following morning – Christmas Day – trying to get them to readmit me, he got short shrift from the staff I'd recently made myself so unpopular with. I could still come in for physiotherapy twice a week and of course they would continue to monitor me closely with follow-up appointments, but basically the message was: "You've made your bed, son: now lie in it. Good luck."

Fair play, I deserved that. After cursing for a while, I got my spirit back. That anger, that rage which has consumed me for much of my life, was driving me forward. I'd been blessed. By a miraculous stroke of luck, I'd dodged paralysis and I wasn't going to get better by lying around in hospital being a patient. And I was going to get back playing even if all the medics dismissed that notion. I never doubted it – ignorance of what might lie ahead was bliss. I was down to just under nine stone, I was skin and bones and my legs were like chopsticks. There was only one direction of travel and that was up.

I needed a co-conspirator, though: somebody who shared my dream. Of course, I turned to my best friend. My mum. Dad initially was fully with the medics – a return to playing was clearly completely unthinkable. But Mamma knew me. I was the firstborn, who arrived miraculously when she feared she was infertile. She knew me better than I knew myself. If I couldn't play sport and run free, I might as well be dead. Seriously. Sport was my salvation. She got that, and her strong Catholic faith also allowed her to take a fatalistic view. Whatever would be, would be – the important thing was to at least try again.

We talked a lot during those first few weeks back from hospital. Some of those conversations were uncomfortable for me as they rammed home what a selfish bastard I'd been. How my actions and behaviour had affected not just me but also others who I loved. Shamefully, that had never really occurred to me before.

Mamma found it horrendous when I was in prison; it was like having a limb cut off. The family was incomplete – her golden boy was missing. Between the two of us, we'd weathered my father's batterings and forced him to change his ways. I'd won that battle of wills and there was a certain degree of harmony when I was around. She felt safe. It left me in bits to hear of her suffering while I was away in Aylesbury. Apparently, at every meal for the whole year I was inside doing time, she laid my place at the table, going through the pretence that I was just back late from training and would turn up soon. The mental anguish took its toll. She couldn't sleep, became exhausted, started taking sedatives and anti-depressants to help her sleep, and became reliant on medication. That was all down to me, and it haunts me to this day. Mamma died comparatively early and the extra stress I brought into her life kills me. Her courage and determination inspired me then, though, and still does, long after her passing.

When I was back out of prison, for a short while life had been looking up, both for me and for her, before this new hell presented itself. But she didn't waver. We'd get through it. God would provide or decide. In hospital, she'd brought me a pendant of Saint Camillus De Lellis, the patron saint for the sick and suffering – and nurses as well, I think – and when I got out of hospital, she then presented me with a cross of St Jude (the patron saint of desperate causes) on a chain, which I wear to this day, every day. For the rest of my career, if I was at home in Cardiff, she'd splash holy water on me and kiss me on the forehead before I ventured out for a game and as long as we'd observed that ritual, her mind was at rest. I'd also do my own little routine out the back of the changing room or in the toilets before every game. We had all bases covered with the big man.

I started out with small steps, literally, and took it from there. Girlfriend and wife-to-be Kate, my other great support and crutch at this time, was a Trojan as well and the two of us started going for regular daily walks in Roath Park – slowly at first, maybe one lap. Then two or three laps at a quicker pace. Then striding out for an hour or more. Much more quickly than I'd ever hoped or expected, I felt my strength returning. It was like turning the key in the ignition in a car that had been well preserved but standing idle in a garage for years. The engine was still sound as a pound. I was still only 21 and my body hadn't stopped developing, and it felt like it was going into overdrive. A daily rush of energy engulfed me. Bloody hell, this was encouraging.

We were still on our own, though. Pontypool seemed to have written me off after their one and only visit to my hospital bed. I was an ex-rugby player, one who'd been a decent prospect but not a big name or an International. I was going to be OK in terms of walking again and not being massively disabled compared with others, so there'd been a happy ending of sorts, and in due course I'd find gainful employment somewhere, but obviously I'd never play again... And I was Cardiff, not Pooler. There were a few best wishes and good luck cards but no practical help, no physiotherapy back-up, no expert rehab – they just didn't have the wherewithal to get involved. Not even on a personal basis... I was yesterday's news. Nobody else in the world of Welsh rugby reached out either. I wasn't important enough. I was just a promising 'bad lad' – a recent Youth cap who'd played a few games for Ebbw Vale and Pooler: a very minor figure. Hopefully, I might eventually get to walk again properly, settle down a bit and perhaps get a job somewhere. Take up golf, all being well. And if I didn't, I would probably end up back inside for a long stretch. That was the word on the streets.

Rugby wasn't good at looking after its own back then, so it was down to me, Mamma, Kate and a few close friends. And my vivid imagination. The *Rocky* films were big around this time – *Rocky* and *Rocky II* had recently come out – and, being a boxer myself, I shamelessly modelled myself on the Sylvester Stallone character, Rocky Balboa. I'd work my way back to fitness just like Rocky, and the *Rocky* music became the soundtrack, in my head, that accompanied my rehab.

My walks in Roath Park became gentle jogs, and then one day I started lengthening my stride and running flat out. Bloody marvellous. Now, I'd never given a second thought to running as a means of training and improving myself as an athlete. I kept fit by playing sport 24-7 – my fitness was a participant's fitness – but now I started to look forward to my runs. Around this time, *Chariots of Fire* was also released and another brilliant, inspiring sport anthem started swirling around in my head: another soundtrack to my comeback. What with *Rocky* and *Chariots of Fire*, I was starring in my own little film, if you like. Ridiculous, obviously, but whatever mental tricks it took to fire me up and give me belief. I was going to play rugby again if it killed me – literally.

Miraculously, my muscle bulk returned and by early summer I had a base of four or five months of walking and running in my legs. I'd thrown away all my neck collars and supports and it was time to step things up, so I took myself down to Driscoll's Boxing Gym, which was something of a Cardiff institution, above the Royal Oak pub. Jim Driscoll, as I mentioned earlier, was the great hero of Irish Town, an underdog who reached the top, and this was apparently the very gym where he put all the hard graft in. Back then, the place was littered with the memorabilia of his incredible life, and I took inspiration from his story. The whole boxing thing fitted in perfectly with my mindset. This was a no-holds-barred fight that I simply had to win. To lose was to die, as far as I was concerned.

I was back in my element at Driscoll's. Speed ball, heavy-bag work, shadow boxing, skipping and circuits. Press-ups, burpees, squats, star jumps, tricep curls, bicep curls, neck-strengthening exercises, stretches, ropework and all the rest of it. Two hours every other day, often with music blaring out. None of it felt like hard work. I was a free man, not imprisoned. I was walking and running, not paralysed for life. I had nothing to complain about. I was alive again and beginning to buzz. When could I play rugby again?

The medics were thoroughly alarmed at that prospect. It was complete madness, they said. Dad and I had a very tense encounter with Professor McKibben, who remained in overall charge of my case and was a man who commanded instant respect. He didn't pull any punches. He had better things to be doing than waste any more time and energy on me and my so-called comeback. I'd come within a millimetre of complete paralysis and another bad knock to the neck would kill me instantly. If the new, grafted vertebrae snapped, it would be with a mighty wrench and I'd be dead before I hit the ground. I needed to be grateful and just get on with my life. Everything from this point onwards was a bonus. "Don't waste your second chance, David." He agreed I could continue, under supervision, with my running and gym work but on no account was I ever to do kamikaze stuff like playing rugby or diving. He was angry.

"Diving? You mean scuba diving on the coral reefs, and all that? Surely that would be OK, Prof? Or would it put pressure on my neck?"

"No, David, I didn't mean scuba diving. That's probably OK up to a point, although don't go too deep. I mean high-board diving down at the pool, that kind of stuff. You're never to even think of it."

My dad was nodding enthusiastically in agreement and diplomatically said what the Prof wanted to hear: "David's very grateful for everything you and the surgical team have done for him and realises that he's lucky as hell not to be in a wheelchair. He'll be sensible from now on and repay your hard work and dedication."

I kept quiet but inside I was bloody fuming, absolutely raging. The Prof was writing me off, but he didn't know me. I wasn't his normal sort of patient – that was my arrogance or self-confidence kicking in. I would now show him. The medics aren't always right. They deal mainly in theory, not practice. Dad had to get back to work so I went straight home and told Mamma of the conversation.

"What are you going to do, David?" she asked, knowing that I would never take no for an answer.

"What am I going to do, Mamma? Where are my bathers? Can you dig them out? I'm going straight down the Empire Pool and I'm going to fucking well dive off the top board. Now, today, this afternoon. That's what I'm going to do. Then we'll know, one way or the other."

And that's exactly what I did. Mamma didn't try to stop me; she just blessed me with holy water and found some loose change for the bus and the pool entrance fee.

"Good luck. I'll say a prayer while you're gone."

I got to the pool, changed and sprinted up to the top of the 10m tower. The shallow end of the swimming pool was quite busy and noisy but there was nobody in the diving end. And nobody watching by the diving boards that day would have realised the significance of what followed. This was crunch time. Would I live or die? That was the bottom line.

I was sick with nerves. I knew I might lose my bottle at the top if I stopped, so decided to jog straight to the edge of the board and go for it. It was my Hail Mary moment. Although I was a strong swimmer, there'd never been time to concentrate on that, what with my other sporting passions. I hadn't been down the pool since I was 13 or 14 and hadn't dived off a board since that day at Lake Garda. I was good off the high board but thought nothing of it. A box ticked, if you like, and bragging rights with my mates.

This time I was ticking the most important box of my life. I launched myself into space with a prayer and somehow pulled off a nigh-on perfect swallow dive, a perfect 10 from the non-existent judges. But how would I break the surface moments later? Would the lifeguards be diving in to drag out a corpse? As I plunged into the deep end and slowed down, with the water flooding up into my nostrils, I waited for something to happen. I wasn't quite sure what, but perhaps the paralysis of those first few seconds on the day of the accident in Aberavon. Or perhaps the moment of death Professor McKibben had warned me of, the moment when the lights simply went out.

I waited and waited and held my breath – both metaphorically and literally – but still nothing. Finally, I broke the surface, shook my head in amazement and then swam gently over to the steps, dragged myself out and sat down. Bloody hell: I was OK. I was alive and absolutely buzzing with joy, energy and renewed hope. I punched the air and screamed – well, swore! – very loudly.

One more dive, just to prove it wasn't a fluke and my return to health could be confirmed. This time I was much more deliberate. I walked slowly up the steps. I stopped at the top and then walked very slowly to the edge before standing as still as a statue, just like Tom Daley and those guys do. I collected my thoughts and stared down. If I could pull this second dive off, I really could do anything. This one wasn't about adrenalin, it would be measured and controlled. No more mental barriers. Complete this dive and it would be 'game on' for the rest of my life.

For the second time in two minutes, I took a leap of faith. Same result. Cracking dive, clean entry, no reaction, no pain; just a massive smile coming back to the surface. I was very animated and pumped up. I craved a round of applause, really, but of course nobody appreciated what they'd seen – that's if anybody had even bothered to glance over. I marched to the showers, towelled off, got dressed and hopped on the bus home, smiling all the way. It was probably the most joyous, triumphant moment of my life outside the birth of my two beautiful daughters.

Reliving this now, it might sound like I had a death wish, but there was logic to my madness. I wasn't going to settle for a life without sport and I had to get over this hurdle first for that to come true. If I died in the process, well, that was the price I was willing to pay, and with Mamma's blessing I'd found the strength to carry it through. God knows what she'd gone through in the hour and a bit it took me to get to the pool and back. I never really asked.

"I'm back, Mamma," I shouted as I rushed through the front door and threw my kit bag in the corner. We both knew exactly what I meant as I rushed to give her a hug.

"Well done, David. I've got some nice liver and bacon for tea: special treat," replied Mamma as she gently kissed the figure of Christ on the cross on her rosary beads and slipped them into her pocket.

***

Onwards, ever onwards. It was July 1982 and some of the lads at the Old Illtydians suggested I drop in and do some fitness work with them a couple of nights a week. Brilliant: great set of guys, many of them old mates from school, and I'd also played a year for their Youth team. So I did that and of course there were touch rugby sessions, and one night – without really giving it a thought – I found myself doing a contact session. No problems. I was really fit, and my body seemed to absorb the knocks with no issues.

The phone rang. The jungle drums had been beating. I was back in training, and it was British Lion Rex Willis. Did I fancy a run out for his team at the Aberaeron Sevens at the weekend? Did I ever! I loved sevens and Aberaeron was a cracking, high-quality summer tournament and a bit of fun out west down by the seaside… Just for the first couple of minutes in the first game I felt anxious, but then I was off and running and we won the tournament comfortably.

I got home and quickly discovered that my dad had got a whiff of what I was up to – he had contacts everywhere – and had also travelled down to Aberaeron and watched through binoculars from a great distance. We had heated words, as you can imagine, but he was a brilliant rugby mentor and as well as being angry, I could see he was also proud. He wasn't going to give me his full blessing yet as he was still on the medics' side, but he was definitely thawing.

More rugby at Old Illtydians. They had a couple of tidy scrum halves who I didn't want to take game time off, so I filled in mostly at flanker, where they were a bit short. Loved it. Late August and most of September I played, getting my confidence back. There must have been five or six games, and I was beginning to get the itch again. With all due respect to a great bunch of blokes, at this stage of my life, having been granted a second life, so to speak, I needed to be playing at a higher level.

Things began to happen very quickly. Pooler got absolutely thumped 33-9 down at Swansea one Wednesday night and looked set for a troublesome season. The following morning, I had their skipper Eddie Butler on the phone. Eddie was to become a great mate, my staunchest supporter and ally during hard times and just a bloody good bloke, but at that stage I only knew him a little from my very short, undistinguished spell with Pooler nearly 12 months earlier – although there had been a good rapport. Apologies in advance for the language!

"The Bish: how are you?" said Eddie. He always called me 'The Bish' as opposed to 'Bish', as if to confer some higher status on me.

"I see you're back playing again. Well done, mate. How do you fancy a game for us? We're struggling a bit. We were dire down at Swansea last night – I expect you heard about it. In fact, how do you fancy coming back for good, like straight away?"

"About fucking time I heard from you, Snooty! Where the fuck have you been all this time, hiding from me?" I replied, as I went off on one. I called Ed 'Snooty' because, despite being a chap from Monmouth School and Cambridge University, he was the least snooty bloke on planet Earth. Others at Pooler called him 'the Prof' or 'Bamber', after Bamber Gascoigne the quizmaster, but he was always Snooty to me.

"Not a bastard word from anybody. No help, no encouragement," I continued, venting as the built-up tension and frustration of the previous ten months came pouring out. "When did I become the fucking invisible man? One mangy basket of half-rotting fruit. Is that all I meant to Pooler? Back playing again? I've been playing for the Old lltydians for six weeks and you only get in touch when those

Swansea bastards make idiots of you down at St Helen's. Fuck the lot of you!"

I really let Eddie have it. A bucketload of resentment at the club came pouring out, but having got that off my chest, I felt a lot better. I was, in truth, ready for the 'big time' again. It was actually perfect timing from Eddie, and as I calmed down, we both knew it. Within five minutes, I'd committed to Pooler again. It was the start of my career proper, and I sometimes wonder if Pooler's great loyalty to me in the years to come was down to some kind of guilt complex about having pretty much abandoned me after my injury and during my rehab. My Lazarus act had taken them completely by surprise. They'd written me off. Everybody had, except for Mamma and Kate.

There was still one last fence to clear. Myself and Pooler soon kissed and made up, and I was back training. Then one night Tony Simons came over. Tony was the very hard-working team manager and match secretary. He did all the First Team logistics during his coffee- and lunch-breaks at work. One of the great men of Pontypool.

"Bish, the WRU have been on: we can't play you unless you're insured – bloody regulations – and to be insured, you'll have to get a specialist to sign you off as fit to play. It's not looking good, but let's see if we can find anybody."

So we were back to that again. The specialists in Wales seemed adamant I shouldn't play, so Pooler sent me off to Farnham Park in England, a state-of-the-art sports injury clinic (run then by the RAF, I think) for assessment. But their neck man took scarcely five minutes to refuse to sign on the dotted line either. I was a hopeless case. I could die. In fairness, I suppose it was too risky to their hard-earned reputation.

Back at Pooler, we looked at the WRU small print. It didn't specify that the insurance document had to be signed by a spinal or neck specialist, just an experienced orthopaedic surgeon and practitioner. That offered a shaft of light.

So, armed with a bottle of 15-year-old Glenfiddich and all my X-rays, I took myself off to see Doc Edwards, who was an old friend of my dad's from Glamorgan Wanderers. He was very wise and an orthopaedic specialist, a rugby man who was well-acquainted with my case. And, before anybody starts pointing fingers, he gave me a very thorough examination for an hour or more – every test known to man – and after studying all the X-rays in detail, eventually pronounced that my neck had healed stronger than ever and that the muscles supporting it were in great condition, which was true enough. I suffered many injuries throughout the rest of my career, but my neck was solid as a rock, absolutely rigid. I couldn't move it much to the left or right and had to move my torso when looking in either direction, and it can hurt like hell some days, but it's just about the only part of my body that hasn't subsequently let me down.

Doc Edwards also gave me the mandatory official warning that if I did ever get a similar neck injury, it would kill me rather than paralyse me. But, miraculously, having had his say, he then, with a sudden flourish, signed on the dotted line and I was free to play elite rugby again. I produced the bottle of Glenfiddich from my training bag, handed it over, shook his hand and said, "Thank you very much, Doc – you've saved my life."

Many years later, I spoke to him about it, and he told me candidly that he'd decided before our meeting to look at the positives rather than the negatives. Reasons he could use to justify me playing, rather than reasons to ban me once and for all. He knew me a bit, and he certainly knew the family and my case, and he was pretty certain that to turn me down was as good as signing my death warrant one way or another, and he was very reluctant to do that. He weighed up the odds – my neck had repaired in remarkable fashion, and he thought the percentage call was to officially let me play. He knew I needed that chance to fly again. For me, good doctoring isn't all about scans, tests and accepted norms. Sometimes you have to treat the psyche of the patient, and Doc Edwards knew exactly what I needed to heal myself. If he gave me the green light, I would do the rest myself. It took some ticker from him to be the medic who said I could play again when others, possibly more expert in the field, had denied me that chance. There'd have been all sorts of grief if it had gone wrong and I suffered that one-in-a-million second broken neck, but he made the decision anyway. Doc Edwards tops the list of those, some no longer with us, who I belatedly need to thank properly.

Only twice in the rest of my career did I feel nervous on a rugby pitch on account of my neck. There was the first game I played back down at the Talbot Athletic Ground against Aberavon, when the events of that day came rushing back to me. Then, much later, there was a brutal League game in Papua New Guinea with Great Britain, when two of the local boys decided to tip me up and looked to pile-drive me head first to into the ground. I threw the ball away, went into the crash position and writhed and wriggled to make sure I landed on a shoulder or the top of my back. Luckily it worked and I survived to tell this tale.

To this day, the muscles in my neck can suddenly lock into a fierce, painful spasm and I have to sit there with a hot towel to try and ease it off, but actually the most painful reminder is the chronic arthritis on occasion, from where they quarried out a lump of my pelvis. That can feel like a deep hole in my back, but even when it's horribly uncomfortable and I'm fidgeting away, trying to find a comfortable position to sit, I consider it a small price to pay. It could have been so much worse.

CHAPTER 10

Cup Glory with Pontypool

IT'S EARLY OCTOBER 1982. I'm back in the fold, and this is when my Pooler story starts in earnest. I arrive back there with steam coming out of my ears and all I want to do is play rugby. A year in prison followed by a fortunate parole, 11 months out with a broken neck and a miracle recovery. I'd come through all of that, and now was the time for action. I was a man in a hurry.

Pross was there backing me. He never doubted my ability, he just didn't think he'd see me playing rugby again after the neck injury and that depressing visit to hospital. I was incredibly fit. I'd taken the intensity of my neck rehab into all my overall fitness, and what with games at flanker for the Old Illtydians, workouts in the boxing gym and pre-season sevens tournaments, starting with my playing comeback at the Aberaeron Sevens, I was ready to go. I was nervous but confident at the Old Parish, where we faced Maesteg in my comeback game, and personally it went very well, with a try from me rounding off our 30-3 win. A big mental hurdle successfully cleared. With my mind cleared of all doubt, and a full bottle of holy water in my kitbag at all times, I looked forward to our next game: at home to Gloucester.

Cup Glory with Pontypool

I may possibly have played better in my career up to this point, but I don't think so. I was on fire from the start, Pooler generally were on it, and we thrashed the normally formidable Gloucester side 52-15, one of the heaviest defeats in their history at the time. I scored two tries and made a couple more, including a 75-yard break from under our posts to create a try for our wing, Bleddyn Taylor. That was the night the Pooler fans truly adopted me, and they stuck with me through thick and thin thereafter. I seemed to dominate all headlines the following morning. Peter Jackson in the *Mail* waxed particularly lyrical about one of the best individual performances he'd witnessed, and others were also lavish with their praise. I felt great, invincible. When you're really in shape, you reach a state of grace where nothing is a physical effort: the only exertion's in your mind. If you need to sprint 80 yards or whatever to make a try, you simply do it; if you need to sprint 80 yards back to make a try-saving tackle, ditto. No sweat, no raising of heart rate, no huffing and puffing. Totally in control of mind and body. You anticipate everything, you're where you need to be all the time, the game unfolds exactly as you dictate. If that's what being in the zone is, I was in the zone that night for sure – and most of the season, to be honest.

It was also the night that Pross decided to give me my head. Up until the Gloucester game, his plan, I think, was to get myself and the pack working in close harmony and dominating games that way. It was the modus operandi Pooler had perfected in the past, but with a dangerous strike-runner and try-scorer at scrum half to up the ante. I'd add a sharp cutting edge around the fringes to cash in on the forward dominance we normally enjoyed in the final quarter. But after the rout of Gloucester, he had a rethink.

Mind you, not before he'd taken me aside straight after the game and given me a bollocking for running out from under our posts to make the wonder try for Bleddyn.

"Bish! What the fuck were you doing? That's madness. What was your thinking? With the boot you've got, you can get us 50 to 60 yards upfield with ease from a clearing kick. No risk involved. Build the pressure. Keep things simple, Bish – save the flash stuff for their 22, that's where you can unleash the fireworks."

"Pross, I've got no idea what I was thinking and why I do what I do most of the time. I just play on instinct and how I read the game," I protested. "If clearing's the only option, my instinct will say to clear, don't you worry about that. But if there's something else on, I'll go for it. We're the fittest team in the bloody country! Let's make that count: let's attack the opposition when they're blowing out of their arses. We can hurt them more that way."

He considered me and what I'd said for what seemed like a very long time indeed, as if he couldn't quite find the words to express his rage and disgust over this, and I was getting ready for another bollocking when he finally smiled. "You're right, Bish. You've got three legs to every other bugger's one, so you see it different. You can see different things. Just do what you need to do and we'll follow."

And that was that. For the rest of my Pooler career, I never had any instructions as such from Pross, just a licence to play heads-up rugby. The shackles came off, and I flew. That's not to say that we didn't still sometimes wear the opposition down in what was perceived as the old-style Pooler way – there were games when that was the correct tactical option, not least in some of our Cup matches later in the season – but on many occasions we opened up in pretty spectacular fashion, even if some in the media were in denial and gave us little credit. We scored many tries that would have graced the Barbarians, but they were barely acknowledged. I remember one length-of-the-field effort, midweek against Aberavon a couple of years later, which was as good as any I've seen. Bleddyn was again the man to dob it down. I might have been on a bonus payment per try, but our wings, Goff Davies and Bleddyn, were consistently amongst the top try scorers in Wales, which hardly supported the claim that we were a nine- or occasionally ten-man team and that Lord Lucan was alive and well on the Pontypool wing. People just lazily bought into the myth.

With a couple of exceptions, that 1982/83 season was a golden time for me. We finished second behind Swansea in the Merit Table, I scored 33 tries in 35 games and was the highest first-class club try scorer that season, and I got called into the Wales squad just a couple of weeks after my return to Pooler as one of three scrum halves in the Wales set-up – Terry Holmes and Mark Douglas being the others. Mark was a pretty decent, strong player but I knew I could see him off, so in my mind, I felt this was the chance to nail down my position as Terry Holmes' deputy and his obvious successor. I'd be on the bench for the Five Nations and hopefully in contention for the Lions tour of New Zealand, which I'd been sounded out for.

We endured a small hiccough – reaction, more like – to that incredible win over Gloucester just a few days later, when we travelled to Bedford and somehow managed to lose 16-15, I think it was. Goldington Road was not a happy hunting ground. Doc, Peter Lewis, wasn't available, and we travelled without any recognised goalkicker and butchered seven or eight shots at goal. Eddie Butler even took two kicks, can you believe – one from halfway. His dad might have been a footballer for Wycombe Wanderers but Snooty hadn't inherited his kicking genes. Nobody seemed to know or remember that I could kick, but eventually I suggested I had a go and I put a couple of kicks over. But then, with a simple last-minute penalty to win the game, I slipped and fell on my arse as I was kicking, and sliced it miles wide. It was a very long ride home; we'd let ourselves down and were determined that wasn't going to happen again.

It was just a minor blip, though. Pooler didn't look back after that. No, my only other major disappointment of the season was a game for Monmouthshire against the New Zealand Māori, which cost me dear – not least my place in the Wales set-up. Wales were playing the Māori ten days later in what was being treated as Test match, and my performance against them for Monmouthshire saw me fall out of contention. I'd scored 14 tries in the seven games since my comeback and was bossing every match save for the trip to Bedford, but that purple patch of form came to an end at Rodney Parade when we lost 18-9.

I wasn't completely disastrous – in fact, plenty of my tactical kicking and long touch-finding was good – but the Māori had been doing their homework and targeted me defensively. And I was a bit slow to appreciate that and didn't mix my game up enough and give Paul Turner at fly half more options. I was naive, and very disappointed afterwards. Media expectations – and mine too – had been high, but I failed to deliver.

I knew it would cost me in terms of my Wales prospects and the Five Nations, as only established players were given any leeway, but I bounced back quickly with Pooler. I talked it through with Pross, who told me not be impatient. Slightly less than a year earlier I'd been bolted to a neck brace in hospital, wondering if I'd ever walk properly again, let alone play any kind of rugby. I'd made remarkable progress, all things given, and I was still young, both in years and experience. With that year in prison and nearly a year out injured, I had virtually no miles on the clock at senior level since leaving Youth rugby. I was raw, still learning and there would bumps on the way. In future I'd know that if a side were targeting me and virtually man-marking me, that meant there would be more scope for the fly half. I needed to learn game awareness and management and how to adapt, and consistency of performance was another thing I needed to work on.

With my mind eased by our chat – and in fairness Dad made all the same points when we had our normal match debrief – I immediately picked up with Pooler from where I'd been before the Māori game. Noting was going to stop me, and from the off I was telling everybody this was Pooler's year in the Cup. That was received with a bit of a raised eyebrow because, for all their success in the Seventies under Terry Cobner, when the Pontypool Front Row reigned supreme and they smashed everybody up front, the club had never done itself justice in the Cup. Pooler's USP was consistency of effort and intensity over a 50-game season, whereas others – notably Cardiff, Swansea, Bridgend, Llanelli and Aberavon – seemed able to go up another level in the Cup. They were great Cup teams and Pooler weren't, and we needed to change that.

We started with a gentle run out at Pontypool Park against junior opposition from west Wales – Pontarddulais, from down Swansea way, who we beat 52-0, with me scoring three of our ten tries. The opposition immediately got much tougher in the second round, when an in-form South Wales Police visited the Park. The Police were a funny team at the time, and it annoyed many on the circuit that you sometimes only needed to play a handful of games for them to get a Wales squad call-up. Funny that. But at various times they could be pretty useful, especially behind the scrum, where they were headed up by Bleddyn Bowen and Richie Donovan. They really took the game to us, and it was just 15-13 on the hour before we finally nudged ahead – through the boot of Peter Lewis – to win 27-13. Goff Davies and I scored tries, but essentially it was one of those Cup games where you just have to roll your sleeves up and get over the winning line. Most of our Cup games in this season were like that, to be honest.

Come the third round and we were on the road to South Glamorgan Institute at their Cyncoed ground. For me it was virtually a home fixture, being just a mile from The Retreat pub, which Dad was running and where we lived at the time. We had the entire Pooler team back for drinks and food afterwards, but first we had to do a job of work against the students. As ever, they had a few promising backs – Geraint John, who was considered a top prospect at the time, Phil Steele, Chris Hutchings, Shaun McWilliams – but could be dominated upfront. Our pack also got to Geraint early in proceedings, which dented his confidence, and my memory is of a much bigger and more comfortable win than the 28-8 scoreline suggests. I scored a try for the third consecutive round and also popped over a drop goal, getting my eye in for later in the tournament.

Next up, the first big one and a home fixture against Cardiff, who'd won the last two Schweppes Cup Finals and always relished the tournament. This would be the acid test as to my conviction that it was Pooler's year. Despite a strong run of form, I could sense Pooler still had a hang-up regarding Cardiff in the Cup, probably dating back to a tie before my time when Pontypool dominated proceedings, only for Gerald Davies to clinch a famous win for the visitors with four brilliant tries. The media also made Cardiff strong favourites. This was going to be tricky.

It should also have been a much-anticipated showdown between myself and Terry Holmes at scrum half, but that got derailed. Terry had injured his shoulder the week before, playing for Wales at Murrayfield, and was very doubtful all week before eventually withdrawing, while I was struggling with a tight hamstring as well. Shit! I was living for that one-on-one with Terry: a good game against the incumbent Wales scrum half would count heavily with the Big Five, surely, and even if they weren't watching, perhaps the Lions selectors might stand up and take notice. There was so much to love about Terry's game but the thing I admired most – envied, as well – was that you couldn't get at him. Opposing packs could try all sorts, but you could never ruffle his feathers and he was stronger and tougher than most of the opposition's forwards. And he was an absolute menace breaking around the fringes. Alas, our little one-on-one wasn't to be.

I was eventually declared fit for a game that quickly developed into an old-fashioned arm wrestle. We didn't want to let Cardiff play wide so put a stranglehold on them upfront, and of course it got very physical.

Clive Norling, the best ref I ever encountered by some distance, was in charge and tempers were fraying early on. I got caught at the bottom of one ruck in front of the Bank and John Scott gave me a right good shoeing, a thorough working-over. Scottie was a hell of a player, a really hard man but talented as well, and I'm amazed he didn't win 50 or 60 England caps. He should have been on the 1983 Lions tour as well. For an English player to be as respected and feared as he was, playing week in, week out in Wales, says all you need to know about the man. We got on very well, me and Scottie, but not on the pitch.

The Pooler fans went mad after the ruck incident, baying for blood. Five minutes later, my opportunity came to plant a retaliatory punch on Scottie, which I considered fair retribution. It wasn't a haymaker or knockout punch, but it needed to be done and Scottie wasn't amused. Norlo called us both over for a chat.

"I see what you done, Scottie, and I saw what you did, Bish – now cut it out, the two of you. You're no bloody good to your side sitting in the stands, and that's where you're going if there's any more of that. Now get on with the game." And that was that. I'm not sure he even penalised me for the punch – it was just, "Stop being idiots."

Norlo was a great communicator, although in my experience he rarely called out players like that and lectured them in public. What he liked to do as we ran around the pitch was have a whispered word on the hoof, nipping things in the bud before a situation erupted. "Calm down, Bish. I can see what they're doing, and I'll ping them next time," or "That's enough, Bish. I saw that little dig: not necessary. No more nonsense." It was brilliant game management. Even back then, over 40 years ago, he much preferred to keep the game ticking over and flowing. For some reason – possibly his tight shorts? – Norlo had a reputation for trying to be the centre of attention, but I found him quite the opposite as a ref: he just took quiet control. It was the game that mattered; the game had to be the only thing fans and the media were talking about. He was another who was treated badly by the WRU down the line, which only increased my respect and liking for the man. I was always pleased to see Norlo's name in the programme before a game.

Anyway, back to the Park and Cardiff. The game simmered most of the 80 minutes but Norlo was on top of it and, despite the close 13-9 score, I felt we had control most of the time, and Cardiff kept shooting themselves in the foot by missing penalty attempts. Our pack had won the war of wills and was in charge in the last quarter, and we had another gear if we needed it. We should have won more comfortably, but who cares: Cardiff were considered our bogey team in the Cup, and the bottom line is that you win most Cup matches ugly. Rarely do you get to put on a show.

Pooler were sniffing it now and beginning to believe my confident predictions. Next up, it was Bridgend at the Talbot Athletic Ground, Aberavon, which felt like a home ground for them. I think we even objected and asked for a Cardiff venue, but the WRU weren't interested. I wasn't too bothered about that; I *was* a bit worked up, though – in a good way – about returning to the scene of my broken neck. Now, Bridgend were an interesting team: Cup specialists who'd appeared in the last four Cup Finals, winning the first two and then losing those two matches against Cardiff. They had a tasty back division with Gerald Williams and Gary Pearce at half back, good gas on the wings with Mark Titley and Glen Webbe, and a fast, mobile pack. We had to be at our very best.

We were. Our 16-3 win was our best performance of the entire Cup run, and a much more commanding victory than the scoreline might suggest. Gary Pearce, my old mate from Youth rugby, gave them the lead with an early penalty, but we tore into them after that. I was wide with a 50-yard drop goal attempt, but then came tries by Bleddyn Taylor and myself. After the break, we polished them off with a drop goal from Mike Goldsworthy and a second from myself – with a kick direct from a line-out which caused a big stir, with none of the greybeards in the press box recalling ever having seen such a thing before. We were some 30 yards from the Bridgend line and Steve 'Junna' Jones threw to John Perkins at the front of the line, who fed me. As I was setting myself up to receive the ball, I could see out of the corner of my eye that their back-row tail gunners were out of the blocks very quickly, looking to get Mike Goldsworthy, so I instinctively checked, shifted my weight and balance and – without looking – hit a peach of a drop goal with my right foot. Pross was beside himself when he saw me after the game. He couldn't get over it; like the scribes, he'd never seen that before. I was always on the lookout for a drop goal but, straight up, had never practised that particular one from that position, or even rehearsed it in my mind.

Ever since watching Gareth Edwards drop a goal against Ireland in the Five Nations on the TV when I was a kid, I was determined to make it part of my armoury even if most scrum halves steered clear of it. A few days after the Edwards effort on TV, I hit the crossbar with a belter against St Peter's Primary School, aged 8! In senior rugby I kicked a few – I remember one monster against Newbridge at the Rec – but only replicated the kick direct from a line-out once more, away to Abertillery one night. I should have used it even more as a tactic and I'm annoyed I didn't, I think it was considered a bit selfish for a scrum half at the time. It's a neglected part of the game. When I'm watching my old VHS tape of my solitary cap – which we'll get to in due course – I often shout at myself to have a pop. Just to break things up a bit and keep the scoreboard ticking over. Back then, though, winning my first cap, I was subconsciously frightened it would be thought overindulgent and that I should feed the fly half, who could make the decision as to whether to drop kick or not.

It's probably worth reiterating at this stage how much I based my whole game on Edwards, and what an influence his game was on me and how I viewed the role of a scrum half. I watched him live on the TV, and then I studied the tapes of his Test match appearances obsessively until they were worn out. It started with his passing technique – even to the extent that, although I could spin it as well off my left and as my right, I sometimes did that thing he perfected when attacking left to right, of turning my back and spinning it off my right hand. I used it sparingly but found I could get a much better view of our options behind, and on other occasions I used it as an opportunity to throw a huge dummy and nip back down the blindside. His kicking game was much overlooked. I particularly like the way he fired grubber kicks to find touch when it was all getting frantic and there wasn't time to lay back and hoist a big conventional kick. He took on the responsibility for touch-finding and tactical kicks much more than was usual back then – in Britain, anyway. The French scrum halves like to call the shots as well.

I did my fair share of what we now call box kicks, but I always tried to box kick into space, a bit more infield than most of them these days. Now they mostly try to work the tramlines, a much more conservative option. I liked to put the ball further infield than that, to sow confusion between their full back and his wings. There's a triangle of space between the fly half, full back and blindside wing, and if you can put it right in the middle of that, you're going to cause chaos, more often than not. The other advantage of that approach is that after two or three kicks like that, the blindside wing will automatically start creeping in two or three yards to anticipate your kick until, without them knowing it, they've left you with the opportunity to beat them on the blindside if you sprint off the base of a scrum or ruck. I used to love those kind of mind games, moving players around like pieces on a chess board.

I explained my thinking on this to Pross one time. He'd called me into the ref's room for a chat before training one night at Pontypool – he used the room to conduct little one-on-ones and pep talks with players. He wanted to talk through my kicking game and what my plan was when I put boot to ball. I gave him quite a lengthy explanation and at the end he just shook his head. "Bish, I've got no idea what you're doing, but it seems to be working so carry on. I trust you."

I was given the Man of the Match award after that Bridgend game and looking back, it was one of my best. I was breaking strongly, kicked and linked very well, and made some important tackles. Were there any Welsh or Lions selectors in the crowd? Probably, but were they checking me out? Who knows. My focus on Pooler winning was so great that for once I wasn't that bothered.

All of which brings us to the final. The biggest day out for the town in decades, possibly ever. Swansea lay in wait – and they were going for the double, having beaten us into second place in the Welsh Merit Table and in fact kick-started Pooler's revival with that big early-season win at St Helen's. They were stacked with quality players across the park, but our pack fancied they had the beating of their eight, even if Swansea had some hard cases in their ranks. And our confidence proved right. The build-up, as if it wasn't emotional enough, took on extra poignancy with the death of Ray Prosser's wife, Nancy, between the semi-final and final. Pross and his daughter had been caring for her for a good while, but it still came as a shock, and the whole club and town was grieving with him. They were devoted as a couple, and it didn't even have to be mentioned amongst the team how much Pooler's first ever Cup win would mean to him. "Whatever it takes," was our attitude.

Personally, I thought we could probably beat Swansea no matter what the nature of the game. We were a much more 'all-court' team than anybody else would give us credit for, but as mentioned, Cup rugby is different. The percentage call, the game plan which gave us the strongest probability of winning, was an old-fashioned stick-it-up-your-jumper effort upfront, augmented by myself at scrum half and Mike Goldsworthy at fly half. It wouldn't be pretty but we weren't bothered, and frankly I couldn't actually ever remember a pretty Welsh Cup Final up to that point. Even the so-called entertainers like Llanelli, Cardiff, Swansea and Neath had always kept it very tight. Swansea would be hoping, praying, that we'd allow the game to become an open, all-singing, all-dancing affair, and if that's what they wanted... we'd take good care to do the exact opposite.

Pricey was flying out with the Lions a few days after the final, but didn't once think of dropping out – he'd made two Lions tours before that, anyway – but Staff Jones was injured and Bobby Windsor took his place. Bobby was injured as well, but wild horses wouldn't have stopped him at least starting a Welsh Cup Final, and Mike Crowley was standing by to come on when Bobby inevitably conked out. Then

Eddie Butler dropped out on the eve of the final and Martin Jones came in at lock. That could have been very disruptive – in my experience, the few times the Pooler pack failed to perform came when Eddie was absent – but such was our focus that nothing was going to disrupt us.

Whatever it took. Our pack went to work, I snapped away at their heels and barked out orders for a full 80 minutes until I was hoarse, we didn't give Swansea and inch to breathe or to think, and we squeezed the life out of them. Doc, Peter Lewis, kicked four penalties and then later in the game, when we were leading 12-6, came the game's only try, when Peter went for a fifth successful kick, hit the post and Bleddyn Taylor followed up quickest to score.

Happy days. Pontypool's first – and still only – Welsh Cup win. I won the Man of the Match award, voted for by the Welsh journalists' association – although I'd probably have given it to Madman, Chris Huish, myself – and a big night of celebration followed. Sweet moment? You'd better believe it. Pooler had finally broken their Cup hoodoo and I – well, it felt like I'd come back from the dead, to be honest. I was overcome with emotion most of that night. And we'd given Pross a little bit of joy at a very sad time. A day for the ages.

Such was my appetite for rugby at this time, though, that I'd barely grabbed an hour's sleep after getting in when Mamma woke me with a cuppa and breakfast, handed me my kit – she'd got up at dawn to clean my boots and wash and dry my shorts and socks – and I was out the door and up the motorway in a minibus to play for The Tavistock pub in the Richmond Sevens!

That Sunday up in London, we had a decent squad. From memory, we had a good Bridgend contingent – Mark

Titley, Steve Penry Ellis and Gary Pearce – and we also had Spikey Watkins and David Fryer, who played a lot of sevens with Ebbw Vale and Newport, and a talented English playmaker, Ged Glynn from Sale, who we'd clocked at various tournaments. He met us at the ground. The craic on the way up was fierce and I got the impression I wasn't the only one who was short on sleep, but we were on fire in the tournament. We beat Blackheath, London Scottish, Met Police and Borough Road College before I got a try in extra time to help us to a 20-16 win in the final over a star-studded Wasps team. What a weekend!

Wasps' star man that day was Huw Davies, no less – my half back partner from Cardiff Rags. I really do need to reiterate what a hell of a player he was. My all-time pecking order at fly half is 1. Ringo, 2. Huw and 3. Jiffy, with an honourable mention for 4. Neil Jenkins, who's hugely underrated and also one of the very top blokes on the planet. England – thank God! – didn't have a clue what an outstanding talent they had on their hands with Huw, and kept messing him around and dropping him, or playing him out of position. Like John Scott, he should have won 50 caps or more. For a couple of years, we knocked into each other a lot at sevens tournaments and were teammates for the Public School Wanderers in 1984. His was the first telegram I received when I won my cap. A top player and a very amusing guy.

It might have been this year that my dad entered an Admiral Napier team in a tournament for pub teams held at Harpenden. We had myself, Ringo, Glen Webbe, Pablo Rees and Eddie Butler for sure, and a couple of top Old Illtydians. Although they were all bona fide drinkers at the pub, I felt a bit guilty about our star-studded line-up – until we encountered a London pub side consisting almost entirely of England Internationals. Anyway, we won, and the trophy had pride of place at the pub for few years before Dad suddenly had some 'liquidity problems' and sold a load of the trophies I won.

I couldn't get enough rugby that spring. I was a regular for the Steepholme sevens team at many tournaments over the years, and we always contested the Amsterdam Rugby 7s, where we won four years out of five. Amsterdam was probably the biggest sevens competition outside of the Hong Kong Sevens and the Middlesex Sevens at the time. The Steepholme team was an invitation all-stars team, if you like, run and funded by Stan Thomas, brother of Peter 'Pies' Thomas, the hugely successful businessman who bankrolled Cardiff for decades. We had a lot of fun and for local Welsh or English tournaments I might be bunged between £100 and £150 expenses, but for something like Amsterdam I acted as the recruiting manager as well as skipper, and would pocket nearly £400. I make no apology: This is how rugby players survived in the 1980s. We couldn't live on fresh air and pats on the back from admiring fans. From memory, this was the year we lost 28-24 in the final at Amsterdam to a team called Kemp & Hawley, who were packed with sevens talent from the top London teams.

I didn't want the 1982/83 season to end!

CHAPTER 11

One-Cap Wonder

I'VE FAMOUSLY, OR infamously, got just the one Wales cap, so you'll have to bear with me as I recall my single day in rugby heaven in minute detail. Even if we did get our arses kicked by probably the best-ever Australia team, the 1984 Grand Slam Wallabies. For me, they were a cut above their World Cup-winning teams of 1991 and 1999, mould-breakers and innovators... Of course, I didn't know at the time it would be my solitary Test appearance. I assumed it would be the first of at least 50, maybe way more, but happily the memories are still seared in my brain.

I'd been disappointed not make the Wales squad for the 1983 Five Nations and, despite being sounded out about my availability, I didn't make the Lions squad for their 1983 tour of New Zealand either, even when Terry Holmes was forced to come home with a wrecked knee. I was green with envy when it was Nigel Melville and not me who got the call-up. I was ready to roar. I've never been fitter and could have made plenty of noise down there.

As I've mentioned previously, despite my huge ego and self-confidence, I fully acknowledge that Terry was a magnificent scrum half, the best I played against or saw in my career, and it was clear that I wouldn't make the Wales spot my own until he'd retired, endured a loss of form with injury or decided to cash his chips in and go North. I was basically OK with that: time was on my side, although that wasn't going to stop me trying to topple him on merit as soon as I could. He was the hare, I was the hound, and I was closing fast. I reckon by 1983 we were level pegging, but he was the man in situ and until he messed up or declined, I'd have to stay patient.

That knee injury from New Zealand was so bad that Terry missed most of the 1983/84 season, so I assumed I'd be next in line for the starting spot as scrum half and was crestfallen when Mark Douglas got the job for the 1984 Five Nations, with Ray Giles on the bench. I couldn't even get a start with Wales B, where Robert Dyer seemed to be a permanent selection. No offence meant to Robert, but really? That was just plain ridiculous, and frankly vindictive and odd. For the first time, I started to properly appreciate that Welsh rugby had a love-hate relationship with Pontypool – mainly hate – and that playing for the best club in the land wasn't necessarily an advantage, for a back anyway, if you were chasing Wales honours. And of course, I was still only three years or so out of jail. Many still objected to me on that score alone, not least WRU committees groaning with serving police officers.

I had a lot of time for Mark Douglas, a more than decent player who at least tried stuff around the fringes and used his strength, but I knew I could take him every day and twice on Sundays. I felt I'd proved many times that I was head and shoulders above any other contender. It was all pretty frustrating, but I was still young and not yet a complete cynic. My time would come. And there were other distractions. I'd started playing for the Public School Wanderers and in March 1984 was the only non-International they selected for their sevens squad for Hong Kong, effectively the world championships in those days. What an experience that was, with Andy Ripley, David Cooke – the flanker, not the centre with the same name – John Jeffery, Roger Baird, David Johnston and the multi-talented Huw Davies.

It was a memorable, eye-opening trip, rubbing shoulders with the world's best players from all the big nations, many of whom made a point of travelling to Hong Kong. We lost 10-4 to Fiji, two tries to one, in a semi-final we should have won – but sevens is like that. Rippers, God bless him, was one of the great men and we hit it off immediately, but twice in that semi he made what looked like decisive breaks and should have passed to his support players. Instead, the years caught up with him as he ploughed on and got tackled and Fiji cleared their lines. Ten years earlier, with younger legs, he'd have scored both tries. The Fijians only mounted two attacks all game and scored both times – we had them well-shackled for the rest of the time. They slaughtered New Zealand 28-0 in the final. We could have won that tournament, but hey-ho; we'd enjoyed a brilliant ten-day run ashore.

Wanderers did things in style – we travelled out a week early to acclimatise, as they call it. We trained and played hard and gave Hong Kong a good seeing to. As a 24-hour city, it was my kind of place, with as much happening at four in the morning as at four in the afternoon. I thought there was a drinking scene back in Wales, but some of the lads out in Hong Kong were in a different class. There was also a fair bit of weed doing the rounds for those who wished to indulge, and myself and Rippers bonded over a crafty spliff here and there. Nothing too dramatic!

So, a brilliant time all round – which also reinforced my confidence that I could thrive against the best. Most of the legendary Aussie backs we were to meet again in the autumn were out there, putting their reputations on the line, and although they were excellent players, I felt I belonged to that level of rugby. I saw nothing to frighten me.

Come the autumn and I was playing exceptionally well again, but assumed I was still down the pecking order for reasons best known to the so-called Big Five and of course J B G Thomas, the veteran *Western Mail* journalist and unofficial sixth member of the selection panel. Many thought his voice was the most important of all.

About five weeks out from the Australia game, Pontypool played Cardiff in a massive midweek clash down at the Arms Park. The kick-off had to be delayed to get the capacity 17,000 crowd in. Terry had returned to action in the final Five Nations game of the previous season so was back in the box seat, but this was a chance to go up against the main man and state my case. Unfortunately, all that happened was that Terry went on an early run, looking to bump 'Madman' Chris Huish out of the way, which isn't something I'd advise anybody to do. Terry, who was a tough bugger himself, came off second best and copped a dislocated shoulder. That shoulder had troubled him ever since it forced him off the 1980 Lions tour.

His Test place was suddenly up for grabs again. No way would he recover in time for Australia. Neither Mark Douglas nor Ray Giles had really taken their chance in the previous year, so I didn't know what to think. I was in the squad but had no great expectations, preparing myself for another let-down. They would find a way of not picking me.

We drew that game in Cardiff 9-9 – it was a ferocious affair – and I finally got my Wales B cap against France in early November, at Rodney Parade, when I partnered another young, uncapped player called Jonathan Davies at half back. I wonder what happened to him, by the way? The French had some lively characters. Éric Champ was in the back row and spent most of the match trying to knock my head off, Denis Charvet was playing centre, Marc Andrieu wing and my opposite number Henri Sanz was pretty tidy as well.

Then, about ten days before the Aussie game, I was in town and bumped into Bill Davey, who ran the travel agency that did all the Wales team travel. He was a near neighbour to us at the Admiral Napier, where Dad was now mine host, and was very well-connected with the WRU top brass and management. Wales is a small village sometimes... He called me over, looked around conspiratorially and then whispered, "David, you're in: you're going to start against Australia."

Bill knew his stuff; he wouldn't have got it wrong and would never have told me unless he was absolutely sure. Suddenly I was flying on a magic carpet back to the pub – my feet didn't touch the ground. I burst into the Napier bar, which was quite busy, and shouted over to Dad that I needed a word with him straight away.

"What trouble are you in now?" he barked back at me, looking worried.

We went out the back of the bar and Mamma came as well, and I told them I was in the team to play Australia – Bill Davey had just slipped me the word. Instant tears all round. I lifted Dad in a massive bear hug and marched him around the pub. Mamma was sobbing, I was sobbing. Nobody can ever take that moment from me or them. I'd waged a war – mainly in self-defence – with Dad for much of my teenage years, but my God: as a rugby player, I was his creation. He made me the scrum half I was. This was his cap as much as mine. As for Mamma, I'd have packed it all in had it not been for her perseverance, belief, prayers and weekly blessing... We shared the moment together and it makes me cry every time I recall that lunchtime in the pub. Family life had been pretty bumpy and torrid at times, but we kept going and came through it all. And it seemed so hopeful for the future. I honestly believed it was the start of something wonderful and lasting. There'd be many more days like this. I'd make my family so proud.

The news became official a few days later and I could share it with all my mates and other family members. I was issued with all my official Wales kit – tracksuit, blazer and tie, bags and odds and sods. Anybody who's ever played rugby will know how ridiculously, illogically good it feels when you get the official First XV stash and its totally yours: you've earned it, and it's not imitation or replica stuff. By the Thursday before the game, I'd split my tracksuit bottoms – they were like tight wetsuits back in the Eighties and they weren't man enough to cope with my oversized thighs. John Dawes on the touchline noticed and promptly ordered up another couple of pairs for me. Once you made the team, you were treated very differently.

We were staying and training up at St Mellons, not far from Llanrumney, so a posse of friends and old mates dropped in and held me up for ages, looking for autographs and getting me to sign balls and bits of kit. I was loving the rock-star treatment: it was all good for the ego. Everywhere we went in the team bus, we got a police escort, which brought a quiet private smile given my mixed history with the South Wales Constabulary. I got an early glimpse of the programme on the Friday evening and there was my name on the line-ups page, although I was a bit disappointed that

One-Cap Wonder

they'd chosen a picture of me in Public School Wanderers kit, much as I love the Wanderers. Would it have killed them to use a picture of me in Pooler colours, perhaps from the 1983 Cup Final?

The night before the game presented a massive dilemma. My routine throughout my career every Friday night was to head out into town about 10.30 or 11 p.m. for a tour of the nightclubs and music venues, a couple of drinks – but, contrary to legend, very rarely more than that. A couple of spliffs, perhaps, but never anything harder at this stage. I just enjoyed being part of the scene and striking a pose – to be honest, I never particularly enjoyed hash or smoking spliffs that much, I just got into the habit and did it mindlessly. It relaxed me, but not because of the dope. Well, perhaps that helped a bit, but it was more of a case of being out late and being myself... That was the relaxing bit. I have no idea if being a night owl was nature or nurture, but it was real for me. Perhaps it harks back to my childhood, lying awake fearful of what might happen next. Like I said earlier, I wet the bed until I was at least 14: the anxiety was ever present. When you're like that, when you're hyperalert and hypervigilant and can't sleep, you might as well be up and doing something and burning off some energy. Being up late was hardwired into my system. In my ideal world, big games would have kicked off about midnight!

The fact is, I felt the need for company, and at that time of night the only places to go were the nightclub venues. I wasn't chasing one kind of music or vibe – although there were a couple of smaller black music dives down by the docks (whose names I can't even remember right now) which I really enjoyed. Reggae and soul. But mainly I just wanted to be out and about.

Cardiff was and is a buzzing city full of such spots, many of them what today you might call pop-up venues. Here today, gone tomorrow. Popular briefly, and venue of choice for the in-crowd, before another place came along to claim that title. The tourist brochures call Cardiff the City of Arcades, but it's actually the city of nightclubs and dens.

When those of us of a certain age get together, it can be an entertaining half an hour trying to recall them all, either from first-hand experience or word of mouth. Sometimes when I can't sleep, it can rock me off, trying to remember all the names. The absolute premier venues for me were the old Casablanca of blessed memory, which had great music and an exotic clientele and was probably the best live music venue, along with The Moon Club. Dropping in on the Casablanca was like dropping in on the best party in town. When it went off, it went off. Magic. Nero's was always a great night but so were many others, some of them long gone. Let me rack my brains: Revolution, which I think became Smileys; The Terminus, which became Sam's Bar; Bogiez; The Hippo Club – how could I forget the Hippo?; Panama Joe's; Lloyds; Jacksons, of course, right next to the Arms Park, which was a favourite with the rugby boys; Chicago's; Bowie's; Berlins; Glee Club; Chapter; The Square; Coco Savannah's; The Toucan Club; the Stage Door... the list's bloody endless. I'm sure I've missed out some big ones there. Cardiff was the perfect city for insomniacs. There's a book to be written by somebody from this era – it was nuts.

And let's be honest, when I was out and about, I got a buzz. For the time being, I was somebody: a local celebrity. A face the doormen recognised. I'd usually be ushered in without charge, or into the VIP area, where there'd be some familiar faces. What's not to like?

One-Cap Wonder

Most Friday nights – and Saturday as well, for that matter – I'd grab some very late food at Patrice's all-night emporium in Roath about 3 a.m. Mixed grill and skinny fries, cheap as you like, some decent music but also lots of pissed guys looking for fights after being thrown out of nightclubs, and night owls who generally considered 3 a.m. too early to head for home. Very edgy. I loved it. About 4 a.m., typically, I would call it a day, but sometimes later... Empty streets, Cardiff in slumber but lights still ablaze. I felt like I owned the bloody place. It was my town. I bloody love Cardiff, couldn't live anywhere else... I'd sleep like a baby until noon, brunch with Mamma, blessing with the holy water and then the drive to Pooler or wherever with the aim of arriving about 45 minutes before kick-off. Any earlier and I'd get stressed and fidgety. I was incapable of killing time and relaxing before a match. I couldn't do that small talk thing or staring moodily into the distance or endlessly rereading the match programme. Not for me. In, get changed, rub-down with Eddie Mogford – always the last one – and then sprint onto the pitch.

That was my tried and trusted modus operandi, so what to do on the night of Friday 23 November 1984, all banged up in Wales camp? I decided not to change the habits of a lifetime, so arranged for a mate, Danny Keating – a taxi driver in town – to pull up quietly at the hotel about 11.30 p.m. and off to town I'd go. I was sharing a room with Perky (John Perkins), and he was livid as he was all ready for bed when he realised I was heading out. "If you get fucking well caught, Bish, this is all on you, I know nothing about this. You'll get me dropped, mate. You need to stay in, just for one night."

I was in no mood to listen to such common sense. I was off and away. There was a great sense of freedom in the back of the taxi on my own late that night, heading back into town and down into the Docks area, where I'd arranged to be let in the back door of the Dowlais Club, one of the smaller, more out-of-the-way establishments, which I reckoned would be fairly low-key and quiet. I started to relax the moment I walked into the nightclub, and chilled with few friends who were in on the late-night deception. I sipped away at a vodka and orange, listening to the sounds, and although I was wearing a baseball cap and trying melt into a corner with a few mates, eventually I started getting a few looks of recognition. Damn. I brazened it out for a while, pretending it wasn't at all odd me being there on the day of my Wales debut, but in the end decided it was probably best I headed back to St Mellons with Danny. And not via Patrice's. As we went, somebody slipped me a couple of spliffs, "just for the drive home, Bish. Good luck tomorrow!" Very considerate, the Welsh are, like that.

I didn't smoke them there and then in the taxi but, somehow, I got through the hotel foyer without being noticed and, after tiptoeing back into our room about 2 a.m., I couldn't get to sleep. It was still ridiculously early for me, and I remembered the spliffs, so went and sat on the bog for what seemed like hours and quietly smoked them, contemplating the day ahead. I suddenly realised I was very nervous, and no amount of bravado could disguise that. It was now late; I pulled myself together and flushed the butts of the spliffs down the loo. Or so I thought. I finally hit the sack – but a few hours later, soon after Perky stirred, I was woken by hollering from the bathroom.

"Bish, you Cardiff shithouse, what the bloody hell are you thinking of? Are you trying to get us both drummed out the team? What are these spliffs doing in the loo?"

"Relax, Perky! Just hit the flush again, they'll go down." And they did. Panic over, although the bathroom smelt strongly of dope. I jumped out of bed and opened all the windows wide.

All sorts of conspiracy theories have appeared over the years from people who either did see me out that night or thought they did at other venues, and the story began to evolve. I was out on an all-nighter, up on the tables dancing, doing drug deals, losing the shirt off my back in an all-night poker school, consorting with organised crime, up to no good. The truth, to be honest, is that it was one of the quietest, earliest, most restrained Friday nights of my entire career.

Match day was emotional from start to finish. The hundreds of good luck telegrams hit me harder than I thought possible – from family, schoolmates, prison inmates, boxing friends and rivals, baseball colleagues, David Daisey, English and Scottish teammates at Public School Wanderers, and many people I didn't even know – from old guys on the Bank at Pooler to two young sisters who went to all the Pooler matches together and made a day of it with a little café lunch in town first. I was their favourite, apparently, and the joy I seemed to be giving a lot of people gave me a warm glow.

I was pretty humbled, and then when I saw the jersey hanging on my peg in the dressing room, I was gone. The same peg as Gareth Edwards and Terry Holmes. I kissed the jersey, had a quiet sob and then tried to get myself together as the singing outside in the stadium started. Just before we ran out, I had to find a quiet corner to do my holy water ritual, and of course that got me thinking of Mamma again and how I owed so much to her, as well as Dad. My father had constructed me as a rugby player but he'd given up when I broke my neck. Mamma alone kept believing that I had a rugby future. All this was swirling around in my head when suddenly we were running out and belting out the national anthem. I was in floods again and could scarcely manage to sing a word, but I felt amazing. This was me; this was where I belonged. This is where I could finally bring purpose to my life.

We lost 27-9 against a brilliant Aussie team, who were clearly inspired by the Arms Park and played at a level none of us had really experienced before. Their pack was much stronger and tougher than some were willing to give credit for, and laid the foundation for their brilliant backs, who did the rest. We could and should have got closer. We squandered a few chances and then started playing catch-up, and certainly gifted them their final try. But let's be clear – we got taken apart upfront and finished a distant second.

Despite my bravado and front, I was always self-critical – that's the bit people didn't see. We had little or no technology in those days to assist our analysis, but I always talked through every game in minute detail with my dad and coaches I rated, and I was as hard on myself as anybody. Dad had taught me that. If I'd done something wrong, made a silly decision or failed to execute, there was no hiding place from Dad. Never had been, all the way from the patch to the Park.

So when I analyse my performance – which I did many times over the years because I had a VHS recording of the game – I'm pretty objective. And proud. During my one Wales Test appearance, I was bloody good in adversity. A solid 8 out of 10 in a struggling team. I didn't let myself or my family down. Coming off, I had the same feeling as when I'd dragged myself off at Pontypool Park that time when Ebbw Vale had been routed but I'd produced a game to remember, the performance that convinced Ray Prosser he must stop me joining Newport.

The other thing I remember is never before or since feeling so battered and tired. And exhilarated. It was two or three levels up from anything I'd experienced, and I loved it. I knew I'd adapt, acclimatise and be even better next time out. No question.

We got an absolute tanking upfront, but I kept it together and produced some quality moments. Save for one nervous loose pass, my service was really sharp, and it's interesting to see me employ the classic dive pass so often, showing exactly the same style and technique as in the Ray Williams training book from just over a decade earlier. I was on the back foot for much of the game and the ball was often slippery and wet – the weather was fine but the ground sodden from a week of steady rain – and the dive pass was often the best option. You almost never see it these days, which tells me (amongst other things) that scrum halves are overprotected – they're allowed time to set up for the big wind-up and spin pass every time. I made a couple of sharp breaks, took my juggling try well down in the corner where our dogs used to do their business, tackled my heart out and feel I can hold my head high.

I was never a particularly 'lucky' rugby player – everything that could go wrong went wrong for me over the years – but I definitely enjoyed one stroke of good fortune early in the game. The Aussies were attacking blind, and I sprinted over to cover what I suspected would be an inside pass to their powerful wing, Peter Grigg. I read their move correctly, but the adrenalin was pumping, and Grigg's step was a strong one. I instinctively flung out my right arm as he sped inside and caught him in the neck, I think, and he fell to the ground. Shit. It was completely unintentional, but the sort of challenge the TMO would be all over these days and, even back then, you'd occasionally get into trouble for. Grigg, to his credit, didn't milk the situation and nor did the Aussies, which earned much respect and thanks from me. No complaints from them and the ref just blew for a simple penalty. And I started to breathe again.

That Aussie team was something special. The thing I marvelled at was the speed and precision of their interplay in midfield between Michael Lynagh, Andrew Slack and the great Mark Ella. It was pinball-quick and almost impossible to defend. It was rugby's equivalent of the tiki taka football Barcelona were to produce many years later. Throw in the genius of David Campese and the strength and poise of Roger Gould, and they were some unit. And that pack of theirs served up a constant stream of quality possession. We were comprehensively outplayed on the day but, in fairness, we weren't the only ones that autumn, as they swept past England, Ireland and Scotland as well. 28-9 was harsh on us. It was an eye opener as to how good you needed to be at this level, but also an inspiration. And I'm still really proud that my try was the only one they conceded in all four Test matches on that tour.

Following the game, despite the defeat, I was chipper and after the official dinner at the Angel, just wanted to spend some time down the Admiral Napier with friends, family and regulars. Strangely, I wasn't on for a big night on the town. I was utterly exhausted – fatigue like I'd never known before in my life – and as I looked to make my escape from the hotel, I caught Roger Gould's eye across the bar. The Aussie full back motioned, did I want a pint? Up until that point, I hadn't had a chance to speak to Roger. We'd played against each other in 1981 in the Pooler game, when I was downright poor and feeling sorry for myself, but I'd enjoyed some good banter and a pint with him after the match. Roger was a very laid-back, citizen of the world sort of character – a bit like Rippers and David Cooke from the Public School Wanderers team in Hong Kong – and I always seem to get on with that type. I fought through the crowd to him and shouted over the noise, "I'm just off to our pub over in Canton – do you fancy a pint there?" Roger's eyes lit up. That sounded like a splendid idea. A surf dude at heart, he could only handle so much formality and rubbing shoulders with committeemen and management.

So off we marched into the Cardiff night in our official team blazers and ties. We stopped at a couple of pubs en route but soon we were settled back at "my place", and he was good as gold with the all the regulars, who were delighted to talk through the game with one of the Aussie stars of a few hours earlier. Roger was one of the last toe-punting kickers, so everybody wanted to know about that, which required multiple demonstrations of the technique in the bar. We toasted my debut – "the first of many" seemed the consensus. It was a very pleasant couple of hours, and I could see how proud Mamma and Dad were that one of the most celebrated Aussies should choose to spend time with us straight after the game. In fact, the bush telegraph started beating loudly, because in no time we were joined by a few more of the tourists.

That Aussie side was not only the best team I played against, but the guys were a good bunch socially. They finished the tour a month later with another week in Wales – Pooler at Pontypool Park on the Tuesday, the Barbarians at Cardiff Arms Park on Saturday – and a few of them, including

Roger, adopted the Napier as their local. They were amongst friends and could relax. We entertained them most evenings. Their coach, Alan Jones, spent time with us in the bar and of course Dad happily discussed tactics and methods as if they were complete equals. It was a cool scene.

Pooler gave a much better account of ourselves against the Aussies at Pontypool Park than three years earlier, and it was neck and neck until they sneaked the 24-18 win with a late try, although the Bank were convinced there'd been a knock-on from the Aussies in the build-up. I had no view, but in all honesty, it didn't feel like we were robbed – they deserved the victory, as well as we played. For the second time inside a month, I was up against Nick Farr-Jones – their young gun at scrum half – and on this occasion, I thought I shaded it. What you've got to realise with scrum halves, by the way, is that even though rugby's the ultimate team game, scrum halves always look on our clash with our opposite number as an individual battle or fight. It's the only position, along with hooker, where you're in direct competition for the full 80 minutes – and, regardless of the match score, both of you always know when you run off at the end who the individual victor was on the day.

Nick was a year younger than me and was in his debut season. We were absolutely of equal ability and potential, and it's always haunted me how his Test career went off in one direction and mine in the other. He won 63 Aussie caps, captained his side in a Lions series and led his country to a World Cup in 1991. And what did I achieve in comparison?

In some ways, I'm touchy about the 'one-cap wonder' label. Part of me rebels against it, looking on it as a thinly veiled insult even when it wasn't intended like that. I remember being at a dinner one time when Cliff Morgan came over to me and my dad, introduced himself (as if we didn't know who he was!), and asked how the one-cap wonder was.

It was meant as a quip to start the conversation. But just for a second, I flared. I was a bit touchy about it. But we sat down and had a good talk for 20 minutes. We were sitting with Gerald Davies, who's always written fairly about myself and Pooler. Cliff told me I should be proud and that now – decades later – I could walk down Westgate Street and still be stopped and asked for an autograph. Which was true.

The truth is, like Cliff said, I'm immensely proud to have won 'just' the one Wales cap. When I played against Australia, I was cap No. 819, and at the time of writing there have still only been 1,215 rugby players in Wales to have represented their country in a senior International in 144 years. If time travel was a thing, you'd still only need one decent-sized marquee to house us all for a reunion lunch. And that'd be a session for the ages.

Some pretty good players have 'only' been capped once by Wales. Roy Mathias, Laurie Daniel, Clive Griffiths, Barry Clegg, Ken Waters, Mike Knill, Rex Richards (who became a Hollywood stuntman and got to the final two in auditions for Tarzan, missing out to Gordon Scott), Roger Michaelson, Neath flanker Phil Pugh (who was one of the best I ever played against) and fellow scrum halves Chico Hopkins, Clive Shell, Billy Hullin and Handel Greville. Many of them had outstanding games on their debut, making match-winning contributions. Hopkins came on as a replacement for Gareth Edwards to win the match for Wales against England in 1970, and was also a standout for the 1971 Lions, winning his one cap once more as a replacement for Edwards in the First Test and again nearly walking off with Man of the Match honours.

I'm not quite sure what the moral is here, but if I find myself feeling bitter and twisted, I try and remind myself that I'm not the only one-cap wonder to have been hard done by in rugby history. It helps a little.

Back to 1984. Three days after the Pooler game, I watched as the Aussies signed off with an incredible match against the Barbarians, which some observers think is up there with the 1973 game. It was outstanding rugby from both sides, and I'd have given anything to be involved. Still, time was on my side. I was knocking on the door and would be part of these occasions very soon.

Strange to say, I've never seen Roger since that tour. I assumed there'd be other opportunities to bump into him as a player, especially as we both played sevens, but I was wrong. I'm not a Facebook man so I've never tried to track him down when visiting my daughter in Australia, and it seems he's not on Facebook either. But regardless of that, to this day I appreciated him coming back to the Napier that night to help celebrate my first cap. If it could feel so special in defeat, I can only imagine what it must have been like to have won Grand Slams and titles in a Wales shirt. I still dream it, though.

CHAPTER 12

The Punch That Ruined My Life

RELIVING THE JARMAN incident – or the Newbridge Incident, as I call it for reasons that will become apparent – is depressing, although barely a week goes by when I don't torture myself by doing just that. It's where my career fell off a cliff, just when it was about to take off. I'd endured my time in jail, overcome a broken neck and established myself in the Wales squad behind Terry Holmes who, by the autumn of 1985, everybody including the WRU knew would be going North the moment he'd enjoyed a big send-off at the Arms Park against Fiji in the November. He needed to cash in his chips with Bradford Northern before his knee went completely. My time was close. I just had to be patient for another month or two and I could start the 1986 Five Nations campaign as Wales' undoubted first-choice scrum half. With the back division I could see mustering, Wales were going to do some serious damage. I had my eyes on the 1986 Lions tour of South Africa – although that was eventually cancelled – and there was a Wales tour to the South Pacific Islands as well, should I miss out on the Lions. Then there was the 1987 World Cup on the horizon.

It was time for my career to fly. I was convinced, and so was Pross.

I was on fire as a player. John Billot, the doyen of Welsh sports journos, wasn't a noted lover of Pontypool but had written more than once in the *Western Mail* that I was the best Welsh scrum half he'd seen since the war, which was pretty eye-popping praise, considering Gareth Edwards would be in that mix. Nothing was going to stop me. I'd been to Wales squad training the previous weekend, we were meeting up again on the coming Sunday and I'd be on the bench behind Terry for Fiji. After that, let the good times roll. I was highly motivated and perhaps a bit full of myself, although nobody ever accused me of lacking confidence to start with.

What then happened was the defining incident of my rugby career and life, so excuse me if I dwell on it a little. It's Wednesday, 23 October and it's a 7.30 kick-off at the Welfare Ground, Newbridge, where the home side lay in wait for a big Gwent derby. Traditionally Pooler v. Newport was the big Gwent clash, but the Black and Ambers were nothing special at this time. Newbridge, on the other hand, were dangerous mavericks with a talented back division led by Paul 'Tommy' Turner and a physical pack of real street fighters who Pooler thought got away with murder. At Pontypool, we always maintained Newbridge were the dirtiest team in Wales. Not the hardest and most physical – that, apart from us, would have been Brian Thomas' stormtroopers down at Neath – but the dirtiest. The team that niggled and got away with the most cheap shots. A lot of the lads knew each other and our matches could get proper nasty and out of control, and the two clubs cancelled games altogether at one stage. Bad blood everywhere. For a

The Punch That Ruined My Life

midweek game, there was a big crowd at the Welfare, which had just one stand with everybody else standing behind the goals and along the far touchline by the cricket pitch. The atmosphere was intimate and intense. The floodlights were absolutely useless up in Newbridge, so it felt like you were playing in the dark in certain corners of the ground, and by candlelight in others.

All our matches were Cup matches for the other team, with Pooler's scalp as good as lifting silverware. It would make their season. Newbridge had steam coming out of their ears and right from the start it was pretty tasty. There was a young kid in their second row, Chris Jarman, who seemed to fancy himself. One or two of the lads had heard on the Gwent grapevine that he'd been a bit of a tearaway up at Tredegar, where he'd played for a couple of seasons, but the truth is, none of us really knew much about him. As we were soon to discover, he was a biggish unit – 6 foot 5 inches and touching 17 stone – and right from the off he started putting it about, looking for a fight. He gave Mike Goldsworthy a clip, clouted Kevin Moseley and some of the boys thought he was responsible for Staff Jones needing to be helped off, injured. Then he was right in the middle of a general brawl between the forwards which caused the referee – Ken Rowlands – to call us all in for a warning. Everybody had to calm down. Gwent derby or not, he was going to start sending people off. Everybody, Ken? There was only one player out of order here.

The Pooler pack was half asleep that night: off the pace, lacking intensity and dog and, frankly, the boys were beginning to piss me off. We were making bloody hard work of this. I called them round quickly What the fuck was going on? Why were they letting this young punk run riot? Sort it out, lads – or do I have to bloody well do it myself?

Then I caught Jarman's eye and gave him a mouthful. "Hey, you: wind your bloody neck in a bit, pal, or else you're going to get your bloody arse slapped."

He replied, "Bugger off yourself, before you get your own arse slapped."

Right: the gauntlet had been thrown down. I don't necessarily blame him for a bit of attitude. He would have been pumped up – over-motivated? – knowing he was taking on the 'mighty' Pooler forwards that night. And I'll concede it takes a bit of ticker – or stupidity – for an individual to deliberately provoke a team like Pontypool. Fair play, in that respect. But if you stick your neck above the parapet like that, there will be consequences. Welsh club rugby in the Seventies and Eighties really was a jungle. Was he man enough to handle it?

All this was happening as we gathered for a line-out. I was raging. Jarman was really annoying me and my pack had gone AWOL. As the adrenaline started pumping, I reverted to type. Remember when the big bully arrived on the patch all those years ago? I took the fight to him and he backed off, bloodied and bowed, never to be seen again. Remember when my father's beatings and attacks got too much? I took the fight to him and he was forced to concede he was second best. He was no longer top dog and never threatened me physically again. Remember the so-called hard men in prison who wanted to make life a misery for the new kid on the block? I stood up to them and they melted away. All bullies are, deep down, cowards.

People have asked for nearly 40 years now why I punched Jarman that night and, frankly, who knows? I'm not a shrink, but my best guess is that it was my instinctive reaction to dealing with a bully. Somebody who was clearly overstepping the mark and was getting away with it. The punk needed sorting and being taught a quick lesson. Then we could get back to the rugby.

I never really had any trouble with genuine rough and tumble in rugby: players trading honest blows and punches here and there, and even occasional violent play if it was spontaneous and just flared up from nowhere. It was a man's game. But I was hardwired never to accept any premeditated nonsense from bullies. It was a very personal thing that made me see red.

So I decided to dispense a bit of his own medicine. I had zero intention of badly injuring the young thug, but he needed a slap to calm him down.

From memory, it was our line-out and, believe it or not, we sometimes had a call when we just didn't jump – we let the opposition have the ball, with the intention of all piling in simultaneously and causing absolute havoc. A bit of muscle-flexing, really, and upping the intensity. What's that modern-day mantra: sometimes it's easier to play rugby without the ball? We were well ahead of the game on that score.

Anyway, up goes this Newbridge kid and as he comes down, it's mayhem as he's dragged down to the ground and a ruck forms over him. He's there right in front of me and the ball's close by as well. In a split second, I bend down as if to get the ball but instead seize the opportunity to connect with the sweetest, shortest right jab I ever landed, either in a boxing ring or fighting in the street, or anywhere else for that matter. I drew back my right fist three or four inches, maximum – it was almost like a flick of the wrist rather than a jab, and he went out like a light. Blink and you'd have missed it. Just about everybody did. Within a second or two, he was snoring away, just like my old man when he threw scalding tea over me and I retaliated with a big haymaker.

I was pretty sure nobody on the pitch had seen it. None of the Newbridge team seemed to know what happened. None of them came at me. None of them were demanding that I be sent off, nor that any Pooler player be sent off, for that matter. Everybody was in the dark. The referee obviously suspected something had gone on in the ruck but neither he nor his touch judge that side had seen anything, so he couldn't send anybody off. It all seemed a bit of a mystery. It was probably one of those hard cases in the Pooler pack, but he'd seen nothing.

If I could have my time again, it would be my earnest wish that Ken Rowlands had seen the entire incident, sent me off and it had been dealt with there and then. A routine month's ban and it would have been onwards and upwards, and I'd have returned to action a wiser man. But nothing. We played on, eventually hit our stride and won 29-13, with Goff 'Sheets' Davies scoring four tries.

As we ran off, I copped some barracking from Newbridge fans in the grandstand, but I always got shouted at and abused wherever I went. I still wasn't quite sure how this would pan out, although my gut instinct told me there could be trouble ahead. Damn, if it hadn't been such a good punch and he hadn't gone out like a light. Why couldn't I just have caught him a glancing blow?

When we got back into the changing room, there was no bollocking for me from Pross. I wasn't sure if he'd seen anything. He never missed a thing so I assumed he'd witnessed it, but if he did, he didn't seem too bothered. He did, however, tear into the forwards for their sub-standard performance. He was livid, and I'm told the fans up in the bar and in the Newbridge clubhouse could hear most of his tirade. Nothing was being said about the kid, but I had an uneasy feeling. Quite how badly things were to escalate was beyond my wildest imagination.

At this point, just before my world went mad, I need to put this in perspective. Welsh club rugby in the 1980s was brilliant and ultra-competitive, but could also be brutal. Punching incidents – whether a mass brawl or isolated punches of retribution for some unseen offence – were bog standard. It would be very unusual indeed not to witness at least one incident in any game between the 18 old Merit Table sides, and often an undercurrent of violence would simmer from start to finish. Pooler weren't angels, obviously, but we were not the only sinners. Far from it. More of which later.

On a Richter scale of foul-play incidents in Welsh rugby in the Eighties, I reckon mine registered a modest mid-table 4. I'm talking about the norms of the time. Obviously, such incidents would be policed and dealt with much more severely these days.

Who knows exactly why my punch was considered so beyond the pale back in October 1985, but I accept there were a few elements which might have ramped it up a bit. It was unique for such an incident to involve a scrum half punching a big second row and, for some perverse reason, that didn't go down well. Macho forwards sorting things out amongst themselves was absolutely OK and expected – in fact eagerly anticipated by most fans, who felt deprived if there wasn't a bit of a biff at some stage of the game. Forwards dealing with pesky, stroppy upstart backs: yep, people totally got that as well. Comical almost – a clichéd encounter and all good fun. Scrum half on scrum half: bloody hilarious, handbags at ten paces from the little men. But for some bizarre reason, David giving Goliath a slap, a scrum half decking a hulking second row, didn't go down at all well.

Other factors kicked in. The overwhelming majority of fans had totally missed it, despite what the 40,000-odd supporters who now claim to have been at the match say. My dad, who had X-ray vision and never missed a thing, missed it. But Rob Cole of the *Western Mail* certainly hadn't and detailed the incident in his match report the following morning. That had a snowball effect, with other papers taking their cue from Wales' authoritative national newspaper. They had to follow it up, although nobody else had definitively seen anything and there was no evidence. Remember, there was no TV footage of these midweek games, no fans with smartphones capturing bad challenges and foul play. No still pictures of anything.

Then it escalated out of all proportion. It was quickly reported that Jarman's father Alun – a recently retired policeman, by all accounts – was going to bring a prosecution because his son had suffered a broken jaw. Talk about going for the nuclear option! It was a staggering development. Resorting to the courts was unprecedented in Welsh rugby, and I often wonder if some individuals in the WRU – with its strong police connections at the time – in any way encouraged that. Everybody seemed primed and ready to go. The South Wales Police Force back then was not the most scrupulous of organisations and the WRU weren't Pooler fans. Was this the green button they'd long been waiting to push?

I would add, incidentally, that I've never seen any proof – scans or medical reports – that Jarman's jaw actually was broken. It's always just stated as a fact, with no corroborating evidence made available to the public. It didn't feel like I'd broken anything – it was just a sweetly timed shot. It's like when you play cricket and a simple defensive push pings off the middle of the bat and races to the boundary. I noticed he was back playing for Newbridge against Neath four or five weeks later, which seems very quick indeed for a broken jaw to heal up. In boxing, you'd be out of the ring for three or four months with a broken jaw.

It was a seismic development, though. The likelihood of court proceedings changed everything massively, got the gossip mill going and made the case into something that it really wasn't. Without that threat, it's probable that Pooler, under heavy pressure, would have organised an internal inquiry and slapped a month's ban on me, which the WRU would have endorsed, perhaps suggesting adding a week or two. I would have gone along with that. But a court appearance for assault, given my previous conviction and time in jail? That was an entirely different matter. I suspect very few of you reading this have ever been in jail and for all my flippancy when writing about the year I spent banged up in Aylesbury, I can assure you it was horrible. What might we be looking at here, if I was found guilty and my two previous convictions taken into account? Another three or four years? Longer? It was completely uncharted territory, but going back to jail for any length of time, with my career finally poised for take-off, would unquestionably kill me. Caged up again like an animal, I'd have found a way of ending it all. I'd unhesitatingly have taken my own life rather than serve another jail sentence.

So with my back to the wall in a way I'd never anticipated, I took a calculated gamble – perhaps ill-advised, but I was desperate. There was no film or any images of any sort of the incident. There was no evidence in the referee's report. It seemed very few people had actually seen it, at one of the poorest-lit grounds in the country. Rob Cole had, yes, but I don't recall that any other press reports from that night had named me, and I seriously doubted if arman's father had actually witnessed the punch himself. Would he claim under oath that he had? There was a lot of hearsay flying around and various people telling the world what they thought had happened, but could they stand up in a court of law and describe events accurately? Could Jarman prove it to the satisfaction of a Crown Court, on just his say-so and that of a single journalist, when so many other reporters and witnesses had seen nothing? I wasn't going to plead guilty to something which happened virtually every week in Welsh rugby. Why should I? If I was in the wrong, so were scores or even hundreds of others every year.

It went berserk. I seemed to occupy the back or front pages for at least the next fortnight and ultimately it rumbled on for nearly two years. I could easily have shot three people dead in Westgate Street in broad daylight or blown up the Arms Park and got less coverage. To repeat, it was a single punch in a dirty rugby match, a Gwent derby that had seen hundreds of punches in its muddy history. I myself had been the target of scores of punches and deliberately stray boots during my career, sly digs at the bottom of the ruck or in the confusion of a maul. Sometimes it was a knee in my back or a boot in the head rather than a punch. Anything went. I walked around with a large X on my back every time I ran out. Very rarely did I retaliate, because that's what they wanted. Mostly the way to get back at them was to pile up the points and humiliate them. I was speaking to the old Bridgend hooker Wayne Hall at a dinner a while back – he's also a member of the 'one-cap wonder' club, by the way – and after a few beers, he rather shamefacedly told me that when they played Pooler, he was detailed to get me; rough me up. Punch, kick, stamp – whatever it took. He started to apologise but I stopped him right there. "Every team tried to get me all the time, Hallie." It was always open season to get David Bishop, but I wore that as a badge of honour. It didn't bother me; I could look after myself. It was part of the game.

In the days after the Newbridge game, the media were following me everywhere. At training at Pontypool Park, Pross said he was going to rest me for the game on Saturday, to get me out of the firing line. Looking back, I can see his point, but at the time I was furious. In my agitated state, it seemed Pooler weren't backing me, and that night, in a blind fury, I phoned Bridgend. I was a builder's mate at the time and my boss basically ran Bridgend. I told him if they picked me for their game on Saturday, I would drive over this very minute and sign for them. They were very tempted, but he got back to me the following day and said they'd already picked the team and it couldn't happen this week, but long term they would be very interested indeed. By that time, I was beginning to calm down just a bit.

That was the Friday. Come Sunday, it was a Wales training session at Cardiff Arms Park ahead of the Fiji Test, and I turned up as instructed by my official WRU letter. I spotted Ray Giles there as well, which was a bit odd. I was the back-up scrum half to Terry Holmes, Ray wasn't in the squad that had been announced, and we didn't need another scrum half. Then Terry Cobner came over when I was getting changed.

"Stop right there, Bish – I need to speak to you. Listen, John Bevan needs a quick word." Bev, by the way, was the very best of men and a brilliant coach, who I'd like to have worked with much more.

Bev said, "I'm really sorry, Bish, but we've been told by the Big Five that while all this court case circus is going on, they can't consider you for the Wales team. They said it would look bad."

I knew it wasn't down to Bev, and I just said, "Whatever happened to innocent until proven guilty?" That has a hollow ring, I know, but I was convinced it would be thrown out if it got to court. It should never have been going to court and I assumed that, at some stage, somebody in authority would step in and end the nonsense. This was going to take ages to sort out and, in the interim, I should be allowed to play on for Pooler and Wales. If I was available for club, I should be available for country. In retrospect, I should have been contrite, wised up, fessed up, served a short ban and been done with it. Let the bully win just that once, much as it went against my natural instincts. But I still hadn't really clocked how my misdemeanour was going to be treated so very differently to everybody else's, nor how vindictive some people could be.

The rest of the season was the strangest of times, although another hugely successful season for Pooler. We won the *Western Mail* Welsh Club Championship yet again and lost just five of our 40 games in that competition. The police continued their investigation into the Newbridge Incident, trying to find witnesses, and I understand that one of the delays was that Rob Cole declined to give a witness statement. As a reporter, it was his job to report what occurred on a rugby pitch, but it was sport and he didn't consider it part

Old Irish Town by the Cardiff Docks, before it was flattened. Ellen Street was home until I was 5 years old.
Newtown and the Irish in Cardiff Facebook group

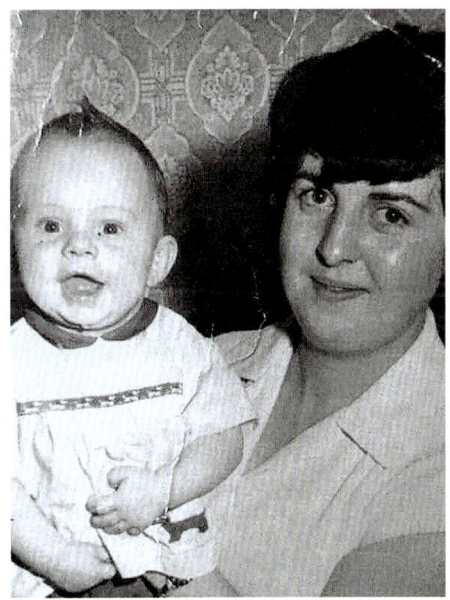

Mum had given up on having children before I came along. On Halloween, would you believe?

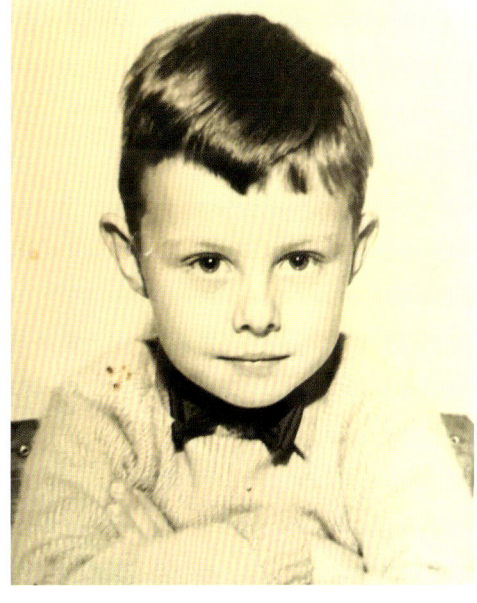

Angel with a Dirty Face, to borrow the title of my favourite film, starring Jimmy Cagney. Pretty sure this is the morning of my First Communion.

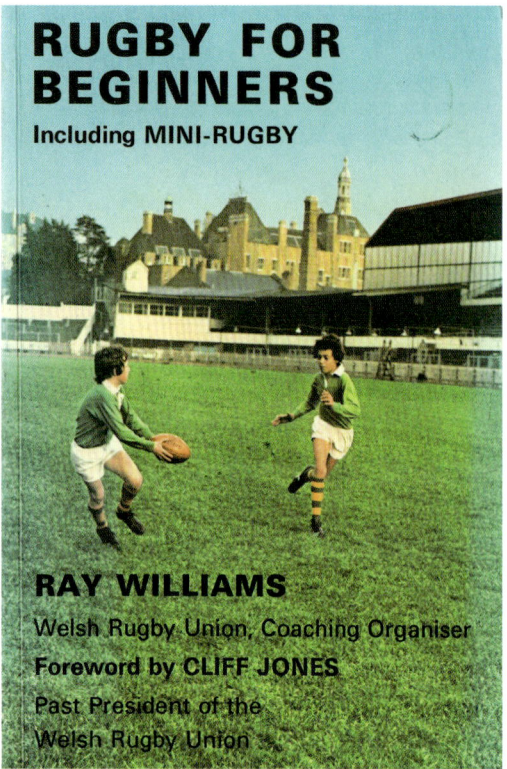

Dewar Shield triumph for St Cadoc's. John Actie lifts skipper Paul Trebilcock. Douglas Actie far left, with me squatting.

Rugby for Beginners. I spent endless hours one summer running around the old Arms Park to help illustrate Ray Williams' trail-blazing coaching book. That's me on the left.

Now, this is how you do it. Swoop low, stay even lower, eyes on target, extend those arms, spread those fingers. Simple.

Roy Agland and his merry gang at Splott YMCA boxing club. We'd just won the Driscoll Shield – again – which he's holding. I'm in the middle in a Wales top, looking very pleased with myself.

Roy Agland working his magic with my boxing and rugby mate Stephen Franks, who many years later became the British unlicensed heavyweight champion.

Touring with Cardiff, and the last known picture of the teddy bear mascot that I sent to the bottom of Lake Garda.

Fresh-faced Youth. Full of hope before my Wales Youth debut against France.

HMP Aylesbury, where I was prisoner A79816. My 'home' for a year. It still sends a shiver down my spine.
Cliff Hide General News/Alamy

Pross. A great man, a loyal friend and a massively underrated coach.
Jeff Morgan/Alamy

Australia taught Pooler a rugby lesson in 1981. Here I'm trying unsuccessfully to stem the flow. Veteran scrum half John Hipwell schooled me on the day.
Mirrorpix/Alamy

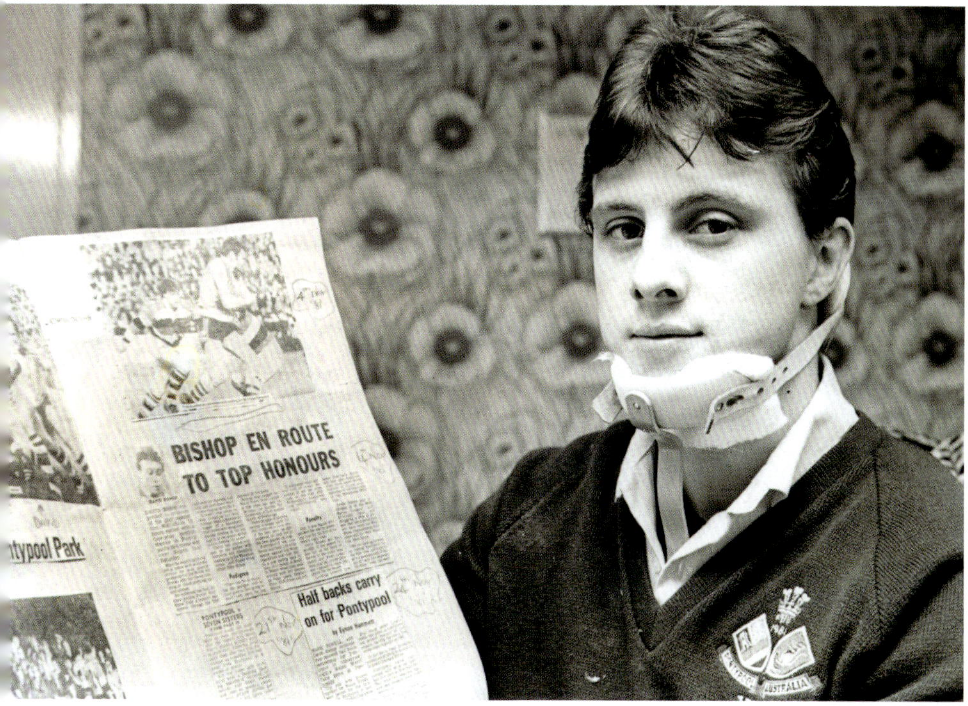

On the comeback trail. I'm through the worst here after my broken neck, and dreaming big again. I was still going to conquer the world.
Mirrorpix/Alamy

On red alert for Pontypool. Something is going down and I need to be ready for action!
Jeff Morgan/Alamy

With Jeff Squire, celebrating Pooler's Cup success in 1983, when I was named Man of the Match.
Mirrorpix/Alamy

I've always loved this picture and would love to say it's from my solitary Test, against Australia… but in fact it's from the B International with France at Rodney Parade two weeks earlier.
Mark Leech/Offside via Getty Images

Celebrating my call-up to play for Wales with Dad at the pub in November 1984. Ours was a complex, highly volatile relationship early on, but rugby was our common ground. He was a great coach.
Mirrorpix/Alamy

```
                                                    23 November 1984

TELEMESSAGE LXP          BLACKSMITH
DAVID BISHOP JUNIOR
WELSH CHANGING ROOMS
NATIONAL STADIUM
ARMS PARK
CARDIFF


         WE KNEW THAT YOU WOULD GET IT. HAVE A GOOD GAME.

         MAM, DAD, MICHAEL, TERRY, SEAN AND CECILIA
         PS. DON AND CHARLES OF LONDON-FRENCH SEND THEIR REGARDS.
```

My cap meant everything to my family. It felt like their achievement as much as mine. It should have been the start of something, not the end.

```
                                                    23 November 1984

TELEMESSAGE LXP          BLACKSMITH
MR DAVID BISHOP AND MR MARK RING
WELSH RUGBY XV
ANGEL HOTEL
WESTGATE ST
CARDIFF


         SORRY ABOUT THE ONE CARD BUT WE COULDN'T AFFORD TWO COS WE HAVE TO
         REPAIR THE BASEBALL CUP YOU SO DELICATELY HANDLED LAST WEEK.
         WE'RE VERY PROUD OF YOU BOTH AND KNOW THE WALLABIES ARE IN FOR A
         GOOD HIDING.

         OLD ILLTYDIAN BASEBALL CLUB.
```

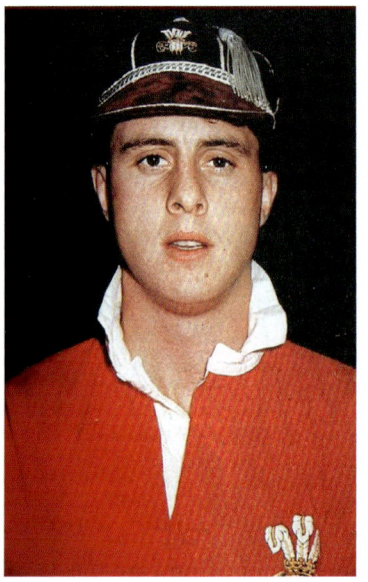

Best wishes telegram from the Old Illtydians baseball boys to myself and Mark Ring. And belated apologies, lads, for damaging the Cup!

Wales cap 819. Nobody can take it away from me... but nobody can give me back the caps that were stolen from me.

A dream come true. Lining up for Wales against Australia. I can still feel it, dream it, hear it.

I spent the entire afternoon on the back foot... but gave a good account of myself in adversity, going toe-to-toe with Nick Farr-Jones.

Mirrorpix/Alamy

The 1984 Grand Slam-winning Aussies seemed to adopt our pub as their local when in Wales. That's Mark Ella next to me, and David Campese on his left.

I'll fight ban — Bishop

By David Facey

WELSH international scrum half David Bishop was today banned from playing rugby for the rest of the season — and immediately vowed to take on the might of the Welsh Rugby Union to get that decision overturned.

Bishop insisted the WRU had made him a scapegoat for the increasing violence in the game, and he would take the matter all the way to the European Court of Human Rights if necessary.

"I'll definitely be appealing. I'm prepared to take this all the way to get some sort of fair play," he pledged.

"I've already told my solicitor I want to take the WRU to court if that's the only way to get them to change their minds. It's a travesty as far as I'm concerned.

"I expected a ban of eight to 12 weeks — not because I deserve it, I've already been punished once — but because of all the publicity over the case, and because the Press called for a ban like that."

PONTYPOOL ARE RAPPED FOR PLAYING WELSH STAR

"But to be banned for a whole season has knocked me for six. My first reaction is one of shock and disgust, but I'm determined not to take it lying down."

The WRU last night decided to ban Bishop until the start of next season in the wake of the court case in which he admitted assaulting Newbridge player Chris Jarman 18 months ago.

The court was told Pontypool scrum half Bishop punched Jarman unconscious while the Newbridge second row forward was trapped at the bottom of a ruck.

Bishop was originally sentenced to a one-month jail term, but three appeal court judges later reduced it to a six-month suspended sentence.

Now Bishop — capped by Wales against Australia two years ago — is determined to force the WRU into a rethink as well.

"They're just using me as a scapegoat," he added. "You can compare my case with four or five district players who've been convicted of assault but are still playing.

"And a couple of years back John Billinghurst got a six-month suspended sentence for breaking someone's nose — and the WRU didn't do a thing about it."

Bishop returned to action for Pontypool while he was out on bail awaiting a chance to appeal against the original jail sentence.

He has gone on the play in five of Pontypool's last six matches, and said: "A lot of players from other clubs have said they were right behind me on this and they hoped I wouldn't get a stiff ban.

"I've worked hard since I've been back to show I can keep my nose clean, but it doesn't seem to have done me any good at all.

"I'm not the type of player who goes looking for trouble. But sometimes when you've had to put up with being provoked and got at, you do things you regret later."

Meanwhile, Pontypool and the Old Illtydians rugby clubs were criticised by the Welsh Rugby Union for playing Bishop around the time of his trial.

Secretary of the WRU Mr Ray Williams said today that letters would be sent to both clubs saying it was most unfortunate that their scrum half was selected when the matter was so sensitive.

"There was no reason why Bishop should not be played but the committee **Turn to back page**

I was punched or kicked in every match I ever played, yet I was the villain of Welsh rugby.

Scrum-halves in the news

BANNED STAR IN LINE FOR EARLY RETURN

PONTYPOOL SCRUM HALF David Bishop — banned until the start of next season — could be playing rugby again within weeks.

The 26-year-old Wales cap was suspended from the beginning of October in the wake of a court case in which he admitted assaulting Newbridge lock Chris Jarman during a game more than a year ago.

But I understand a Welsh Rugby Union panel will hear an appeal against the sentence by the player early next week.

WRU panel to hear appeal

By CHRIS BALDOCK

And the outcome is likely to be announced after the Union's monthly general committee meeting on the Thursday.

It would seem that only one of two possible decisions can be reached:

● Either the ban as it stands is confirmed; or

● The suspension be lifted with the player given a stern warning over his future conduct.

I believe the second choice is the most probable result.

There is a strong feeling that Mr Adrian Owen-Jones — in which the Bridgend skipper was suspended for 21 weeks and subsequently let off on appeal — has paved the way for a return to action by the controversial Bishop.

Denials

"My WRU verdict on Bishop came after he had a one-month jail sentence for the assault on Jarman suspended by three Appeal Court Judges in London.

A statement declared: "The Welsh Rugby Union Committee, having considered the case of David Bishop of Pontypool RFC, who recently pleaded guilty at Newport Crown Court to a charge of common assault on the rugby field, has decided under by-law 28(1) that his conduct was prejudicial to the interests of the Union and the game."

WRU secretary Mr Ray Williams disclosed though that it was the scrum half's earlier denials of his involvement in the incident which prompted the action.

In the weeks since the ban was imposed, the WRU have insisted they would hear any appeal by Bishop and that it was up to him to make the first move.

But the player, after consultation with legal advisers and backed by the Pontypool club, was set to take the Union to the High Court.

The needle for the most part stems shortly after the suspension was announced, Bishop's solicitor Mr Bernard de Maid being quoted as saying: "It could be seen will be an injunction to restrain the WRU from carrying out the suspension."

And he added: "This may be a unique event, but we feel David Bishop has been very harshly treated and we must wonder at the motivation of the WRU decision."

An appeal to the Union has always been the most likely step though, a stumbling block, I understand, being a request for members of any panel to be independent of the original hearing.

Bishop was this week relenting inquiries about the development, but with the Welsh club champions in crisis state on the field they hope for the telephone to ring, refused to be drawn on the action.

The club have been wary of commenting on the affair after being censured along with Cardiff side Old Illtydians for picking Bishop around the time of his trial.

IN TOUCH FOR THE HOLIDAY ACTION

Whitefoot back to face Bath

By Echo Sports Reporter

WALES PROP Jeff Whitefoot (above) returns to the Cardiff team for the match with Bath at the Arms Park...

● DAVE BISHOP — could make an early comeback.

Pontypridd in hunt for new fly half

PONTYPRIDD are looking for a fly half. The two players who have appeared in the position for Ponty this season...

Freedom tears of the rugby player with KO punch

EXPRESS REPORTER

RUGBY international David Bishop cried yesterday after being freed by the Appeal Court.

Tearful 25-year-old Bishop, jailed for attacking a player during a game, said: "I'm happy and relieved it's all over." The Welsh star buried his head in his coat and was surrounded by family and friends.

A one-month sentence imposed at Newport Crown Court earlier this month was suspended for a year. Bishop, who punched the other player unconscious, had admitted common assault.

Lord Justice Neill, sitting with Mr Justice Tudor Evans and Mr Justice Staughton, said Bishop, of Whitchurch Road, Cardiff, was a distinguished rugby player "but those who achieve fame in this way and become heroes in the community do have a responsibility to the game, their fellow players and the public."

The jail sentence "to mark the gravity of what had occurred" could not be faulted.

But the Appeal Court took into account the punishment Bishop had received by not being chosen to play for Wales.

It also took into account evidence of his bravery in disarming a man with a knife who threatened a policeman in a bar, and his rescue of a woman and a child from a river.

Bishop: Attack

'Bishop was victim of a witch hunt'

By CHRIS BALDOCK

"DAVID Bishop was being victimised, he was pulled in because he was wearing our colours," ...

MARKED MAN — Bishop was singled out because he played for Pontypool, say the club.

Eddie Butler's loyalty and approval was a massive confidence boost for me. His friendship never wavered and I still miss him terribly.

PA Images/Alamy

Rugby genius. Ringo was the best player I ever encountered, either code. Our season together with Pooler was a dream come true, a farewell gift before going North. Love you, mate.

Allstar Picture Library/Alamy

Winding it up for Hull KR. League was brutal but with fewer bodies on the park and no flankers living offside, there was occasionally more time than in Union.

I spent most of my League career injured! Feeling the pain after the GB game v. Taranaki in 1990. Those ribs trouble me to this day.

Somewhere in New Zealand on tour with GB. John Devereux was a really good player in both codes, and a top bloke.

Playing baseball for Wales against England with Ringo. I think this is Liverpool in 1988.

A family photo from the mid 1990s, with wife Kate and daughters Natasha and Samara. Very special women, all three.

The Bishop clan scrubs up well when it has to! L–R: me, Michael, Phil and Cecelia, Dad, Terry and Sean, at Cecelia and Phil's wedding.

My daughter Samara, who lives in Australia, with my grandchildren Thalia and Joseph.

My other daughter Natasha, with my grandchildren Amara and Ezra.

Mike Phillips, the best Wales nine of modern times, and Rupert Moon – a fine player, a battler, and a top guy.

Spinning a few yarns, some of them even true, with old Pooler mates. L–R: Eddie Butler, Paul Crabtree, yours truly, Peter Lewis (Doc) and the great Jeff Squire, who was over visiting from South Africa.

Chilling with two of my favourite players: Jiffy and Neil Jenkins. Did you know that between us we have 125 Wales caps? (I'm here all week!)

Craig Bellamy. Great footballer, Welsh legend, top bloke, brilliant Wales manager... but most importantly to me, a staunch and loyal friend. Love you, Bellers.

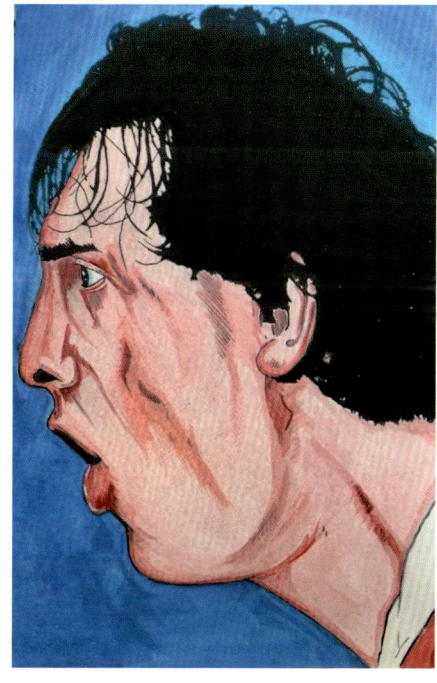

A fan sent this in one time and I've always liked it. I wish I remembered who it was to say thank you. I love the intensity and rage.

The Crazy Gang. Class of '83, who won the Welsh Cup Final against Swansea. Back row L–R (team only): Chris Huish, Graham Price, Mark Brown, John Perkins, Martin Jones, Goff Davies, Steve Jones, Peter Lewis. Front row L–R: David Bishop, Lee Jones, Lyndon Faulkner, Jeff Squire, Bobby Windsor, Mike Goldsworthy, Bleddyn Taylor. *Staff Jones and Eddie Butler were absent, injured. Mike Crowley came on for Windsor.

of his remit to provide witness statements for criminal prosecutions for events that happened on the field of play. That would have set a very bad precedent for sports reporters generally – in fact, it could have been professional suicide. His contemporaneous report of the game was there for the court to see and assess, but that was it.

I was eventually charged in the New Year. But the court system works very slowly and there seemed no prospect of a hearing in the short term. The WRU weren't able to formally discipline me but they still refused to consider me for Wales, which was the greatest penalty of all. In the meantime, I was free to play for Pooler pending the police inquiries and then the court case.

It was bittersweet. Playing was my salvation and kept me sane. I could run free and Pooler were going well, so it lifted my spirits a bit. I was squeaky clean and playing some of the best, most controlled rugby of my life, in the hope that something could be sorted out. Perhaps the court case would be dropped, and we could get back to normal.

But it was also a desperate time mentally, as reality kicked in. My dream of becoming a Wales regular was going down the pan. The WRU, encouraged no doubt by their good friends in the police, were out to get me and make an example of me. And now we reach the real crux of this matter. Suddenly, the whole weight of the WRU's accumulated disgust at the violence in Welsh rugby – which they'd allowed and tolerated for decades – was going to be thrown at me. I was the scapegoat they'd been looking for. They'd make an example of me and those pantomime bad boys Pontypool in an attempt to cleanse Welsh rugby. It would paint the WRU in a much better light, generally. Chief Inspector Rod Morgan, the chairman of the Big Five, had it in for me, as did Chief Constable David East, another influential WRU committee man who would become the WRU Secretary in 1989. This was the open goal they'd prayed for, and they had no intention of missing it.

It was bizarre and totally depressing. Every week, I'd witness some violent incident or other – to my eyes, more savage than the Newbridge Incident – and still they were just allowed to pass unmentioned and unpunished. One evening down in Neath, Mark Brown – not normally a fighter, by the way – ended up slugging it out toe-to-toe in the stands with opposite number Mark Jones after their on-field run-in spilled over, and nobody thought anything much of it. Just two forwards letting off some steam. The crowd roared them on; the press stayed quiet.

Despite the distraction of still playing and excelling for Pooler, 1986 in many ways was the worst year of my life. I felt helpless, but eventually the court case was set to be heard at Newport Crown Court on 1 September 1986. Crown Court, for God's sake. What was a case like this doing in Crown Court? I'd by now convinced myself that it was a formality – Crown Court would surely not be interested in a mere Section 45 assault? At worst, it would be a fine, I thought, and I arranged to meet Kate for lunch afterwards. But the judge, who looked at me as if I was some kind of child molester, took a different view and sentenced me to a month's imprisonment. I was stunned. Instead of going into town for lunch, they led me downstairs and off to Cardiff Prison, where I was processed by the duty officer before he asked for an autograph. Another officer was an old school mate, Tony Wheeler, the son of my old Splott boxing coach Paddy. I obliged with the autograph before being led into a communal holding cell, where my old mate John Actie was also being detained for some reason. That was comforting, but I could feel rising panic and claustrophobia and an overwhelming urge to get out of this hell-hole. My dad and my brief, Bernard de Maid, called in and insisted they could get bail pending a Court of Appeal challenge in London. The Court of Appeal in London for a punch in a dirty rugby match in the Valleys? This was completely mental. I went to bed that night feeling close to ending it all.

I was up early the next morning – Tuesday – for the obligatory jail porridge, and Tony Wheeler asked me if I fancied turning out for the prison football team on Sunday morning. I suppose it must have been an indoor five-a-side team on the premises or something, but I told him to fuck off. I was strictly here for the day: there had been a serious and gross miscarriage of justice, and I would be out of here by lunchtime. He laughed and I joined in, but I was crying on the inside.

I asked John Actie if he could track down a transistor radio – he always knew someone who knew someone – because I wanted to listen to the latest news but, as we were discussing it, a screw came in and told me I was going home. Bernard had done his stuff. I was out on bail pending an appeal, and went straight to a pub and discussed things over lunch. There was a mob of photographers and reporters in tow, and I played up to them a bit by ordering a bottle of champagne, although I didn't feel much like celebrating. This was just another skirmish in a very long war of wills.

17 September was the first slot available for the appeal, and getting off that one-month sentence had become my Holy Grail. My brother Michael and I travelled up the night before and stayed with some friends in Essex, where we went out on the town, larging it and getting pissed down a local

nightclub. I was dreading what might happen. The following morning, I presented myself at the Court of Appeal. I was feeling very delicate and was taken to the downstairs holding cell, from which they lead you up to the dock. There were three hard cases there, one serving 14 years and the other two doing ten stretches. They were looking for a good parole outcome, having served over half their original stretch. I got talking to the chief hard case, the one serving 14 years – I can't remember now what for, but presumably something bad – and he asked what I was up for.

"A month for punching a bloke on a rugby pitch," I shamefacedly told him.

"A month, a fucking month? I spend a month on the pisspot inside most years. Seriously, what are you doing here, mate?"

Indeed.

They started being wheeled in and one by one they all got their parole. After the second 'result', the screw took great pleasure in informing the two of us left that he'd never known three of us get off in one sitting, so don't get your hopes up. Nonetheless, the third one up made it a hat-trick, and then came my moment. "See you in ten minutes. You've got no bloody chance," advised the ever-helpful screw.

I was up in front of a high-powered trio: Lord Justice Neill was sitting with Mr Justice Tudor Evans, who was a Cardiff man, and Mr Justice Staughton. They were read a lengthy account of events and a summary of the finding of the Crown Court a couple of weeks earlier, and I was re-examined briefly. They seemed in businesslike mood at the end of a busy morning, but not unfriendly. It felt like my entire career, in fact my life, was in the balance, despite the modest sentence under review. Another jail sentence and I'd be tarred for life – it would be impossible to challenge for Welsh honours again.

There was also a lot of interest generally about the whole principle at stake over the incident. Rugby players didn't get sent to prison for a fight on the pitch – this was new territory that could create a precedent and affect players throughout the land. That was certainly a strong line from my counsel, Mr Peter Griffiths, who stressed the overall picture and how what was decided today would affect rugby players throughout England and Wales at all levels. This would be a landmark ruling, argued Mr Griffiths, who deliberately wanted to up the ante.

Careful note was made of character references from my old headmaster and the severely disabled rugby player I'd spent some time with as he dealt with his disability. My counsel also reminded the court of my Royal Humane Society award for bravery, and my Police Commendation for disarming a man who was wielding a knife dangerously in a public place. Lord Justice Neill gave just the very slightest nod of approval on hearing that. He struck me as a fair bloke who might try and give me a break, but it was touch and go.

They retired briefly before Lord Justice Neill delivered the verdict. He started promisingly, noting that "the charged atmosphere of the game had to be taken into account", but then things took a less encouraging turn. "Bishop is a distinguished rugby player, but those who achieve fame in this way and become heroes in their community also have a responsibility to the game, their fellow players and the public. The original Crown Court decision to send him to prison is sound," – my heart sank – "but we take the view that being denied the opportunity to represent his country throughout this year is punishment enough. The sentence will be suspended for a year."

I almost collapsed with emotion, and burst into tears. I'd got myself so wound up over this. As we rushed for the car – I fully intended to play for Pooler at home to Newport that night – my counsel spoke with the waiting press. "What's happened to him has rattled the windows of every clubhouse in the land. David Bishop has been humiliated and has suffered enough."

But – freedom. It felt good. We crawled out of London down the A4, then raced down the M4, pulled over at the services to phone Tony Simons to say I was good to go for the match, and then headed for Pooler, arriving in good time. This was going to be sweet. Newport had been shaping up well at the start of the new season and we needed to put those bastard Black and Ambers firmly in their place. It was a ferocious, tight game which we won 13-10, but I felt great and was in the zone. At one stage, it all boiled over and there was a big outbreak of fighting with punches connecting everywhere, but I theatrically walked away with my hands raised up high to signal no involvement. Butter wouldn't melt in my mouth. This was the match, incidentally, at a key stage of which there was a tannoy appeal for a doctor because a man had collapsed on the Bank, and Peter Lewis – Doc – sprinted from the pitch and vaulted into the crowd to do what he could.

Anyway, we squeezed home and for a fleeting moment I fondly thought I was through the worst. The presiding judge at the Court of Appeal had been quite clear in his summing up: I'd "suffered enough" and the WRU had already had their pound of flesh from banning me from International rugby during the entirety of the Five Nations and the summer tour to the Pacific Islands. But the vindictive bastards wanted more. Whatever happened to the idea of double jeopardy? No, they wanted to destroy me, and teach Pontypool a lesson. This time they ordered me to appear in front of them for bringing the game into disrepute. Again, we fought them hard but on 2 October they announced that I was now, additionally, banned from all rugby until 31 August 1987. So, in case the maths is defeating you, I would have served a ban of one sort or another for 22 months and copped a suspended one-month jail sentence for something that was happening on pitches across the country every week. Why was I being singled out? Unbelievable – and also, for me, totally soul-destroying. These guys were stealing my dreams.

The reasons the WRU gave for coming down so hard on top of everything was that I'd played a couple of games between being released after my appeal and the WRU's decision, although the WRU had given me no timeline as to how long they might take nor any guidance as to whether I could play in the period leading up to me appealing their new ban. I played in that Newport game, and then again against Ebbw Vale and a midweek game against Munster. Nobody at the WRU had said that I shouldn't. If it was an issue, they could easily have said so. The Court of Appeal judge had been specific – I had "suffered enough". But that wasn't enough for the WRU. They wanted more blood and were also unhappy that I hadn't been sent to prison. But it was an incident that was commonplace throughout Welsh rugby: either put everybody in court, or nobody.

The local Gwent paper, the *South Wales Argus*, and their rugby correspondent Robin Davey organised a huge petition and delivered it to the WRU offices. We also contemplated taking the case to the European Court of Human Rights – Bernard de Maid was a great fighter for what he believed were miscarriages of justice and was willing to do that for me – but I was exhausted from dealing with this, running out of funds and motivation, and I doubted that anything would change the narrative. There were things that were out of my control.

My off-the-field reputation went ahead of me, but equally there's no question that there was a massive amount of score-settling going on between the WRU – which we perceived to be a west Wales organisation, mainly – and Pontypool. Pooler had inflicted too much pain over the previous years, played a none-too-romantic version of the game that the WRU didn't appreciate, and they wanted to find a way of getting at the club. The incident at Newbridge was a case of all their Christmases coming at once.

But it was the sheer bloody hypocrisy that stuck in the craw. You'd think Pooler were the only team who'd ever thrown a punch or trampled on a player in Wales. Two days after the WRU finally announced my new 11-month ban, the *South Wales Echo*, God bless them, decided to take the ball and run with it for a minute, and actually establish the facts. Using the WRU's own official statistics, they compiled a league table for sendings-off in senior Welsh club rugby from September 1980 to 4 October 1986 – dates which incorporated the entire span of my senior career thus far, including the considerable periods when I was injured or otherwise engaged at HMP Aylesbury.

To the surprise of the vast indoctrinated brainwashed majority, but absolutely nobody at Pooler, the so-called free-flowing Newbridge – our 'innocent' opponents back in October 1985 and media darlings in the wake of the incident – were by a very large margin indeed the worst offenders and the 'dirtiest' side in Wales. They absolutely bossed this particular table. It was probably the only table they ever topped in the Seventies or Eighties! Newbridge, those choirboys and WRU favourites, had accumulated 15 sendings-off for foul play during this period, which was nearly double the number us 'villains' at Pooler had clocked up. Newbridge's total was also six more than Neath, Newport and Pontypridd, who all tied for second place, while Cross Keys and Aberavon joined Pooler in a comparatively well-behaved joint fifth place. This is one of the reasons I call it the Newbridge Incident. But it was all Pontypool's fault, apparently – we alone were the boil on the backside of Welsh rugby that had to be lanced.

Of the 125 red cards during this period – I'm still quoting from the article and the league table the *Echo* drew up – Pooler were responsible for just over 6%, yet the Cardiff and west Wales media and the WRU seemed to think we were the only offenders. Correct me if I'm wrong, but wasn't it WRU blue-eyed boys Newport who caused referee George Crawford to march off in disgust at Bristol in September 1985, when he accused both sides of street fighting? Wasn't it Newport a few weeks later who spent most of the afternoon in ugly running fights against Fiji at Rodney Parade, and who had no fewer than three players sent off away at London Welsh the same season? Unbelievable. Where was the comeback and police investigations on all that?

Wasn't it Swansea's Dick Moriarty who the WRU made Wales skipper in 1986 despite numerous previous dismissals for foul play? A few years earlier, wasn't it a Llanelli forward who virtually scalped England lock Chris Ralston while playing at Richmond, leaving him needing 32 stitches?

Neither Llanelli nor the WRU wanted to get involved and the Scarlets reluctantly banned their entire pack for one game – one bloody game, for nearly killing a bloke – only to overturn their decision. And that was it. Case closed. Unthinkable that a west Walian club could be such thugs. When in doubt, stick the boot into Pooler. Again, unbelievable.

And then, halfway through my WRU ban, I'm watching Wales v. England at Cardiff and all hell breaks loose. Wade Dooley sprints 15–20 yards to land a haymaker on Phil Davies, breaking his jaw, and he gets a one-match ban and is playing against Wales at the World Cup just weeks later. No police investigation or court case. If the WRU were being serious and consistent, there was a much stronger case against Dooley than against me – it had been caught live on TV and witnessed by 55,000 fans. Three other England players also got a one-match ban but, let's be honest, I watched that match closely and England weren't the only team throwing punches and putting it about. Wales were no innocents, but the WRU were mute on the subject. You could drive yourself insane trying deal with the WRU around this time.

If you asked supporters from that period who the dirtiest players in Wales were – week in, week out – I doubt if anybody would even have me in their top 20, certainly not before the Newbridge Incident and all the surrounding publicity. In my entire senior career, I had one sending-off against Saracens for stamping early in 1984. I was at the sharp end and can't recall a single game when I wasn't punched, kicked or tackled ridiculously late, and I reckon that's an OK record. Not without blemish, but decent. And I was under the microscope from referees more than anybody after the Newbridge Incident. Some of the holier-than-thou stuff from our friends in west Wales was laughable. They've bred some of the dirtiest players in all Christendom down there, as well as some of the best and most talented.

I got my kicks in rugby – and money, such as it was – by scoring tries, kicking goals, landing drop goals, making big legal tackles, being better than my opponent and rubbing their noses into the dirt by outplaying them, and winning games with Pooler. That was why I played rugby. I'd never stand for any nonsense, never ever took a backward step, but for 99.9% of the time, I had much better things to do than go battering people.

But here's the thing. The same people who objected violently to Pontypool for our alleged crimes are the same people who were happy to include four or five of our forwards in the Wales team – though they did somehow omit the hardest man of them all in 'Madman' Chris Huish, who was the toughest individual I played with in either code. The WRU craved hard, physical, allegedly dirty players in the Wales team, but then hurled insults at us when we sometimes played hard against the top Welsh clubs.

After the ban, it was open season on me. Everybody piled in. I'd been asked to play a bit of Sunday morning football to keep in trim, but the Football Association of Wales stepped in to ban me from doing that. Why? Sorry: what on earth did it have to do with them? Stay in your lane. How was that even legal?

It was just unreal. It was suggested that perhaps now was the time go North, but the Rugby Football League announced they wouldn't allow a player to sign until bans incurred in another code had been served. Aussie Grand Slam coach Alan Jones, who'd really rated me on the 1984 tour and was an occasional visitor down our pub, got in touch to see if I wanted to play Down Under – "We traditionally welcome the criminal classes down here, mate; in fact it used to be obligatory" was his wisecrack – but my visa request was blocked, so that was a non-starter. I'd been reduced to a non-person. All I could do was get down the boxing gym to work out and keep putting in the road miles and play a bit of baseball in the summer – although the authorities initially tried to ban me from that as well. Opposition teams, however, let it be known they'd be very happy to see me back playing, and I enjoyed a good season with the Old Illtydians as the baseball authorities turned a blind eye.

It was a very dark period, which included the 1987 World Cup. I'd set my sights on that from the moment it was announced in 1985. As it turned out, I looked on from afar in despair, hypercritical of what I felt were some bang average performances from Robert Jones, who offered no threat of his own. I should have been there. I could have made a difference.

It ruined my life, basically. Enough said. To finish this painful chapter, I'm going to quote Ray Prosser's entire press release, which he issued at the time of the ban and which, increasingly, I looked on as a lifeline. Mamma still religiously kept all the cuttings on my career, good or bad, and I used to re-read the Pross verdict to stop myself going mad. It became like a prayer. The very fact that he took the trouble to issue a press release was remarkable in itself, as that wasn't his style. The normal fruity language is mostly absent, of course, which makes me think somebody at the club gave it the once-over before it was released, to ensure the club wasn't criticised further But I can hear his authentic voice, and also his despair at realising that this was the final straw and I would, surely, be heading North sooner rather than later. His dreams were also being stolen.

Anyway, indulge me. Here it is in full:

I will make no comment on the length of the ban, and I do not condone his action, but I will say this – David Bishop has been unlucky on two counts.

He has been judged to a large extent on his behaviour off the field and secondly, he has been judged by the club he plays for.

I will say one thing straight away: "Let he who is without sin cast the first stone", and I haven't seen a bloody ripple yet.

If this is how David Bishop and Pontypool are going to be treated. so be it. But every player in Wales and every club in Wales must be treated exactly the same.

I've seen worse than the Jarman 'incident' in hundreds of games from hundreds of players.

I feel a great sorrow for David Bishop. Our success in the last three years has been largely down to him. There have been times when he has played out of this world.

It's a sad loss for Pontypool and a sad loss for Wales. He has the talent to play in any position in the backs for Wales, that's the calibre of the man.

He's a competitor and we are going to need competitors in New Zealand at the World Cup.

Myself and fellow coach Ivor Taylor stand by the man's rugby-playing ability. I hope he comes back an even better player, if that's possible, but it will be a tragedy if he decides he's had enough.

It has always been a privilege to coach the lad and I feel deeply for him at the moment.

CHAPTER 13

The Crazy Gang

THE KEY TO Pooler during the 'glory years', or at least those I was involved in, is that we always considered ourselves underdogs. And we took that mentality and mongrel attitude onto the pitch, even when we were notching up big wins. 'Train like a contender, not the champion', as the old boxing saying goes. We really nurtured that chip-on-shoulder mentality. We were never one of the big clubs, blessed with incredible facilities, a large regional fanbase and an array of wealthy sponsors or sugar daddies. It was all about bloody-mindedness and bonding with loyal fans. Pontypool and its surrounding area wasn't one of the wealthier parts of Wales. It had been struggling for a while and, with the big industries closing down, life was bloody hard. Many of our fans also saw themselves as underdogs in life, looked down upon and forgotten compared with folk down the road in Cardiff or Newport. We – the players – were their representatives in the big bad world. They loved it when we gave any of the established clubs a bloody nose – and that included the aristocrats of west Wales rugby, such as Llanelli, Swansea and Neath. We represented a deeply working-class industrial town, but Pooler were more than that. It was a club full of contradictions. A couple of miles out of the valley and that part of Gwent is very rural, beautiful and agricultural, and we were their side as well. England's just over the border and although there was a big rivalry with the English clubs, we didn't see them as the out-and-out enemy, as was the case in other parts of Wales. Many people in the area had everyday dealings with the English – at work or socially – and Pontypool was never consumed with the traditional Welsh rugby hatred of them. We still loved beating them, but it felt more like a local derby than a big Anglo-Welsh clash.

As I get older, though, I see clearly what a freakish gathering of sporting egos and talent we were – a sports psychiatrist would have a field day digging into what made us tick. Contrary to the stereotype that people like to draw, there was an enormous amount of brain as well as brawn at Pooler. We were a clever side with some massive rugby intellect, making the best of what we had and solving problems on the hoof in the heat of battle. Pooler was always so much more than the group of headbangers we were usually portrayed as: highly talented but damned near psychopathic squaddies when let loose on a rugby pitch. That's how we allegedly battered opponents – and how the WRU liked to portray us – but it was a long way from being the whole truth. Pross himself was as wise a rugby man as I've ever met, and he was just the tip of the iceberg.

At full back, our kicking machine – one of the very best I ever saw – was a particular mate then and now: Dr Peter Lewis. He was also a very tidy all-round player. Peter was a highly rated surgeon at St Joseph's Hospital in Newport and rose to become a big cheese in the Gwent NHS generally. He was exactly what you'd expect in the 1980s: a busy young doctor rushing from shift to shift, who still managed to play 35+ rugby games a season and finish top or near the top of the list of leading points scorers in Wales, and Britain.

I don't know how he fitted it all in – other than that he learned to be very focussed when he had to be, which I suppose is THE secret of being an 85%+ goal kicker. Right up to about 42–43 yards, 'Doc' was the best I've ever seen. But that was his range, and not a foot more. If we needed somebody to get the driver out and have a pot from long range, that would usually be me.

Doc was good company off the pitch. We shared a brilliant run ashore in New York once, when Pooler were ostensibly touring Canada. We disappeared over the border and spent 48 sleepless hours partying in the company of Genesis, who we went to watch in concert, and then Hall & Oates, who we bumped into backstage and got on with like a house on fire. New York in their company was party central! We blew a decent hole in the tour kitty getting back to Niagara Falls by taxi to play our scheduled match there, arriving an hour before kick-off. Great touring days. You'd get fined by the club or savaged on social media these days, but we were young amateur sportsmen living our lives. Pooler shrugged it off. The summer tour was our reward: the lads were meant to enjoy themselves. The rugby was pretty incidental.

Then we had Goff Davies, our prolific wing. He was known as 'Sheets', for reasons I can't really think of other than that he was as pale as pale can be. Anyway, he was a dedicated career teacher and even at a young age, when he was playing for Pooler, was a deputy headmaster at Blackwood School. After retiring from playing, he was a much-respected headmaster at Hartridge High School, a challenging appointment. Sheets used to clock up a huge number of tries every season, and I always looked for him down the blindside when the opposition was expecting me to make the break. He also enjoyed one record-breaking season as assistant coach with Bobby (Windsor), but had to step down as his schoolmastering duties increased. He was badly missed. A clever, regular guy – the adult in the room on many occasions, and a great steadying influence in a very maverick team. 'The designated driver', as somebody once called him.

In the centre we boasted, at various times, all sorts of exceptional individuals. Where do I start? Well, there was our hard-as-nails centre Lyndon Faulkner – nephew of legendary Pooler and Wales prop Charlie, who we've encountered already. In the early and mid Eighties, Lyndon was as good defensively as any midfield player I've seen, especially when teamed up with Lee Jones, a tough and skilful west Walian who won a Wales B cap. Both were an integral part of our Cup-winning team. They were going well in tandem the following season too, until a bad knee injury in a charity match for Public School Wanderers up in Guildford wrecked Lyndon's rugby career. However, that unfortunate injury was probably the making of him as an off-the-Richter-scale businessman – one of the most successful Wales, and indeed Britain, has produced in the modern era.

An engineer by training and working with Nimbus, Lyndon was frustrated at that early end to his sporting career and poured all that anger and manic energy into his job. He also brought his winning mentality, confidence and focus from his time at Pontypool. He became an absolute force of nature in his specialised field and his big break was his early championing and developing of CDs and related technology ahead of vinyl and cassettes. It wasn't taking off as hoped and things were looking pretty grim until he manged to wangle a slot with *Tomorrow's World* and Raymond Baxter at the BBC. After that show and the demonstration of what the CD was capable of, the world went mad for the CD and, soon afterwards, Lyndon was headhunted by an emerging new company in California called Microsoft. Whatever happened to them? In America he became Lyndon J Faulkner and took a leading role in developing their Windows, Microsoft Office and Xbox technology before setting up his own Nasdaq-listed company, Pelican. He also appeared as a guest on *Shark Tank*, the US equivalent of *Dragons Den*.

It's actually very difficult to get your head round the success Lyndon made of his career and business interests in California, and exactly how our mate from the back of the bus became such a world-beater. We always kept in touch and now he's back in Wales for good, hopefully, he comes out with the boys regularly. Nothing's changed: the banter is the same – no airs and graces. Hand on heart, I can't say that when he was forced to retire as a player, I'd have predicted the glories that lay ahead for Lyndon, but there was always something a bit special about him. When injury struck, I knew he'd be successful in something, just not that successful. We're very proud of him.

The list of Pooler characters continues. In the 1985/86 season, three lively itinerant young Kiwis turned up – have boots, will travel, etc. – and club chairman Peter Lawlor put them up in a house in Usk and provided a weekly food and beer kitty. There was Lyndsay Raki, a talented if erratic Māori at fly half; Scott Pierce, a long-legged wing who could really shift and played a bit of sevens for New Zealand; and then there was a lean, almost fragile-looking young centre called Sean Lineen, who at the time was trying to track down some Irish grandparents and prove his qualification for Ireland.

Sean, at centre, was the class operator of the three. He'd been picked for the 1985 New Zealand tour to South Africa which was cancelled because of apartheid, and he decided to travel to Wales instead. There was in fact nothing fragile about him: he was wiry and tough, but he possessed some silky skills and really added to our back division, especially when teaming up with our emerging homegrown product of Roger Bidgood. Sean was a thoughtful, intelligent player but, alas, we only saw him for one season. Having investigated his family lineage, it was discovered that one of his grandparents was actually from the Western Isles of Scotland, not Ireland, and that it was Scotland that he qualified for. Lucky them. He left us for Boroughmuir and was soon in the Scotland side and, to the surprise of nobody at Pooler, played a starring role in their 1990 Grand Slam side. After retiring, he became a highly respected coach.

Roger Bidgood was a fireman and often arrived hotfoot from a call-out. He was as steady as a rock for us and always good in a crisis, practical and unflappable both as a player and an individual. He was quietly amused by some of the wilder characters in the side – such as me – but enjoyed our company. And 35 years on, he hasn't changed. The nicest man in the world, along with Goff Davies.

Two other backs I must mention are Mike Goldsworthy and Bleddyn Taylor. Goldie was often my half back partner and had a big boot, kicking from hand, and a neat all-round game. He was also a reliable short-range penalty kicker when Doc was absent – like Doc, he had a very fixed range and immediately lost form and shape if he tried beyond it – and was something of a drop-goal expert. He was one of those players who perhaps hadn't made the impact he'd wanted at his previous clubs (Penarth and Newport), but suddenly found his niche at Pooler and was mightily effective. He was from Penarth and, with me in Cardiff, we became good mates travelling up to training and matches three or four times a week together. Mike was and remains a top bloke. Bleddyn was west Walian, short, stocky and very explosive. He also had the very valuable habit of popping up on your shoulder to finish off great team scores. Bleddyn was often the man to dob down our very best tries.

Now the forwards. First: Eddie Butler, no less. 'Snooty' was a very bright man but also the salt of the earth, which was an unusual combination. English dad who was a semi-pro footballer, educated at Monmouth School, Cambridge Blue, modern languages degree, star BBC trainee, Wales captain, *Guardian* columnist and the future voice of rugby, taking over from Bill McLaren. Bloody hell, that's some CV! But he wore his talents lightly and there was also always a bit of a rebel lurking in what appeared to be an Establishment background. Eddie was one of the most intelligent rugby men on the planet, but also hard as nails and a key forward and leader at Pooler who was in charge for three of our Welsh Club championships in the 1980s. As a player, you might think he wasn't quite big enough for lock or fast enough for the back row at elite level, yet somehow it didn't matter with Snooty: he read the game so well, he was always where he needed to be. And he punched above his weight.

Eddie was about as far removed from the Pooler stereotype as you could imagine. We hit it off pretty much straight away. I never felt I had to prove myself with Eddie, or be somebody I wasn't: he accepted me warts and all. I envied his intelligence and social ease; he envied my street cred and loved my streak of madness. It was Snooty who was big enough to break the ice and get me back involved with the club when there'd been radio silence during my recovery from the broken neck. And we didn't particularly know each other at that stage, as we'd played just a few matches together – he just took it upon himself. I got a huge kick and confidence boost from the fact that somebody as accomplished as Eddie rated me and valued my friendship, and that friendship and support never wavered, no matter what scrapes I got into. He was no fair-weather friend. He 'got' me, and knew there was a good, loyal and kind side to me, even if I mostly did my best to hide it.

Flanker Mark Brown was – is – another impressive man and formidable rugby talent: one of the two or three quickest men I've ever seen in Welsh rugby. When I needed to sharpen up my speed, I teamed up with him at sprint training, especially for the pyramids and snake runs, as we called them. I reckon I pipped him one night – he must have had the flu or something – but that would be about it. He was always a couple of yards ahead of me, and chasing him ensured I was working flat out at 100% all the time, when he was probably only at 90%. Mark was a seriously good athlete with both speed and endurance, a nice man and model citizen. He was a quantity surveyor, another highly qualified professional and another who didn't fit the so-called Pooler mould. With a father from Jamaica, Mark was actually the first black player to play Rugby Union for Wales when he made his debut in 1983, pipping Glen Webbe, but I don't recall anything much being made of that. South Wales was such a mixed, multiracial society that it just washed over most of us, to be honest, and Mark was modest to a fault. He'd have hated any fuss or claims to fame. But he was that man who officially broke the mould. A player of his athletic calibre would be priceless in the modern game.

Mark was always known as 'Shaft'. Pross named him after the Hollywood detective John Shaft, played by Richard

Roundtree, when Mark arrived at Pooler the same autumn as me, sporting a big Afro hairdo. You'll know the theme tune even if you don't remember the films. It probably wouldn't be allowed or encouraged now, but to me it's yet another example of how we had no racial hang-ups back then in the early Eighties. Nobody for a second saw Mark as any different to anybody else at the club and, at Pooler, everybody needed a nickname. You didn't get picked unless you had one and 'Shaft' was a pretty cool one – certainly better than 'Fatarse' (Staff Jones) or 'Pimplehead' (Pricey).

Shaft was tall, thin and wiry – a bit of a basketball dude in looks, and that made the so-called Big Five suspicious – but he was tough and could keep going all day. He was a bit raw, having played football until he was 17, but he picked up the basics very quickly. In Shaft's ideal world, a game of rugby would last 160 minutes, two halves of 80 minutes apiece and the pitch 160 yards long... Wales didn't appreciate what a talent they had on their hands – but, let's be honest, the WRU had previous in that respect. His bad luck was to make his debut against Romania in Bucharest in 1983 when the entire team had a collective nightmare, and I think that was always held against him. He worked his way back into contention for the Wales tour of the Pacific Islands in 1986 and was by all accounts brilliant, particularly against Western Samoa in the final game, when he was the runaway Man of the Match and gave his opposite number at openside flanker a torrid time, both in the loose and at the line-out. And who was that? That would be a youngster by the name of Michael Jones, the future All Blacks great. Shaft could have been our Michael Jones, but Wales at the time had no idea how to use him and play to his strengths. I'm bitter and twisted at my one cap but Mark has every right to be fuming at his total of six. It should have been so many more. Another road not taken.

We've kept in touch, and we were comparing war wounds during Covid when I had my stroke. Mark had something similar – he has a slow heartbeat and apparently, one night when he was sleeping, it went so slow that the blood started pooling in his brain and clotted, which causes a type of stroke. As he discovered when he woke up, it had badly affected his peripheral vision. The fittest of men without a spare ounce on him even in his sixties – it just shows it can happen to anybody.

It was always the mix at Pooler that made us special, so let's look at some of the other talents you might think are more typical of the club. Chris 'Madman' Huish – some called him 'Rambo', but I prefer 'Madman' – was and is a big mate. We still FaceTime regularly now he's living in Australia, where he's the main refuse collector for Bondi Beach. It's a tough job but somebody's got to do it! Madman is the strongest pound-for-pound rugby player of either code I've ever encountered. One-on-one, you just couldn't better him. And many tried. The possible exception would be Bobby Windsor, although I only played with Bobby at the tail-end of his career. Madman knew no pain and was often too brave for his own good, so picked up a lot of knocks, which he shrugged off. There are scores of old players around Wales right now with aching bones nagging away and interrupting their sleep courtesy of Madman and his big hits. Wales never had a look at him (probably too small for their liking), and I think – like Shaft, actually – he had an England qualification as well and there was talk at one time of perhaps going down that route. He should have been playing International rugby, that's for sure. For me, as with

Snooty, he was a key man in our pack. We were never quite so strong or invincible upfront when they were missing: that's when we became vulnerable. And personally, he was a godsend – he was brave as a lion in the loose and soaked up a lot of punishment on the ground that I'd probably have been getting otherwise. Ask any Welsh forward from the mid and late Eighties who the hardest, most enduring player and their least favourite opponent was, and I suspect Madman will top the list.

Frankie Jacas was an interesting character – a legend of a player, to my mind. If I had to nominate the player with the most unrecognised potential and talent, it would be Frankie. I didn't realise until recently that he was a Londoner originally, before moving to south Wales and settling in Tredegar, where this athletic giant of West Indian extraction developed a belting Gwent accent. Frank was a labourer, a hard-working physical guy and, my God, what an athlete – right up there with Shaft, but a bit heavier and more muscular. I've seen him going from stationary to top speed in a flash and leaving opposition backs in his wake. We occasionally managed to get him, Shaft and Madman teamed together in the same back row – with Eddie going up to lock. That was the most fun-packed Pooler breakaway trio we ever had and my favourite, although I appreciate if we're talking about the 'best' Pooler back row, Terry Cobner and Jeff Squire probably take precedence.

I didn't really know Terry or Jeff well, although one of my very first games for Pooler before my broken neck was, I think, the game at Abertillery where Terry copped a bad cheek injury and was forced to retire. We clashed a bit, if I'm honest: both at Pooler training, when he would often organise the forwards, and then with the WRU later when he was a selector and worked closely with John Bevan. As individuals, we were very different and I can see now how Terry, being the heart and soul of the club, might have been suspicious of me. His club Pooler, his pride and joy, hadn't become one of the powers in the land by importing brash Cardiff scrum halves with a high opinion of themselves, as yet unproven in the heat of battle. None of this lessened my admiration for him as an all-court hard-as-nails flanker, for what he did for the club – along with Pross – and for his achievements with Wales and the Lions. Behind Gareth Edwards, he was one of my favourite Welsh players. He was the only forward I really watched intently, as I devoted most of my attention to Gareth Edwards growing up, and of course my dad purred over his skills. Terry could pass and kick as well as any back and there's no question: he could have played Test rugby at centre if his career had taken another course. He was Dad's identikit all-purpose forward.

Jeff was a legend of the game with Newport, Wales and the Lions and became a huge figure at Pooler when he joined in the late Seventies and skippered us for three years. I only got to play a couple of seasons with him before he retired, but he was some performer. Jeff was so incredibly strong and commanding he could take on the opposition pack on his own and give the rest of the Pooler pack time to regroup. When in possession, he just controlled games at his pace and he was such a big hitter as well. It didn't matter who you were playing and how pumped up they were – if you had Jeff on your side, you couldn't be intimidated. The only time I ever felt I got an armchair ride behind the Pooler pack was when Jeff was having one of his mammoth games. When he was in that mood, he totally bossed proceedings. We were different generations and I never got to really know him before he moved to South Africa, but was delighted to catch up with him at a recent reunion when he was back for a while. My God, what a player. We were never quite the same upfront after he moved away.

John Perkins was one of the smaller second rows around at just under 6 foot 2 inches, but he was a proper hard case and a very good operator at the front of the line, who played like a much bigger man. Perky was a local Blaenavon/Pontypool guy and the hardcore emotional centre of the club along with characters like Pricey and Steve 'Junna' Jones, our hooker who took over from Bobby (although Bobby, despite allegedly being retired, used to turn out regularly at prop). Perky was a real old-fashioned scrapper and enforcer – he had no fear about taking anybody on and, like all the Pooler forwards, never complained when somebody fought back. He once said that for every stitch he'd inflicted on the opposition with fist and boots, he'd probably picked up two stitches himself, and that sounds about right. When I was serving my interminable ban for punching Jarman and was up there as public enemy number one, I used to watch the likes of Perky with envy. He and many other players like him at all the Welsh clubs used to consider a fight and punching an almost essential part of a rugby game. It was expected from them, the crowd wanted to see it and generally a blind eye was turned unless they went completely OTT, in which case they might occasionally get sent off and serve a short ban, no questions asked. Life seemed so much simpler for them.

Perky, Pricey and Junna would be among the guys who were most suspicious of me when I parachuted in from Ebbw Vale and then reappeared after my broken neck. I had to earn their respect, and it took a good while.

Junna and Pricey were fitness fanatics who, like me, did most of their fitness work away from the club. Pricey was a proper athlete and runner – his natural weight was probably only 13 and a half stone and he ran all day. I'm no front row expert – and I only played with him during the final years of his career – but it struck me that it was his fitness and endurance that as much as anything made him the prop he was. In terms of sheer raw scrummaging power, there were others in Wales who could match him – the place was awash with good props – but none of them could do it for 80 minutes. And remember: back then, replacements were only for injuries. Pricey worked away at his opposite number and, like the Pooler pack generally, he came into his own in the final 25 minutes or so when the other guy was dying a death and he was still full of beans.

Junna was a gym bunny who discovered weights in his mid twenties, which apparently transformed his physique. Club folklore had it that he'd also do 500 press-ups every night while watching the TV. He certainly led an enthusiastic gym group three or four times a week at the leisure centre by the ground. One of his co-trainers was prop Mike Crowley, 'the Bear', sometimes called 'Biffo'. Now, with Pricey and Staff Jones around – and Bobby in the wings if needed – getting a start at prop with Pooler was not easy, but there are some who think the Bear could have been as good as any of them. He was certainly the strongest and a complete animal in the gym, and he used to make a huge impact when he did get a start or come off the bench. One year, despite being theoretically a second team player for us, the Wales selectors were having a serious look at him before he got injured.

We only had one properly big guy – we were a pretty small team, more like a League side in stature than Union – and that was Kevin Moseley. 'Boris' (don't ask, I have no idea where that came from) was a middle-of-the-line-out jumper, who later on became Director of Rugby down at Cornish Pirates. He could be pretty docile in some games and very fiery in others – you were never sure which Boris was going to turn up – but he unquestionably enjoyed some really big games for us, when he looked like a proper Test second row. Despite that, he wasn't always an automatic first choice. For some of the big games, we tended to move Snooty up alongside Perky, because we had so much strength in the back row.

Then we had the fringe players – and I don't mean anything disparaging by that, because they'd be automatic starters at most clubs, but they chose to stay at Pooler because they loved the club and the whole ethos of the place.

There was Alun 'Spring' Carter – again, I can't remember where that nickname came from, sorry – who was an all-purpose back-rower who went on to win a couple of Wales caps. Alan died recently aged just 59, another sad funeral. There have been too many recently. Alun was another rangy athlete. He always excelled on the Grotto Run alongside Shaft, and could play anywhere in the back row. He even moved up to lock on occasion. Getting a regular start in the back row we had was a tall order, but he played a good few games for us before he eventually went down to Newport. He was, by his own admission, the worst policeman in the Gwent Constabulary for most of his time with us, but he was a rugby man through and through and had a good rugby brain. He'd done a PE degree down at South Glamorgan Institute and was very interested in what was then the new 'science' of video analysis and incorporating data on the opposition into your gameplan. So much so that, when he hung up his boots, he spent ten years or more as the main analyst for the Wales national team. He was at the absolute forefront of that side of the game and I used to enjoy some pretty detailed tactical discussions with him. Like I say, there were always serious rugby intellects involved with Pooler, from Ray Prosser and Terry Cobner downwards.

Then there were a handful of other stalwarts who kept all the starters honest in training games and never let the club down when called upon. They were mainly local boys, the kind of characters I had to prove myself to before being totally accepted – but once I'd gone through that process, you couldn't have a tighter bunch supporting you. They had my back. There was utility forward Mostyn Davies, who was officially the skipper of the Athletic but played well over 100 games for the First XV; Haydn Wilmott, another tough old back-row warrior; and then there was the gangly Martin Jones – nicknamed 'Horse' – who moved around in the back five and was a very useful line-out option. Good players, automatic starters and stars at most clubs. Our half-hour full-contact sessions at training (if we didn't have a midweek match) – when the Athletic would line up against the First XV – were often much tougher than the games on Saturday, with Pross urging them to get stuck in and the opportunity to earn a few bragging rights. Martin stepped straight into our Cup Final-winning team in 1983 when Eddie had to drop out with a hamstring injury, and was one of the best players on the park. That was how we rolled at Pooler. You couldn't begin to recreate that player dynamic today.

CHAPTER 14

The One and Only Pross

WHAT A PRIVILEGE and honour it was to play for Pontypool, both in our glory years between October 1981 and May 1988 and then again when life was much tougher between 1996 and 1999, when the club was struggling with the new realities of professionalism and I was dealing with a battered body and advancing years.

The glory years were a blast, with four Welsh Club championships, a Schweppes Welsh Cup, a couple of near misses, a couple of dud seasons and much controversy – a good deal of it caused by yours truly. It was all a bit rock and roll. Although we were a small club, we became, just for a while, big fish in a smallish pond and featured in the papers and on radio and TV most days, which was heady stuff. Of course, pre-1995, most of the squad had proper jobs to go to in the day. The 'bungs' from Pooler helped, but you couldn't live on them. Even I rolled out of my pit some mornings to help my then father-in-law with his loft insulation business. I was the guy who fed the fibreglass into the blowing machine. Not overly taxing, even on Thursday mornings after a tough midweek game. That Pontypool side was full of big characters and individuals, but of course

The One and Only Pross

nobody was bigger than the boss himself, Ray Prosser. We were the side that Pross built – with much loyal help, of course, from his right-hand man Ivor Taylor, the father of future Wales International Mark Taylor. And then, for one brief season, my last before going North, Bobby Windsor inherited the crown jewels, added his own embellishments and we produced another staggeringly good team. The third great modern-day Pooler side, if you like, along with Terry Cobner's side of the Seventies. As many have commented, of all the teams in Welsh rugby you might have expected to embrace the professional approach, Pooler would probably top the list because we were damned near professional in our approach to training, playing and winning. But that was the great mistake everybody made. It was that ultra-professional approach which set us apart as amateurs, and when everybody started taking that approach as 'new' professionals, we lost our main advantage and point of difference. Without that advantage, Pooler reverted to being just a Gwent valleys club with slender financial resources. And Pross was no longer at the helm. For 17 years or so, he *was* the club, so there was always going to be a gaping void when he stepped down.

Pross is fundamental to my story. Obviously, I've mentioned him already, but perhaps now is the time to pull over and pay proper tribute, and put down as best I can what he meant to me.

We connected straight away, from that first evening in the Elm House clubhouse after Ebbw Vale played Pooler, when I was trying to make my escape after finally manning up and telling Ebbw Vale I'd be joining Newport the following week. That was purely on an instant personal level. Even though I had a father – and I've explained that volatile relationship, warts and all – Pross instantly felt like a second father, and I have no real explanation for that. Who can tell why that happens?

He treated me like the son he never had, and I've heard it suggested that he shared a similar dynamic with Terry Cobner when they achieved such great things in the 1970s. But there was also something else whirring away in the background – a kindred spirit, perhaps... From various conversations with him, I learned that Pross was a bit of tearaway as a youngster around Blaenavon and Pontypool straight after World War Two, and rugby, amongst other things, was his salvation. He came to the sport late: like Shaft, he was a footballer to start with (a goalkeeper, which is a pretty scary thought) and only concentrated on rugby in his mid twenties, not playing for Wales until he was nearly 30. He had no real trade as such – he drove bulldozers on building sites and then at the scrap metal yard at Panteg Steelworks – but from the off, he found that the training and discipline at Pontypool helped curb his wilder tendencies and the camaraderie he found at the club offered him a support group he hadn't enjoyed previously. He recognised a lot of wildness in me when we had that first chat in the Pooler clubhouse. He already knew my backstory, though he didn't let on much – in trouble with the police, not that long out of jail, short fuse, a bit gobby, a creature of the night. He knew where I was coming from, but he could also see how running onto a rugby pitch transformed me and brought the best out of me. With just a couple of well-publicised red mist exceptions, I was generally on my best behaviour playing Rugby Union.

He indulged me to an extraordinary extent, so much so that he allowed me to change the way Pooler played. When I joined, he had very rigid views and famously they were almost all formed on the 1959 Lions tour to New Zealand. He'd noticed that the All Blacks' series victory was almost totally down to their superior fitness and narrow game plan. Boss it upfront and let Don Clarke kick the goals. In terms of skill and panache, the 1959 Lions were streets ahead of New Zealand but they still lost the series – although it should be noted that when Pross won his solitary Lions cap in the final Test, they won. Nonetheless, he'd tell you the series was gone by then. He'd arrived in New Zealand as the so-called hard man of Welsh rugby but, to use his own words, got his arse kicked from pillar to post all around the country because he simply wasn't fit enough. He never sugar-coated it. He was on the receiving end when Otago rucked the Lions off the park in Dunedin, and that was another lifelong lesson about the importance of rucking and how there could be collateral damage. If you ruck properly and efficiently, some of your own team would more than likely get caught up in the threshing machine. That was a price you must be prepared to pay. As a team, you had to buy into that.

He took over as Pontypool coach in 1969 after Pooler finished below Penarth at the bottom of the Welsh Championship, and nobody finished below Penarth in anything. When it came to coaching, he unashamedly adopted the All Blacks' style. Pontypool, with their limited catchment area and lowly status in the Welsh game, were never going to attract many of the great natural talents. They had to seek out success by being the fittest and most ruthless side in Wales; all backed up, if possible, by a world-class goal kicker. The 1970s team had Robin Williams; the 1980s team had Doc (Peter Lewis), while Mike Goldsworthy was a pretty handy back-up. "I don't want ball-handlers, I want man-handlers" was one of Pross' maxims at the time, and his dedication to fitness was total. "Rugby is about physical fitness and I'm here to fucking make sure you can't get enough of it," he used to tell us. Pross wanted his teams sprinting through the pain barrier when others were hitting the wall with 20 minutes to go.

He was being entirely practical, working with what he had. I remember attending a social at the club one night – it was a quiz night or an awards night, I forget which – and Gerald Davies was our guest of honour, and he and Pross did a Q & A on the stage. The subject of Gerald's four brilliant tries from four touches in Pooler's famous 1978 Welsh Cup match against Cardiff naturally came up, and Pross started getting all poetic and dreamy. "Gerald, if we'd ever been blessed with you on the wing, you'd have got so much bloody ball, you'd have been begging us to stop and stick it up our jumpers for a while." And he meant it. But Pooler never had a homegrown Gerald Davies or Phil Bennett, so they cracked on and did it their way with the talent available.

He worked you like a dog at fitness training on Monday night – when you would rarely see a ball – and he liked his top players to get into that Wednesday/Saturday rhythm, because there was no substitute for playing when it came to building fitness. To log up 40+ club games before you even thought about Wales training and Test and other appearances was nothing for a Pooler player. We old-timers chuckle today when we hear complaints from the modern generation about overplaying. Really?

At summer training and then fitness training in the season, he was like a horse trainer on the gallops. He stood back and took it all in, master of all he surveyed. Pross had eyes in the back of his head and didn't miss a thing – that's one of the reasons he was so lenient with me. His experienced eye

The One and Only Pross

knew that I was as fit as I could be. There wasn't a single day of the year when I wasn't fit to play top-class rugby – as long as I wasn't in prison, in hospital or banned! I arrived at training at my fighting weight and ready to go. I didn't train to get fit; I got fit to train. Which is possibly why I was spared the Grotto Run, although I always did the pyramid sprints to the bitter end. Being excused the Grotto Run was an extraordinary concession from him because that run – and then scramble on all four paws – up to the high point of Pontypool Park, from where you could see seven counties, was the basis of everything he did and believed in. Going through that pain barrier regularly and the fitness you got from that was what made Pooler so good in the latter stages of a game... I'm not sure what to make of it. I like to think it was a nod to the way I prepared and how he wished others would train away from the club but, to be fair, there were very few slackers at Pooler. Perhaps he just wanted to surround me with a touch of mystique; perhaps in terms of suffering and going to the edge physically, he reckoned I'd already been there with my broken neck and rehab and pushing it again would be counterproductive for me. Or perhaps he just couldn't be bothered to have a huge row with a cocky Cardiff git. I told him at one of my very first sessions that I was a thoroughbred not a Grand National runner and the Grotto Run wasn't for me – he laughed it off rather than make an issue of it. He'd have had his reasons and thought process, for sure. He loved Bobby Windsor to bits but he still made Bobby do the Grotto Run.

Pross was his own invention. He didn't have WRU coaching certificates or spend summer weeks at Ray Williams' coaching camps, but he knew the game inside out. He didn't attend one of the great PE colleges, but he knew everything

227

you needed to know about physical conditioning. He'd have scoffed at the notion of a dedicated sports psychologist, because he thought that was an integral part of being a club coach or captain – being a brain mechanic was a big part of a coach's job. He was a much more complex individual than outsiders thought, although once you got to know the man, that realisation came quickly. He admitted to me that he was a huge mummy's boy: that his mother was the most important person in his life until he married, and it was she who'd instilled "what goodness I have in me". That chimed with me and of course, shrewd man that he was, that's exactly why he mentioned it in conversation. Another time, when I was in the depths of despair over my one solitary Welsh cap, he started talking randomly and very emotionally about the very great privilege of playing for Pontypool, representing the town and area, putting in a proper honest shift every Wednesday and Saturday, which would strike a chord among the many manual labourers among our fans and putting a spring in their steps with our success. He considered that much more important than how many Wales or Lions caps you might or might not have, because selection for those sides was just so random. Wales was a fleeting thing; it was Pontypool that really mattered and it was how the Pooler fans remembered me that counted most... It was what I wanted to hear at the time, hence the conversation, but he truly believed it, nonetheless.

There was also, I feel in retrospect, a hint of guilt in our relationship, or at least the desire to make amends. The look of complete horror and helplessness on his face when he first saw me with my broken neck in hospital has always stayed with me. He thought I was a goner, certainly as a rugby player, yet for the best part of a year Pooler did little

The One and Only Pross

or nothing to support me and I became the forgotten man. I fell off their radar completely. I hadn't made any firm friends in my short time there – I was almost like a permit player, borrowed for a few games from another club. After a while, they knew I'd been spared the worst-case scenario of full-blown paralysis – unlike Pontypool prop Roger Addison, who broke his neck playing against Rugby in 1966, and spent the next 40 years in a hospital bed – and that I'd get to live a pretty normal life once more, but they didn't expect to ever see me at the Park again.

When I returned, Lazarus-like, a year later, fit and raring to go, Pross wasn't expecting it. But it was a chance for both of us to start afresh and, in my opinion, that's another reason – perhaps the main reason – why I benefited from that leeway and leniency that others didn't enjoy. Nobody at the club had believed in me when I lay in that hospital bed, my skull bolted onto a metal frame, nurses having to evacuate my bowels and feed me. But now I was back, Pross for one wanted to rectify that situation. He vowed to afford me every opportunity and to trust me implicitly. That's my take on it, anyway; others from the outside looking in might feel differently.

It was fun and challenging working with Pross, from the off. In that first session – when I made the mistake of going off with the backs after our warm-up laps and he exploded – he sat me down briefly to explain his thinking. Pointing towards his pack, he started saying, "It's them and you, Bish; them and you. Nobody else counts."

We'd argue just occasionally, and my teacher's pet halo would drop. One time he'd got it into his mind that when we did a short line-out move near the opponents try line, it would be better to have Snooty – 6 foot 4 inches and 16 stone

– stand at scrum half to drive the ball over the line after we won the ball. He'd seen the French use that ploy in the Five Nations and liked it – Pooler could do their own version. Feeling personally insulted, I went mad at that suggestion and started shouting at him in the middle of training at the Park. Everybody stopped and listened, including the couple of hundred fans we often got up there, watching us go through our paces. Nobody shouted back at Pross on the training paddock. But, this time, the verbals were strictly one-way traffic as I embarked on a world-class rant.

"Pross, what are you talking about? Who's the best fucking scrum half in Wales? It's me, isn't it? Who's got the best hands and the best break? Me or Snooty? It's me, isn't it? Who's quickest on their feet? Me or Snooty? It's me, every time."

The silence was deafening, but I'd started so I needed to finish. Pross hadn't reacted in any way so far to his gobby Cardiff upstart. Which way was this going to go? I was skating on thin ice. I had no choice but to continue.

"So when that ball comes back from the line-out with one of their flankers three yards offside, who do you want picking the ball up off their fucking feet and going for the line from a standing start? Me or Snooty? It's me, isn't it?

"You wouldn't ask a short-arse like me to jump at the line-out instead of Snooty, or to prop instead of Pricey, so why are you asking Snooty to play scrum half instead of me?

"Enough of this bollocks, Pross. We either do this move with me at nine or not at all."

I finally ran out of steam and braced myself. I could very soon be an ex-Pontypool player... Suddenly, led by Pross and Snooty, everybody burst out laughing, with some even clapping my 'performance'. Smiling massively, Pross strolled over and rested his massive right paw of a hand gently on my head, something which he often used to do in a fatherly sort of way, as if transferring his knowledge to me or vice versa. Perky and the lads thought it was like a Papal blessing, which only heightened the thought that I was the chosen one.

"Fuck me, Bish – you're right. As you were, lads." And the subject of Eddie playing at scrum half at line-outs was never discussed again.

Mostly, there was a quiet, unspoken harmony between me and Pross. We both appreciated what we were doing for each other. From the moment I returned from my broken neck, he backed me all the way. I've mentioned before that, although a night owl, I'd rarely drink much the night before a game. But I did very occasionally fall into bad company and one time I had a massive night on the thrash before a visit to Welford Road to play Tigers. I got home drunk as skunk and Mamma had to wake me up early to cook me breakfast before somebody drove me to the club to get on the coach to Leicester. Within minutes, I was slumped across two seats in a world of my own, with a sick bag in case that dreadful moment came.

I could still hear one or two of the conversations going on in the background, though. Perky was going bonkers. The tirade lasted all the way to Welford Road. "Cardiff shithouse… pisspot… lightweight… irresponsible… totally unacceptable, Pross… it's not good enough… letting the club down… it's Tigers away, not Penarth or Blaenavon at home." And you could see his point, to be fair. All the time, Pross bit his lip and refused to join in, trusting in my powers of recovery. I wouldn't let him down.

And I didn't. We got to the club and I stood under the shower for ten minutes – which seemed to revive me – and then started my pre-match routine, winding up with the blessing with holy water and, on this occasion, a few extra prayers for a quick recovery from my hangover. By the time we ran out, I felt human again and two minutes later, as the adrenaline kicked in, I felt on top of world and had a stormer. We won in style. Pross beamed like a proud father afterwards, no words needed. The next morning, one of the English papers raved about Pooler's SAS-like efficiency in their smash-and-grab raid over Tigers, with David Bishop showing the way. SAS? I sincerely hope the SAS don't turn up three sheets to the wind.

There's a false impression that Pross was always a shouter, a swearer and a Sergeant Major figure, mainly because many remember him driving us hard at the fitness sessions. But although he could let rip and turn the air blue in the changing room, he was more often than not quiet and low key, and moved around offering whispered bits of advice and reassurance here and there. A tap on the shoulder, a knowing wink, a thumbs-up or a last-minute instruction. When he was in this low-key mood, there was no swearing or dramatics. And away from the cutting edge of matchday or training, he was a very relaxed, thoughtful figure, whose favourite pastime was nurturing his small garden where, he insisted, he did most of his thinking. He was always telling me to take up gardening. "Everybody needs a hobby, Bish, otherwise rugby will consume you." A few pot plants is the best I've managed.

Talking to Lyndon Faulkner, I know he credits some of his success to the life lessons he learned at Pooler under Pross. He always mentions how Pross made Pooler a tight-knit family; how good he was in talent ID and making the key signings that could transform a team; the huge value he put on teamwork; and how he got little units working within one big team unit. All that transfers across to the business world. As does Pooler's dedication to the cause and emphasis on supreme fitness, which both breed confidence – that also has a place in the business world, because a company needs to be lean and fit for purpose.

The other thing Lyndon always stresses – and which was a big thing with Pross – was to always be a winner in defeat. If the team or business environment's right, you'll learn your lesson and bounce back from defeat and be even better. An unexpected defeat or setback makes you re-examine what you've been doing and sometimes you spot something that's fundamentally wrong. Nail the basics at all times. We're almost back to my dad insisting I kick off both feet and pass off both hands. At Pooler, a defeat almost always sparked a renewed energy and a run of victories – it awakened something inside us.

Pross was loyal. He was unswerving in his support of me during the Newbridge Incident and its aftermath and saw, straight away. that although I'd transgressed up to a point, it was a blatant attack on his beloved club Pooler as much as it was an effort to make an example of me. They were one and the same. He was outraged at that, and at the hypocritical approach to my punch compared with the many hundreds, possibly thousands, of similar incidents he'd witnessed as a Pooler player and coach. But, realistic man of the world that he was, he also knew how this story would end if the WRU maintained their approach of not picking me. He knew I'd eventually have to go North, and sympathised with my dilemma. "A man must always do what's best for him and his family," he told me. But I sensed an immense sadness as he gave me his blessing.

When I finally signed for Hull KR, I wanted to give him some money but he wouldn't accept it – he said it smacked of payment for services rendered and, old-fashioned rugby man that he was, he felt that was wrong. Pross never took a penny from Pooler, as far as I'm aware, and he didn't condone the bung system – or 'generous expenses' – but, as ever, he was a realist. Back in his early playing days at Pooler, he learned that Benny Jones and Malcolm Price were getting £5 per week expenses and he actually queried it with the committee. He knew it went on back then in the Fifties, let alone in the Eighties, but he insisted on keeping his distance from it. It wasn't his world. He knew that Peter Lawlor had 'made it worth my while', but he wanted to be spared the details so his conscience was clear and he could look the WRU straight in the eye if ever they came knocking. He was convinced the WRU spent every waking hour trying to make life hell for Pooler... and I don't think he was far off the mark.

Anyway, after his refusal to take any money from me, I asked him if there any sort of present he would be willing to accept. He immediately piped up that he'd always wanted a big state-of-the-art TV to watch all the sport and his favourite films on. So I hunted down the biggest and best model money could buy in Cardiff at the time, and delivered it to his house. We enjoyed a big emotional man-hug, and he wished me well and thanked me for everything I'd done for the club – which was ridiculous. It was I who needed to thank him for everything he'd done for me, as a player and as an individual. He could see I'd stuck it out as long as I could, had given Pooler my all, but being excluded from the Wales squad was driving me insane. He muttered his thanks again and with that, he hoisted the TV onto his still massive shoulders and carried it like a sack of spuds into his house. I'd never seen him so happy.

We never lost that close connection, even during my dark days after retiring fully, when I was a lost and troubled soul in the Noughties. He was always there at the end of the phone. The last time I saw him in person was a few years before Covid, when I called by and he was out. I drove into Pooler town and wondered if he might be in the indoor market there – he often used to hang out in a café there, talking to all his fellow pensioners who used to follow Pooler. I parked up, wandered in and that's exactly where he was, dispensing wisdom over a pot of tea, encouraging those who were struggling – the leader of his new team, if you like. Nothing much had changed. I loved the man.

It was a huge shock when he died, although really a man of 93 passing away shouldn't be a shock. But I'd assumed he'd go on forever. It was right at the very height of Covid, with people cowering at home and with big challenges of their own at the time. But I was very angry that he didn't really get the send-off I felt he deserved. I was upset and tearful – both at the passing of this great man and at what I perceived as his lack of recognition from the town to which he brought such honour, although I appreciate times change and it was over 30 years since Pross had been directly involved with the club. Afterwards, when I calmed down, I realised he wouldn't have wanted a huge fuss anyway. It was never about him. He invariably left the clubhouse early after one of our great wins – he never sought the limelight even though, ironically, the media hung on his every word. A great man, who I've missed every day since his passing.

CHAPTER 15

Rugby Heaven with Ringo

THE 1987/88 SEASON was bittersweet for me. Statistically, it was Pontypool's best-ever season, which is saying something, with just two defeats in close on 50 games. Unbeaten away, can you believe? We won the *Western Mail* Welsh Club Championship by a wide margin – which made it four in the last five seasons, the most successful run in the Championship since Aberavon's four in a row back in the 1920s. A word of explanation here for those too young to remember how it was structured back in the Seventies and Eighties. The WRU had always thought a formal league smacked too much of professionalism, and only started pushing for one towards the end of the 1980s. Prior to that, the *Western Mail* Club Championship winners were recognised as the Welsh champions, and we won 35 of the 36 Championship games, losing just once at home to Bridgend. There were doubles over Llanelli, Neath, Swansea, Cardiff and Newport – in fact everybody we played twice, save for Bridgend. We were also 100% against all English opponents, although they of course didn't count towards the Welsh championship. We were unquestionably the strongest week in, week out club side in Britain and Ireland, and possibly in Europe.

Rugby Heaven with Ringo

Under our captain Steve 'Junna' Jones and new coach Bobby Windsor, his assistant 'Sheets' – Goff Davies – and with the now 'retired' Pross always in the stands and never far from Bobby's side when needed, we played an exceptional brand of all-court rugby which ticked all the boxes for me. I got to spend a year playing scrum half to Mark Ring's fly half and, rugby-wise, it was the most enjoyable time of my life. I scored 35 tries, Ringo kicked 357 points and our outside backs were scoring for fun. It was like playing with the Barbarians at times.

I'd seen enough of Bobby from playing alongside him at the tail-end of his career, and then of course all the footage of him in his pomp with Wales and the Lions, to know what an incredible all-round rugby player he was, and what an astute coach he'd be. Bobby wasn't just a front-row hard man (although, of course, he was that as well): he could do everything. I wasn't the slightest bit surprised that Pooler blossomed during his time in charge. He'd seen rugby played at its very best – by two Grand Slam-winning Wales sides and the undefeated 1974 Lions – and that was his template. Bobby was somebody I looked up to immensely. He'd fought for everything in his life and it was impossible to bullshit him or pull the wool over his eyes.

At the end of the season, I also had the privilege of captaining Monmouthshire to their first Welsh Counties Cup for nine years. Small fry, you might think, but for too long Monmouthshire had failed to put out our strongest side and that had to change, given the talent available at the county's seven senior clubs. Another box ticked. I just couldn't get enough rugby – I'd take on any game or sevens tournament, any time. I even answered an emergency call from my old friends the Public School Wanderers one weekend in

December 1987, when they'd arranged a fixture with South Korea up at Old Deer Park. I didn't even know they played rugby in South Korea. That proved unexpectedly eventful – the Korean boys were very fit and physical, and it wasn't the gentle Sunday afternoon jolly after a late Saturday night that some of us had expected. We were leading 29-22 and hanging on a bit towards the end, when Glen Webbe copped a high tackle that injured his neck, and the game had to be abandoned. Glen had only just recovered from a nasty concussion after nearly having his head taken off in the World Cup against Tonga, so he wasn't overly amused.

Somebody from the crowd answered a call from the announcer to attend Glen. They and the physio fashioned a breathing tube out of the solid cardboard tube you wrap tape around, and placed it in his mouth to clear his airway and stop him swallowing his tongue. Later that night, a guy came into the West Middlesex hospital looking for Glen, saying he was a journalist – and suspecting the worst, I'm afraid I told him where to get off. But it was the guy who'd come out of the crowd – David Llewellyn, a reporter from the *Daily Express* – and he'd come to retrieve his coat, which he'd put over Glen to keep him warm until the ambulance arrived. I apologised for my outburst and need to say sorry again all these years later.

I had rugby coming out of my ears. I was in full flood. Yet smouldering away in the background was the certain knowledge that, no matter how well I played, it was all in vain as far as Wales were concerned. They had no intention of picking me – hell would freeze over before they even considered the possibility. By the end of season, the 'Ayatollah' himself – Neath coach Brian Thomas – was calling me the best player in the northern hemisphere. He pleaded with the

Welsh selectors to take me on the tour to New Zealand that summer, when the more observant critics could see Wales might be riding for an almighty fall. Pooler had done the double in regular season games over Neath and I'd enjoyed a stormer when we won 13-9 at the Gnoll, which was a bit of a bogey ground for us. He wasn't one to dish out lavish praise on anybody, let alone a Pontypool player. I have his words after that 13-9 win here in front of me.

> Bishop is the best player in the northern hemisphere. He is a very strong man both in mind and physique. Sometimes a player can be strong in physique but weak in mind. He is strong in both. He has many strings to his bow. He has been criticised in the past for not being a team man but he is a team in his own right, and that says it all. I have seen him play when he has effectively played in five positions in a match, not just scrum half. He knew where to be when our kicks went astray – last night he snapped them up. He's magic. The one game Pontypool have lost this season, he wasn't playing, and look at them last year without him. He has got everything and I find it surprising that Wales keep ignoring him. They would be fools not to take him to New Zealand. Pontypool would have lost to us twice this season without him.

His encouragement was very welcome and I cut the article out and kept it handy to remind myself, occasionally, that there were major rugby figures in Wales who believed in me. But I knew for certain that Brian's plea would fall on deaf ears where it mattered. One thing that had really hurt was not even being considered for the Wales sevens squad to compete in the Australian Bicentenary competition in Sydney in 1986, which was being billed as a Sevens World Cup. Seriously? Nobody in Wales played more sevens than me and nobody was as successful across the board. Even my fiercest critic would have told the WRU I should have been the first name on the team sheet as skipper. Robert Jones was selected, and he was no sort of sevens player at all. That was just plain spiteful of the WRU.

Robert was now the chosen man and for all our so-called rivalry, this was really the only season when we were technically in direct competition with each other for the scrum half spot – a season when I wasn't banned altogether, banned specifically from the Wales team or recovering from pretty catastrophic injury. Except we weren't in competition, were we? In my entire time as a player, I think Gwent only ever had one big Five Member for a short period of time – Terry Cobner. For the 1987 World Cup, Wales somehow managed to select not a single player from any of the seven senior Gwent clubs. No wonder I and others were a little paranoid about what we perceived as a west Wales, or at least Welsh-speaking, 'mafia'. It was absurd then and remains absurd looking back. It still makes me rage. There's nothing that anybody can say to ease that pain.

Quietly, behind closed doors, it drove me half mad with frustration and encouraged a great deal of paranoia, but that was countered by the sheer release of running onto the pitch twice a week and expressing myself in actions, not words – demonstrating time after time what Wales were missing. God, that made me feel good, but it was only a short-term high, twice a week – an ego massage and a boost to my morale. We played rugby with a smile as well as plenty of grunt, but those days between matches and training with the boys were dark. That's probably why I sought out rugby games for whoever would have me – Public School Wanderers, Monmouthshire, sevens tournaments, charity games on Sundays. Anything to keep going and stay sane.

What was going on? I was on top of my game, but right at the back of the queue. My career was hurtling down the road to nowhere. Deep down, I was playing mainly to brandish two fingers at the WRU, but there's only so much satisfaction to be gleaned from that and it doesn't pay the bills, although Peter Lawlor continued to bung me. I knew with nagging certainty this would be my last Union season. I didn't want to go North – in fact, I was extremely anxious about the whole prospect. I was a confirmed homebird who got homesick just crossing the Severn Bridge. But what choice did I have? With the benefit of hindsight, I should have been braver earlier. I wish now I'd bitten the bullet and gone North at the end of the 1984/85 season. Had I known then that I'd played my last game for Wales, I could have turned professional three years earlier at the absolute height of my fitness and form, and enjoyed a few more years learning the League game. I could have forged a much more substantial League career and done myself justice.

At least I signed off from Union on a high. I wanted to leave everybody something good to remember me by so they'd think, 'What a loss to the Welsh game!' Well, that was my emotion at the time – little did I know I would reappear for Pooler seven years later, when Rugby Union unexpectedly turned open and I returned as a player/coach. I was an older, heftier, much injured and extremely battered version of myself, although I like to think I still made a difference and rolled back the years occasionally.

Back in the summer of 1987, before the start of that successful 1987/88 season, I'd convinced myself that once my ban ended, the selectors would treat me fairly and was highly motivated. I'd watched the World Cup with a jaundiced eye, thinking of course that I should have been there, and although Wales came third, the painful drubbing they took at the hands of New Zealand in the semi-final was a true indication of our world standing. Wales had the makings of a decent side and a couple of outside backs – Jonathan 'Jiffy' Davies and Ieuan Evans – who could produce moments of brilliance that disguised serious deficiencies, and a really solid unit in midfield in John Devereux. But we were still a long way off and I knew I could make a big difference.

"One more effort," I told myself. "This could happen yet. Don't give up. Keep your mouth shut, behave yourself and play your bollocks off."

As a compulsive viewer of all the VHS match tapes, I knew what Wales needed was much more of a threat at scrum half. More power, pace, breaking potential, try-scoring potential, stronger tackling, more dynamism and more physicality. Scrum halves need to give so much more than just a good service. As far as I'm concerned, that's a given, surely? If you go out at the start of 80 minutes with the one ambition of just providing a smooth service to your fly half, you're denying your team so much else.

It's the extras that made the difference. Wales couldn't leave it all up to Jiffy to provide the creativity and spark, because he was quickly becoming a heavily marked man. Much better to have both half backs firing shots. I look at the scrum halves I've admired – Gareth Edwards, Terry Holmes, Joost van der Westhuizen, George Gregan, Mike Phillips, Antoine Dupont – and they have every weapon in the armoury. Attacking and defensive lynchpins. A Test scrum half must be more than just a facilitator. And here's the thing. If the opposition have to be wary at all times of an attacking scrum half, the outside half automatically gets more time and space. It's a win-win situation.

The painful shortcomings were there for everybody to see again when New Zealand twice put 50 points on Wales during the summer tour of 1988 – the one Brian Thomas had begged Wales to send me on – scoring 18 tries to one. Watching at home, I could have wept. I should have been there, doing my bit.

And then in December 1988, by which time I'd gone, we only went and lost 15-9 at home to Romania – after which even Jiffy decided it was time to jump ship. At least he'd been given a chance to make a difference.

So to rewind 18 months, I was hyped up and training hard in the boxing gym and out on the park that summer of 1987. I did my usual circuit of demanding sevens tournaments, I gave my baseball some serious attention and put in the hard yards up at Pooler fitness training, especially in the pyramid sprints chasing Shaft, although I still declined the Grotto Run, which had no value for me. I didn't go on the piss all summer like some. I was fit 24-7 – for me, back in my pomp, it was always just a fine-tuning process. I take the view that it's such bloody hard work getting fit that you should do it only once in your career. Once you're there, once you've reached the summit of fitness, then the trick is to tick over and make sure you don't slip down the other side. Binge training is no good for you, just as binge drinking, binge eating, binge anything is no good for you. Take it from somebody who learned the hard way – once you've reached peak fitness, just keep doing a bit of work every day. I've never liked the terms 'off-season' or 'pre-season'. For me, the season lasts all 365 days of the year. That's the professional approach.

That summer, there were changes afoot after a bloody poor 1986/87 when Pontypool had missed both me and the criminally underrated Chris Huish, who'd been recovering from injury. Pooler had finished an unthinkable 14th in the *Western Mail* Welsh Club Championship, behind the likes of Maesteg, Abertillery, Glamorgan Wanderers, London Welsh and South Wales Police, for God's sake. What the bloody hell was going on? We needed to hit back and get inventive or we'd revert to being a small-time Gwent valleys outfit again. It was make-or-break time for Pooler, and I tried to bring some of that urgency to proceedings.

Mark Ring was two years younger than me at Cardiff Youth and I'd only really got to know him socially, through playing baseball. We were mates for a while without being bosom pals, but that summer, playing baseball after he got back from the World Cup, I got to know him better and got the impression he was very unsettled at Cardiff.

Firstly, Ringo was definitely a fly half by inclination – the ultimate playmaker and creative genius – but Cardiff and Wales insisted playing him at centre. He could do a very good job there, of course, because he was class, but his lack of absolute pace was sometimes exposed.

Secondly, from what I could gather, it didn't seem that Cardiff were 'looking after' their big players, as the euphemism of the time went. There were no generous expenses or bungs. Being good enough to play for Cardiff and Wales and filling stadiums was a full-time business, but Ringo, one of the biggest box-office players in Welsh and British rugby, was getting nothing for his efforts. In fact, I think he was still having to pay his club membership just for the honour of representing Cardiff. If Mark was playing today, he'd be a marquee player in the Premiership on £1m a year, or the star man at one of the big Top 14 clubs. No question – he was the Finn Russell of his era, a fabulous player.

So, with Pooler's permission, I started working on him. Did he fancy a move to Pooler? It seemed radical, but why not? In fact, he didn't take much persuasion, though I think London Welsh were also showing an interest and trying to put a package together, including college and professional qualifications. On the table at Pooler was a guaranteed start at fly half all season with a few quid per point, along the lines of the deal I had. Doc – Peter Lewis – was retiring, so he'd also be our front-line goal kicker, and I'd only step in for the long-range howitzers. He could take every other kick. Pooler also offered him a car and petrol, but Ringo didn't drive at the time. So the club organised driving lessons, and he finally got there on the third attempt, I believe. It's funny how some of the most dextrous, coordinated sportsmen are bang average car drivers. And I'd include myself in that!

Then I turned my attention to Pablo Rees, another fellow baseballer. The Cardiff baseball scene was awash with rugby talent, enjoying their summer. Pablo is one of the great characters of the Welsh game and energised every changing room he was a part of. It was Pablo, if you remember, who got me up to Ebbw Vale in my time of need, when Cardiff kicked me out. And it was Pablo who'd bent Charlie Faulkner's ear when he was at Newport and got Charlie to contact me that time, just before I moved to Pooler.

Pablo was a freewheeling character who liked to travel and smell the roses, so I decided to tempt him with the promise of a Pontypool club tour to Fiji the following summer. The summer tour destination – all expenses paid, obviously – was the major unit of currency in the amateur days when players left clubs, way more than the pocket money or expenses most clubs tried to pay. The summer tour was usually the deal clincher.

Of course, no such plans existed: we were actually heading to Germany again to enjoy rides on tanks, drink gallons of foaming beer and to play the Welsh Guards and the British Army of the Rhine. And that was about it, save for the beery weekend in Limerick playing Munster which we normally organised. It was a month or more into the season before my lie about the Fiji tour was fully exposed, and by then Pablo was having so much fun with us he decided to stay put for the rest of the campaign. Although a very successful businessman in retirement, life and sport were never about the money for Pablo – just the craic and the good times.

Pooler fans were rubbing their eyes in disbelief. Yes, we'd always been able to play a more expansive game than we were given credit for, but that tended to happen in the final quarter when we'd worn opponents down and they could scarcely walk, let alone run. With Ringo at the helm, we could travel to the beat of a different drum, attacking from anywhere at any time. Anything was possible and, although of course at times it suited us to keep things tighter, the fact is that Pontypool was a spectacular side for most of that memorable season.

I always knew Ringo was good, but I had no real idea what a rugby genius he was until I partnered him at half back. Save for a lack of real pace, there was nothing he couldn't do. He'd mastered every skill in the book, and he made it look so bloody easy. It was a privilege and a joy to play with him that season and he lifted my spirits, despite all my internal brooding as to where my career was going. He played with a cheeky smile and the Ringo strut, and he was so 'unPontypool' it was almost comical. It was like an alien life form had arrived unannounced at the Park, but the fans took to him instantly.

Rugby Heaven with Ringo

I remember the first time he went back to Cardiff, for our Cup game that season. The first two things he did in the opening minutes was to put a 70-metre touch-finder down the line and then, from the line-out and not my best-ever pass, he stopped, set himself and chipped over a 30-metre drop goal with his wrong foot, from pretty wide out. Then there was the day he masterminded our big win over Llanelli at the Park, when we needed 40 or more points to pass the world record for the number of points in a club season. We were in no mood to declare, and he ran the Scarlets ragged that day. All season he was purring for us. He reeled off round-the-back offloads and no-look passes before we even had a phrase to describe them. He'd slow to a walk or even stop and draw the defender in to take the hit before passing and, if the ball went loose, he'd just bend down and scoop it up one-handed, while running at full speed. It was like Meadowlark Lemon and the bloody Harlem Globetrotters some days. Ringo was born 30 years too early. He'd be rugby's great entertainer in the modern game.

Pross, enjoying retirement but as engrossed in the game as ever, pulled me aside after one game early in the season: "Bish. This fucking Ringo, I can't make him out. He's a trick cyclist, a bloody circus act, isn't he? He can't be for real?"

"No, he's the real deal, Pross, take it from me. Pooler need to trust him, like you trusted me."

I often get asked who the best fly half I played with/against was and I always go with Ringo, even though he only played a couple of games in that position for Wales, at the end of his career when Wales weren't great and his knee had gone. He was a magician and the reason I place him fractionally above Huw Davies and Jiffy is his all-round game. As well as his passing skills, he was one of the best kickers of a rugby ball I ever saw, and that's before you even take into account his jinking and dummying. Jiffy was an extraordinary strike runner at fly half, who could open defences on his own or carve out tries for others, and he had a nose for drop goals as well – people forget that about Jiffy – but as an all-round rugby talent, I'm going with Mark by a whisker.

Pablo was a huge influence as well in this season for the ages at Pooler. Like Ringo, he lacked that extra yard of gas some like to see in backs, but he was so strong and powerful and so positive and attacking in his outlook that he still caused carnage from fifteen.

In the environment we were creating, all our backs began to flourish. Wales B wing Alun Glasson arrived from Cardiff and suddenly Roger Bidgood and Keith Orrell were on fire in the centre. I'd always rated Roger but the selectors were none too kind to him either. The so-called Big Five couldn't believe Pooler could produce such a rock-solid talent at centre. As for Keith, he was highly skilful and opportunistic. A little bit mercurial, but when he was hot, he was very hot – and a natural try-scorer, amongst other things, which is not that common for centres. When I ponder my all-time Pooler XV, which I do often, it's always an agonising toss-up between the unbreakable defensive line that Lyndon Faulkner and Lee Jones offered for a couple of seasons and the attacking capability of the Bidgood-Orrell combo. I normally come down in favour of the latter, but it's a close-run thing and it would probably depend on who we were playing. I'm proud to have played with all four of them.

I'd never had so much fun playing rugby – well, away from sevens, anyway – and I even started staying much later at the Pontypool clubhouse of an evening. In the past, I'd often made my excuses and headed back to the bright lights of

Cardiff, but the feelgood vibe that year was great. We were a tight bunch.

One of the moments the season is remembered for is when we played Swansea in the Cup, in the fifth round in atrocious conditions at the Park. Pooler never ever postponed a game; in fact, I don't think we even bothered with pitch inspections. Rugby was a winter game and you took whatever the Weather Gods threw at you. One time we played Berry Hill with over a foot of freshly fallen snow on the ground. We were the only game in Britain that week. Anyway, the Swansea game was much anticipated – not least by me, with the prospect of Robert Jones in opposition and some of the so-called Big Five in attendance. R H Williams and Derek Quinnell were definitely there, and I believe Clive Rowlands, Robert Jones' father-in-law, was also in the crowd.

We won 29-18, but it was more comfortable than the scoreline suggests. I enjoyed a top game in the mud with my dive pass coming into play – as a scrum half, you don't have to spin pass to deliver a smooth service. The problem with spin passes to this day, even with the much better quality balls they use, is that they take time to wind up and are very predictable. You can read them. This is another reason I sometimes baulk when people go on about Robert Jones' service. Yes, he had a very decent spin pass – I'll acknowledge that – but the spin pass isn't always the pass you want or need. In some weather conditions – rain, mud, wind – it's easier and more efficient, although not so flash, to execute a dive pass or a simple swing-through end-over-end pass. The other thing which nobody ever talks about is that I know a lot of fly halves who didn't always enjoy catching bullet spin passes, especially in the wet and especially with some of the ropey balls that we used. Spin passes can come at real speed, pointy end first – like a torpedo cutting through the water – which can make for tricky catching. There isn't much to grab hold of. The traditional pass, meanwhile, comes at you at less speed, end-over-end or just sitting upright, and can give you an easier pass to catch, especially under pressure. I'm just saying. The spin pass looks great, and much of the time it's the right option, but not always.

I digress. I was on fire and finished things off by smashing home a penalty in midfield from about 45 metres out – given the angle – that was still going up as it went between the posts. I reckon it was worth about 65 metres on a normal day! I was elated, almost more than I can recall at any time in my career. Before the game, I'd told myself that if I did something special or spectacular, I'd pause and give the so-called Big Five in the stand a massive two finger sign – or perhaps blow kisses to them. But, as the kick was signalled good, I vetoed those thoughts. It would almost certainly result in a life ban or another prison sentence. Then I thought I'd do a bum-wiggle for the benefit of the fans on the Bank by way of celebration but, as I was preparing for that, I thought it was such a good idea that I'd do it for the selectors instead. I looked into Pooler's small stand, spotted them, and then turned my back on them and wiggled my arse three or four times in their general direction before trotting on.

Unbeknown to me, this was the celebration that Fatima Whitbread had used to celebrate her World Championship javelin throw the previous summer. So, many apologies to Fatima for that! I thought it was my own spur-of-the-moment invention. Hopefully I didn't breach any intellectual property rights.

It was an undeniably sweet moment, and I think Pross also stood up, shook his fist at the selectors and swore at them about it being bloody criminal that they wouldn't select me. All to no avail, but I knew that anyway. I probably wouldn't have done it otherwise; I was getting a little demob happy.

The 24-carat perfection of that season was spoiled by just two games, our only defeats. The first, at home to Bridgend, I watched from the Pooler Grandstand. I was in trouble again and a meeting had been arranged with Ray Williams, by then Secretary of the WRU, who'd been sent to investigate widespread reports that I might have tried to sign for the Rugby League club St Helens the previous day.

The reports were widespread because they were true. However, the deal had fallen through (more on that in the next chapter) and I'd slunk back to Pooler with my tail between my legs. Luckily, nobody other than Saints officials, whose lips were sealed, had categorically seen me at St Helens – which was important when Mr Williams came up to interview me at Pooler the following day. I decided I'd brazen it out and see if they could prove what I'd done.

Pross had intercepted Ray at the ground and given him an earful about how yet another long WRU ban would kill me – literally. "In the name of God, give the boy a break!" was his message. I think the man-to-man-approach from Pross may have touched a nerve with Williams, and I was more than a little surprised when Ray greeted me like an old friend. We'd scarcely spoken directly since I collaborated with him on *Rugby for Beginners*, although, obviously, he was a senior figure in an organisation I deeply distrusted, and he'd been the man often tasked with the latest media updates on my disciplinary issues over the previous two or three years. We spoke behind the main stand at Pooler and, after the initial pleasantries, our conversation was brief and to the point.

"David, I've read reports that you were at St Helens yesterday, signing for them. Are these reports true?"

"No, Mr Williams, they aren't." Not a lie – there'd been no signing!

"OK, that's fine by me, David. Stay healthy, keep playing well and send my regards to your father if I miss him."

"Thank you, Mr Williams. I will."

And with that unexpectedly civilised and practical exchange, he went back up into the stand to watch the rest of the game. I owe him a debt. Most of the WRU seemed out to get me most of the time. But not Ray Williams, for which I give belated thanks.

Meanwhile, in the game with Bridgend, the boys were going very well without me, leading 15-0 at half-time. But Ringo started getting overelaborate after the break and making things too complicated, and we let them back into the game – so much so that they pipped us. That was annoying. In fact, I give him stick about it to this day. If I'd been on the park, I'd have starved Ringo of ball for ten minutes until we had the game 100% won.

The second occasion we lost that season – and the only time I personally experienced defeat – was when Neath deservedly beat us in the Cup semi-final. It was the single biggest disappointment of my career behind getting just the one cap. I'd set my heart on some farewell silverware and going undefeated individually for the entire season in all games. Great occasion, big crowd at the Arms Park, sunny weather but breezy, and a heavy pitch from rain, although it was fine throughout the game. It was the one day in fifty that season when we collectively lost concentration and focus. We took first use of a strong wind and turned around 9-0 up – it should have been 20-odd, but we failed to capitalise on a lot of pressure and decent approach work. Early in the second half, Ringo missed a kick that was simple by his standards and, from that moment, 50 minutes in – it was all downhill for us. We'd failed to cash in, Neath got second wind and played superbly with the elements to run out 20-9 winners. Their pack really took it to us and all three of their tries came from set-piece moves. They were the one side at the time who could match us for 80-minute fitness and, for once, it was our turn to suffer.

The first half, ironically, produced one of the best tries I was ever involved with at Pooler, and illustrated our new approach that season. We were midfield, 10–15 yards in front of our 22, and Ringo took position on his own, out to my right. The intention seemed to be a simple pass, for him to drill it into the far corner using the wind. Or maybe a high, hanging kick for Alun Glasson to chase. Anyway, it was clear he wanted the ball and had something in mind. We had a telepathic understanding by now, and I instinctively knew he wanted to make the play.

It was a strong, steady scrum and, at the base of it, I dummied expansively – you were allowed to do that back then, to keep their back row honest – before giving him a quickfire pass deliberately aimed to his right, to give him more time for the kick I thought he probably wanted. Except, on the hoof, he decided not to kick. He caught the ball and stepped infield at the exact same instant, as only genius players can do, before tearing off into the middle of the pitch. The move was on. Pablo had read Ringo like a book and steamed up on his outside, taking the ball at full pelt before handing on to Roger Bidgood. Again, everything done at full speed, not faltering or stopping – perfect passing. Roger handed on to Keith Orrell, who then timed his pass to Sean Hanson on the left wing. Sean hit the accelerator and roared into the corner for a try, which had Gerald Davies up in the commentary box raving for weeks. That'll do for me.

The Neath back row were very good and, personally, I didn't get much mileage out of them on the day. When he was 'on one', Phil Pugh was a particularly formidable opponent who often raised his game against Pooler. He had a stormer, but I should have boxed much cleverer and mixed it up more. I'm annoyed with myself to this day. Their coach Brian Thomas, when dishing out his extravagant praise of my play a few weeks earlier after Pooler completed a regular season double over Neath, did mention they had a plan for me in the Cup and he was right. Phil almost did a football-style man-marking job on me. He was my shadow for 80 minutes and, for the only time that season, I couldn't come up with the answer after the break. I should have gone into facilitator mode, fed Ringo as smoothly as possible, sent Phil to sleep a bit, and then maybe struck. If I could have one day on the rugby pitch back so I could do it differently, it would be this one.

I thought we'd got over our Cup phobia – we'd put away good Swansea and Cardiff sides in the two previous rounds – but no. It was a massive opportunity lost. We bounced back straight away in the next game and finished the season in storming style, but it left a bad taste and I'd never get to play at the Arms Park again.

It was soon afterwards that I treated myself to that little end-of-season diversion in the Welsh Counties Cup, when Monmouthshire (Gwent) decided to give it a proper lash. Their chairman, Jim Regan, was a friend of the family and I went to school with his son Chris. Jim cornered me one night at the Pooler clubhouse and asked, "What about it?"

Monmouthshire usually didn't bother, and put in weakish teams. Why not change that trend? I could be the captain, coach, chief cook and bottle-washer, just like with my prison team. And we would make it a bit of fun. OK, I was up for that. Pooler provided the five or six core players, but all the senior teams in the county provided at least one player and I was genuinely excited by the mini-campaign. Our toughest game was probably first up at Sardis Road against Glamorgan, who drew heavily on Cardiff and Pontypridd players – but we won that handily enough, 25-12. We then really let rip against North Wales in the semis, crushing them 50-6 before the final against Breconshire at Pontypool Park. We piled into them, scoring nine tries in a crushing 46-4 win. I enjoyed the responsibility of being captain and soon after that I was asked to be captain of Pontypool for the 1988/89 season – a great honour but, barring something extraordinary happening, I already knew I'd be gone before the first match was played.

Still not quite 28, my Rugby Union career was to all intents and purposes over, at the elite level anyway. During that time, I'd spent a year in prison; the best part of year recovering from a broken neck; 11 months barred from any Wales team, although still allowed to play club rugby pending a court hearing; and then 11 months on top of that barred from all rugby – indeed, all sport, technically, although I continued to play baseball and still worked out with the boxers down the gym. Despite all the chaos, distractions and grief, I'd helped Pooler win four Welsh Club Championships, finished runners-up once, enjoyed two world record-breaking seasons with the club and won the Welsh Schweppes Cup. I'd been sent off once – correctly, albeit a bit harshly, in my opinion – against Saracens, while during that entire time (from 1980 to the end of the 1987/88 season), I'm struggling to recall one single match in which the opposition didn't try to 'get' me with either a well-aimed kick or a punch, and often both at the same time. One night down at the Gnoll, I reckon the entire Neath pack put a stud in me at one hellish ruck, with a couple of them reversing to go back for seconds. I couldn't lie on my back to sleep for a fortnight or more. But that was the game.

It came with the territory and, generally, I kept my cool or the Pooler forwards sorted out the perpetrator. The moment I retaliated or became the enforcer (as at Newbridge), I was instantly installed as public enemy number one and deemed unacceptable in Welsh rugby forever. Off the pitch, I was still not a fully formed human being – I freely admit to that – and had a habit of not being able to avoid trouble in town, where somebody was always looking to fight me and make a name for themselves. But on the pitch, my record was much better than many, including a number of Wales regulars whose dismissals for frequent punching, kicking and incidents of foul play were never held against them. I was being treated differently and, alas, it was time to give up on my Wales dreams. Message received, loud and clear. I wasn't wanted. It was probably time to piss off.

One big regret around this time, while I was agonising before taking the plunge to go North, was the issue of the Pooler captaincy, which I've already briefly mentioned. The Pooler committee offered it to me, which I can now see was a final roll of the dice to get me to stay – a bit like when Ebbw Vale offered me their vice-captaincy at the age of 19. I was honoured by Pooler's appointment, but I accepted reluctantly, doubting if I'd ever get to fulfil the duties. It was a confusing time for yours truly, in retrospect, and I wish I'd handled things better. What I wasn't fully aware of at the time was that Bobby wasn't in favour at all, for the best of reasons. He knew me better than I knew myself and was, rightly, convinced I'd probably be gone by the autumn and didn't want that disruption to his team. He dug his heels in. He wanted Mark Ring as captain and argued his case strongly in front of the club committee. The Blazers eventually voted for me and Bobby stepped down as coach, feeling his wishes had been ignored, although he stayed on at the club as a committeeman and helper. John Perkins was voted in as the new coach. Then, when I did sign for Hull KR, Ringo decided it was time to head back to Cardiff, which I'd have confidently predicted if anybody had asked me. Coach gone, star fly half gone, star scrum half gone. Pablo retired soon after that, I think, and Roger Bidgood and Keith Orrell were soon sought out by Newport. Others departed. The magic spell was broken, a brilliant side and managerial set-up vanished almost overnight, and Pooler endured a very tough season straight after I departed. Happily they rallied strongly for a couple of years under Perky and reached the Cup Final again in 1991, a superb achievement, before the bad times arrived with a bump. I was distressed by any upset I may have inadvertently caused, but I'd given all I could for the club. My main consideration now had to be to try and secure a future for myself, given that Wales wouldn't look at me.

CHAPTER 16

Tough Going Up North

My Rugby League career was ill-starred and ended in unsatisfactory fashion, but I still look back on it fondly and remain friendly with many old Hull Kingston Rovers colleagues and fans, not to mention quite a few opponents. I go back to Hull three or four times a year, which I suspect is more often than some Welsh players who took the money and 'went North'. I didn't remotely achieve what I wanted – and we'll go into the reasons for that – but I'm still proud of my efforts in a team battling the odds. In my two completed seasons with Hull KR, I was voted the fans' Player of the Season on both occasions, and that means more than I can say. They 'got' me and I loved them. I enjoyed their straight talking and bluntness. In fact, I found that refreshing everywhere in the League game and in the north of England generally. I grew to love League as a game but became incredibly frustrated that a dire run of injuries and making the switch too late in my career meant that I never really achieved my full potential. There were days, though, when I felt on fire and anything seemed possible.

It was definitely the hardest time of my sporting life physically because, at least when I was playing, there was simply no comparison between amateur Union and professional League in terms of fitness, physicality and violence. Stuff that would scarcely get ten minutes in League would have earned a six-month ban in Union but, strangely, there was an honesty about it which made it more acceptable. The stiff-arm tackles, punches and scraps were up front and in the open, and often seemed an accepted and anticipated part of a game, like an ice hockey punch-up. They were part of League's DNA, and often expected by the paying crowd. There was no stigma for League 'hard cases' – in fact, there was often kudos, and much-loved characters were sometimes almost expected to do their stuff. I always say the only similarities between Union and League at the time was the ball and the sticks. In every other respect, it was a foreign sport that had to be learned afresh. Never underestimate the achievements of those Union players who made a big success of the switch.

I started on the back foot: my mindset was all wrong. I'd never really wanted to play League, my focus was totally on a glorious Wales career in Union. When that was denied me, I looked to League initially as a last resort and, frankly, a chance to cash in my chips after the bitter disappointment of a thwarted Union career. I wasn't particularly attracted to League, nor was I sure if my particular Union skills as a scrum half transferred easily to League. Terry Holmes, admittedly on one leg by that point, after his injuries, had struggled to make an impact and it seemed to me that Union centres, fly halves and flankers were the most suited to making a successful switch.

But beggars can't be choosers. I was on the road to nowhere in Union. Winning games for Pooler was beginning to lose its appeal – it felt hollow without the reward of a

Wales career – and a few League clubs certainly seemed to be interested. My ideal move – the move most likely to remotivate and enthuse me – would have been to League giants St Helens, and I was genuinely quite excited and flattered that their supremo Alex Murphy had spotted my talent himself and wanted to sign me so badly. The offer certainly wasn't going to be through the roof – £100,000 as opposed to the £120,000 I was to eventually receive from Hull KR – but with St Helens, it never seemed to be just about the money. I'd be part of a star-studded squad that would, inevitably, be challenging for silverware across the board. I'd be surrounded by the very best League talent, and to a certain extent there'd be time to learn my craft and to be eased into the squad. And as a member of a successful Saints team, the expectation was that a decent GB career would follow.

When we first met, at a motorway services outside Worcester, Alex had been very warm and supportive; he spoke my language. Although a League legend, he'd played two years of Union for the RAF and Combined Services during his national service and knew how to explain things and make comparisons between the two games. He had an exact idea of how he wanted to use my talent. He was the sort of coach you would die for – and if I had to go North, this was the club for me. The officials were slick and efficient. When I asked for a car on top of my £100,000, they didn't bat an eyelid – that would be totally OK.

After dancing the dance with St Helens for a few weeks, I finally decided it was the right time to move, and Alex arranged for me to come up for a medical one Friday, with somebody tipping off the northern press boys that there'd be a big announcement late that afternoon. I headed north up the motorway at the crack of dawn, nervous because this was bound to be life-changing, and slipped into the St Helens ground, where their doctors were waiting for a pre-signing medical. Unfortunately for me, Alex wanted me at Saints so badly neither he nor the club had clocked the small matter of a broken neck less than seven years earlier. When it came to the club medical, which I needed to pass for insurance purposes, their club doctor spotted my scar just as I was pulling my shirt back and panic set in when I told them the full story. There was no deception on my part: it hadn't occurred to me they might not know my backstory, given all the publicity at the time and the frequent references to it in the press afterwards. Alex was happy to go ahead and risk it – I'd played a huge amount of rugby since my recovery and had flourished – but the Saints' directors, who were stumping up the cash, weren't happy. It was an unacceptable risk.

The deal was off and, as a final insult, I then had to climb into the boot of a car to be driven away from the ground, to dodge the media that were gathering, with £85 expenses to cover the cost of the day. Alex was upset and I overheard some heated conversations with the club directors, with him saying he'd resign if they didn't complete my signing. But from the moment the medics got involved, it was never going to happen and Alex's threat was futile. It was a big blow for me though. The set-up had felt right – Alex would have given me wings.

My League career felt in tatters before it started, though luckily it wasn't. In tandem with Ringo and a rejuvenated Pooler, I continued to play some of my best-ever rugby that season with Pooler and, soon after Christmas, Hull KR came in for both me and Ringo, the idea initially being a very high-profile joint signing that would certainly have been some coup and caused a stir up North and indeed in south Wales. It was a bit awkward because they were offering me – with my one Wales cap – considerably more than Ringo, who had 20-odd caps at the time and was the undoubted pin-up boy in Wales and a superb box-office player. Their explanation was that they thought I was better suited to League, that I was more robust physically and they'd get more bang for their buck from me – which is more than ironic considering the litany of injury issues I was to encounter when I did switch codes. I'm not sure Ringo was ever that interested, to be honest, and he stepped back from the offer pretty quickly. But I was all in. Almost the first thing Hull KR said was that they knew all about my broken neck but wouldn't have a problem covering the necessary insurance costs and, frankly, there seemed no reason not to move. It was now or never.

The year before I joined, they were mid-table in the Championship but hardly ripping up trees, which did worry me a little. Friends who knew their way around League warned me that Hull KR was an ageing team, possibly on the way down rather than up. But the Board members I spoke to insisted that they had other big-name signings in mind. There was going to be a major rebuild at the club, which sounded promising – although it didn't really materialise. It was far from what I'd dreamed of, unfortunately. In football terms it was like being courted by Manchester City only to fail the medical and be picked up by Burnley. Sorry, Burnley fans, but you know what I mean.

I haggled hard over the contract. I'm not sure why, but deep down I was probably still rebelling against having to 'accept' a career in League. It felt like second best. That was the level of my ego. So, rather to my shame now, I was a bit dismissive of League and not over-careful who I upset when we met at a very upmarket hotel near Hereford.

The basic deal was good. £50,000 on signing, £35,000 in the second year and then £17,500 for each of years three and four. That was the basic – that graduated scheme was how it worked for everybody back then, although I'm not sure why. There was clearly the temptation for players to be less committed in the final two years after they'd trousered the main part of the money on offer. Then there were the add-ons: a £300 win bonus, £50 when we lost and a £20,000 bonus if I was capped by Great Britain. I also somehow managed to sell exclusive stories and promises of future columns to both *The Sun* and the *Mirror* – arch rivals – for £20,000 and £15,000 apiece, and agreed to a third column for *Wales on Sunday*, which also paid well enough, although not in that league. These don't sound like huge amounts now and indeed, compared with Premiership football, they clearly weren't. But in 1988 they were tidy sums – you probably have to multiply everything by at least 10, maybe more. Kate and I bought our first house around this time for £22,000, which gives you some idea.

I really dug my heels in over a car. I'm an almost compulsive haggler; there's probably some kind of psychological explanation about wanting to feel that power and enjoy the victory of getting a deal. I wanted a top-of-the-range BMW – there was no offer initially, but I wore them down. I wouldn't sign until I got the car, and eventually one of the directors piped up that he'd look after the car for me. So the deal was done. I was the flavour of the month, and the power that makes you feel went to my head a little bit. What I didn't realise – because, as explained previously, I wasn't a proper adult human being at this stage – is that my

VIP status was strictly temporary. You're soon yesterday's man. I was determined to spend almost all of the money as quickly as possible but Kate, thank God, got me to buy a few houses for rent with it as well, which came in handy when the bad times arrived.

A big issue from the start was my relationship with coach Roger Millward, a true League legend – one of the best British players ever, who won 29 caps for Great Britain and made more than 400 appearances for Rovers. He was by all accounts an incredible playmaker and try-scorer and a pint-sized warrior, as tough as hell, and when he died in 2016, the club retired the No. 6 shirt.

The problem, though, was that Roger had never seen me play and had no part in my signing. I'd been forced on him and, understandably, he didn't like that much. I wasn't his man. I would have to prove myself in his hypercritical eyes. Plus, the expectation and hype in the press was that I'd play five-eighth, i. e. his old No. 6 shirt, and that I might be the new Roger Millward. All very difficult.

I'd been spoiled by the father-son relationship I'd enjoyed with Pross, surely a once-in-a-lifetime situation, and I just couldn't get on the same wavelength as Roger. We had no real rapport. He was brutal in front of the team and with the media as to expectations of me and assessment of my performances – although, funnily enough, I've learned from various sources over the years that he defended me to the hilt in private and was a strongly influential voice in insisting I be given a chance with Great Britain.

So it's complicated, but on a basic day-to-day level, we didn't get on – although we made it up before he died in 2016. I'll just outline our differences in general terms, as Roger isn't here to defend or explain himself.

Tough Going Up North

Our main area of clashing throughout was over injuries and their treatment. I'd never had my fitness and attitude toward playing questioned before by anybody, at any level, in any sport. Save for the neck injury, I hardly ever missed a game in Union – I was always fit and good to go. In fact I could never get enough rugby, which is one of the reasons I'd play for any old invitation team or sevens outfit. Rugby was my outlet, my happy place.

But, sod's law: the moment I started playing League, it was like my body rebelled at all the miles on the clock, and all the accumulated knocks and strains from the previous ten years visited me at once. In my debut game at Salford alone, I did my ankle ligament, shoulder and loosened three teeth, and over the coming months I also suffered a serious groin injury – actually a hernia, but it lay undiagnosed for a long while – knee issues and busted ribs. My ribs had become fragile and brittle with age. And these are just the main ones. Just when I needed to be at my best physically, I was at my worst. The statisticians tell me I only got to play in 67 senior games of League, which is a modest figure, but frankly I'm surprised it was even half that number.

That was all untimely and unlucky, but I reckoned I was a quick healer and, if I could have been left to get on with the rehab – rest when I felt rest was the key, work like a dog when that was needed – I'm sure I could have been fit for purpose for most of that difficult opening season in the Championship. But I wasn't afforded that luxury by Roger. He didn't trust me like Pross did, and I daresay he was under pressure from the Rovers chairman and directors to get their main investment on the pitch at all times. Put the 'talent' to work.

So began the depressing vicious cycle of injections, mosty of cortisone, but occasionally also of straightforward local anaesthetic. Sometimes I was jabbed during the week so I could train; almost always before a match so I could play; sometimes at half-time so I could continue to play; and then occasionally something to deal with the pain after a game. It was madness, really. The injection might enable you to keep playing in the short term, but ultimately you make your injury or injuries worse. Training becomes difficult, you lose condition, you get banged around at the weekend and the cycle repeats itself. I became a regular POP trainer, i.e. somebody who had to train in plaster of Paris (POP) because of injury. Of course, you start overcompensating. If I couldn't do any running, I blasted the weights for the upper body and arms and developed muscles and poundage I didn't need. It was counterproductive but at least the trainers at Hull could tell Roger and the Board that I was working hard. Somehow, I played 24 Championship and Cup games in that first season and, in many ways, that's almost my finest achievement in rugby. I reckon I was fit to play in about half a dozen of them at best. The most difficult to manage was a persistent wrongly diagnosed groin strain, which reduced my pace and running ability.

Not only was I trying to adapt to a new sport and to fulfil expectations, I was struggling with diminishing fitness and physical capability. What I needed was six to eight weeks off, time to heal, rehab and regain fitness away from the pitch itself. But in Rugby League – well, at Hull KR with Roger in charge – that was just a dream. It was never going to happen.

As if that wasn't difficult enough, it was immediately obvious that the side – three times Championship winners earlier in the Eighties – was in marked decline and heading for a relegation battle. David Hobbs, Roy Powell, Martin Bella and even All Blacks star Zinzan Brooke were confidently expected to sign about the time I signed, but nothing transpired. Nor did their raid on other Union stars come to much. Ringo knocked them back, so did Colin Laity, Glen Webbe, John Bentley, Roger Bidgood and reportedly even Jerry Guscott and Scott Hastings. Nothing happened. I'd been sold down the Humber, if we're honest.

I felt a bit helpless initially, but kept plugging away, determined to give some sort of value for money and at the very least playing for my pride. My debut – with 20 coaches of supporters coming up to Salford from Pontypool – hadn't gone well. The injuries hadn't helped but, additionally, I was off the pace – League literally took my breath away, as did the brutality of it.

For my first four games or so I deliberately turned the other cheek when it came to the rough stuff, despite there being an unwritten rule in Rugby League that everybody got a free pass to have a pop at the new Rugby Union lad. Referees turned a Nelsonian blind eye. The media, especially back in Wales, badly wanted a David Bishop thuggery story, and I was determined not to give it to them. I'd be beyond reproach in everything I did on the pitch – embarrassingly so, to be honest, but so be it. I was fed up with what I considered an undeserved reputation for dirty play. Things were going to be different.

The problem, though, was that with that negative mindset, my play lacked the hard edge and warrior spirit I needed. If I didn't yet have the League skills to set the place alight, my initial contributions needed to be based on fire, passion and spontaneity. I sensed I was disappointing the fans, just as I knew I'd underwhelmed the Pooler supporters during those first seven games before I broke my neck.

I was low and anxious before my fifth game, a big home tie against St Helens, the all-star club I felt I should have joined. Poignant hardly does it justice and, mentally, I wasn't in a good place. Before the match, I bumped into my old mate Phil Ford, who'd dropped in to watch the game and support me – he knew things weren't going well. Fordie had made a big success of his move to League with Warrington, Wigan, Bradford Northern and his club at that time, Leeds. He was a GB regular and much respected on the circuit.

He pulled me to one side.

"What the fuck's going on, Bish? You're making me look a bloody idiot."

"What do you mean?"

"I've been telling the lads you're the best player to come out of Wales in decades, that you're the absolute bollocks and that you'll be a GB star inside a year. And look at you. You're not even hitting the bastards back when they give you a clip. It's war out there, mate. You need to stand your ground. None of these can take you in a fight. They're pussycats. You can deal with them blindfolded."

"I dunno, Phil. I've got a load of injuries. I'm struggling a bit, mate, and I feel I've got to be on my best behaviour. I'm fed up always being the bad guy, the villain of the piece."

"Listen, Bish: this sport is full of hard bastards – or lads who think they are – and you need to stand up to them. The fans expect that, they pay to see that. There's no comeback in League if you stand up for yourself. This isn't Wales.

"You're going to be bumping into Roy Haggerty this afternoon. Roy is proper tough, old-school Rugby League, and he'll be trying to land one on you, take my word. That's a big part of his job. If he gives you a slap, you've got to hit back – do you understand, Bish?"

Blimey. Phil's one of the nicest guys on the planet and one of the fairest players you'll ever encounter, yet here he was giving me a pep talk and telling me to harden up. These were strange times.

I went down into the Hull KR changing room and Roger was soon starting his pre-match piece.

"Bish, they'll be targeting you again today. Good: keep your cool, soak it all up and it'll earn us a few penalties."

"Sorry, boss – it isn't happening today," I said.

"What do you mean, Bish?"

"It ain't happening again, Roger. I'm not turning the other cheek any more. If somebody belts me, they're getting it right back with interest. Nobody's going to fuck me around any more. I've had enough. No more Mr Nice Guy."

When I finished my piece, there was an embarrassed silence, with everybody shuffling their feet and looking at the floor. Roger was obviously completely nonplussed and, after about 20 seconds' silence, just started talking about something else as if our conversation hadn't taken place. What I didn't know back then was that Roger had suffered a couple of very bad facial injuries over the years from foul play and was never over-keen on violent play as a coach, although he had to accept it was part of Rugby League at the time.

I ran out and Haggerty immediately made eye contact and mouthed a few obscenities, along the lines of me being in for a bloody hiding. Sure enough, early on I was heeling the ball back and a massive haymaker came over the top, splitting my lip and dislodging a few front teeth. I exploded, spat blood and shards of teeth back in his face and decked him with a good 'un, and suddenly it's an all-in fight. No more Mr Nice Guy.

A few moments later, I'm in the line and get the ball with only one thought. Bugger the rugby for a minute or two; there's some business that needs sorting. Where's Haggerty? He's getting some more... I spot him, change direction, build up the pace and charge into him, looking to cause maximum damage, making pleasing contact with my shoulder. I get tackled as well by another Saints player and there's a further eruption and a general fight, during which I land another decent punch on Haggerty. Eventually it all calms down. In fairness to Roy, I heard him tell his Saints colleagues, "The fucking Taffy's OK," as they gathered for the restart. That meant a lot, and we called a truce for the rest of the game.

The crowd were absolutely loving it. Even this early in the season, they knew it was going to be a long haul for their creaking, underpowered team, and they were looking for a bit of defiance and dog to cheer them up. I date my great relationship with the Rovers fans back to that moment. We'd go down swinging. We continued to lose on a regular basis. There were a few wins as well, but I don't recall losing a scrap or a fight if the opposition started something, and I remember feeling much better about myself. And, of course, what happens once the word goes out that you won't stand any nonsense is that fewer of the hard men actually try it on. Against that backdrop, my general play picked up markedly, despite the almost crippling injuries. I kept soldiering on and did pretty well, certainly well enough to be voted Player of the Year by the supporters. It was a start.

I was in bloody agony, though. The 'groin' injury was very debilitating and wouldn't settle, and eventually it was New Zealand legend Dean Bell who put me on the right path to recovery. For some reason, despite our troubles, Hull KR played exceptionally well against a star-studded Wigan that season. We drew 16-16 with them at Craven Park in the Regal Trophy, in a match with a fair bit of controversy. I wasn't the only one who thought my late drop goal went over to win it, but the referee wasn't convinced – it was one of those soaring kicks that goes higher than the posts – and we were possibly denied a massive upset win that night. Dean Bell wasn't playing as he was injured, but he was there with their party afterwards, sharing a beer with us. I was playing half back that night. Then a couple of months later I was playing second row when we met them in the Championship and it was another cracker, which we lost 19-18 – again a bit unlucky, if you ask me. Dean was playing centre that night, alongside the Iro brothers, Steve Hampson and Mark Preston in the Wigan backs. Oh, and Shaun Edwards and Ged Byrne as half backs. Not the worst.

Dean came straight up afterwards in the bar and started shooting the breeze. Just as I've always liked and got on with English players and fans, I've always rated the Kiwis – they seem to be top blokes. Dean didn't beat about the bush.

"I've been watching you, Bish, and you're not moving freely. You're not right, are you, mate? What's the problem?"

"Gone in the groin, Dean; at least that's what the doc says. I've been struggling most of the season with it – it's driving me mad. It's only jabs keeping me going."

"You want to cut that out straight away, Bish – does you no good. Listen, are you sure it's the groin? I was struggling a while ago and they told me I had a groin injury, but I insisted on getting a Harley Street doctor to look at it and, hey presto, it was actually a hernia. Pretty similar symptoms and they get them mixed up sometimes. I went in for the op, six weeks' rehab and it's been good as gold ever since. You need to get down and see this guy. Don't mess around: it's your career, mate."

Dean was spot on. I took the details of the Harley Street specialist off him – it was a guy called Jerry Gilmore – and I went steaming into the medical room at training on the Monday morning, demanding I be sent down there. Of course, it wasn't that simple. We had four Championship matches left and still had an outside chance of avoiding relegation, so I'd have to bite the bullet some more. I could have had a broken leg and Rovers would still have expected me to play. They also wanted the local NHS specialist to examine me first, which he did, but he couldn't find anything definitive. By the end of the season, I was going mad with frustration and stormed in again one morning and declared I was off down to Harley Street anyway and would pay for everything myself if I had to. With the season done and dusted and a break before our Division Two campaign started in August, the club were a bit more amenable to trying other avenues, so myself and Wayne Parker, who'd also been struggling with a groin injury, were dispatched down south to London.

The waiting room was like a sportsman's bar, with all sorts of vaguely familiar faces queuing to be seen – one was definitely Steve Archibald, the Scotland striker. The examination took two minutes, top whack. Drop your trousers and a couple of tugs of each testicle to see your reaction. On the left-hand side, I was in agony.

"Acute hernia, serious case. Operation a week on Thursday," said Mr Gilmore to an assistant, who was busily making notes. Wayne was the same, so the following week we were back down in town in a private hospital – more like a six-star hotel – having the operation and being treated and fed like kings in the process. I loved it initially, but after four or five days, I got tired of the rich diet and discharged myself. I'd spent enough of my life in hospitals, thank you... Wayne had a spectacularly good insurance policy which not only paid for the operation but seemed to give him £100 or some such figure for every day he was in hospital, so he stayed a bit longer!

It hurt like hell when I woke up after the operation – nobody had warned me about the acute post-op tearing pain, and I nearly passed out the first time I walked to the loo – but everything had gone well. The key was really getting on with the rehab as soon as the wound had healed up, which I did. It felt like this was my last chance of making something of my Rugby League career. I had to make it work.

CHAPTER 17

Stormy Days with Rovers and Great Britain

AUGUST 1989 AND the start of the Division Two season. Finally, after recovering from the hernia op, I was as fit as a butcher's dog and mad for it. We started with a 50-16 win at Keighley, and we never looked back after that. I was playing half back mainly, with the occasional venture into the second row, and I couldn't stop scoring or making tries. It all started to come together and we ripped the league apart, if I'm being honest. Only Halifax were really in our class – we were both essentially mid-table Championship sides who'd somehow found themselves in the Second Division after a really poor season. Yet again we played brilliantly against a fully loaded Wigan – this time in the Challenge Cup, when they came to Craven Park and pipped us 6-4. It was fun locking horns with Wigan and GB legend Shaun Edwards and believing I gave every bit as good as I got. That match was in the January, from memory, and it was after that I realised I might be in the running for the 1990 GB Lions tour of Papua New Guinea and New Zealand. The perceived wisdom was that Great Britain didn't pick players from the Second Division, but the media were floating the idea and I certainly felt I was playing well enough for consideration.

For once I was briefly relatively injury free – you're always nursing knocks in League, but I was on top of things – and by March I was absolutely flying as we looked to close out the league title. I'd scored a hat-trick against Bramley, and then we had two big wins over Whitehaven – 46-2 at their place and 92-10 at Craven Park, where I got another hat-trick. That last game came at a cost, though. Right at the end, I went up for a high ball, fell awkwardly on an opponent as I came to the ground and felt a couple of ribs crack and ligaments wrench. Shit. Did I not need that!

It was the stupidest injury of my career. What was I even still doing on the pitch, other than the management trying to get every last penny of their investment? Rugby-wise, it made no sense. Many years later, I remember idly watching a match at the 2023 Rugby World Cup where France were thrashing Namibia, and couldn't believe my eyes when Antoine Dupont came out for the second half. I started swearing at the TV: "Get back in the fucking changing rooms, the game's long won! Nobody gives a stuff what you do against Namibia – you've got a World Cup to win!" Let's just say I wasn't surprised five minutes later when he was being led off with a fractured cheekbone. Madness.

Broken or cracked ribs always means a six-week lay-off and is the most uncomfortable injury. You can't breathe without moving your ribs: they're involved when you eat, cough, sneeze, roll over in bed, in fact just shifting in the chair you're sitting in.

My heart sank. We had the final games to complete to ensure our return to the Championship, and I'd heard on the grapevine that I was to be included in the GB squad to play

France at Headingley on 7 April, just over three weeks later. The ante was upped even further as it was made quite clear I had to play in that game to be considered for the Lions tour. Getting a GB cap was important to me – I'd missed out on just about everything in my Union career and a British and Irish Lions cap was top of the list. I wanted to rectify that with League's equivalent, plus there was the small matter of the £20,000 bonus which would allegedly be paid by Hull KR on my becoming a GB Test player.

So, reluctantly, after couple of weeks it was back to the jabs, this time exclusively anaesthetic as there's nothing cortisone can do for broken bones. The GB medics also cut and redesigned a shoulder pad to offer up some protection to my rib cage, although the protection was more psychological than actual. Come matchday, I came on at full back just before half-time and the first thing that happened was that I got double tackled in the ribs. It was bloody agony, but wild horses wouldn't have dragged me off – there was a tour on the line. We lost, but I won my own personal battle to get through and a couple of days later was named in the GB squad announced for the 9-week, 15-game tour of Papua New Guinea and New Zealand.

The 1990 Lions tour was a dog's dinner at the start. We had players missing and unavailable, and then a few big names like Joe Lydon and Martin Offiah were going to fly out just for the New Zealand leg. But at the same time, I was excited. A proper big representative tour, and I was the only Second Division player to play, which was kudos to me and Rovers. That, though, was tempered by the constant nagging pain in my ribs. I was off training for the first week or so and out of contention for the first game, which I felt put me on the back foot in terms of getting into the Test team.

I'd clearly been earmarked for the midweek dirt-trackers, but so be it. I stayed philosophical and optimistic. Just to compound things, I picked up a dead leg in my first game and turned my ankle for good measure. Neither were tour-ending injuries, but neither helped my cause. My body was letting me down badly and ominously. Deep down, I realised my time might be running out.

Papua New Guinea took you right out of your comfort zone. Fierce heat, hard-as-rock grounds, warrior players in opposition who kept coming at you regardless of the score, and rabid fans who threw stones and gravel at you whenever they took a fancy. It became known as the Tear-Gas Tour because the local police targeted the fans with tear gas at most of the games.

I wasn't the most well-travelled guy in the world back in those days, and I found the whole thing very alien and edgy. I remember watching the first match against Southern Zone in Port Moresby and being shocked when two young lads fell at least 20 foot out of the tree they were watching from when a branch snapped. That alone was horrible to witness, but what happened next took my breath away. The police moved in – to help the lads, I thought, and perhaps call an ambulance, but what they actually did was unbuckle their batons and beat the shit out of the prone bodies on the ground. Unbelievable. At just about every game we played, the police would pile in at the slightest provocation with their tear gas, which blew around indiscriminately, affecting the players just as much as the fans.

I was well up for my debut against Northern and Highland Zones in Lae, and so were the opposition. Within minutes I'd been tipped on my head with a classic spear tackle; the only time I ever really feared for my safety after breaking my neck. They tried it again moments later, and this time I fought back. When we got the penalty, I seized the ball and ran full tilt at the player who'd assaulted me. My blood was up and I wasn't turning the other cheek. I got involved in two or three more scraps as they continued to pile into me, until eventually our skipper Mike Gregory shouted to the guys, "If Taffy starts another fight, bloody well leave it to him!" I was pleased with how I went, though, apart from picking up the dead leg. I must have lost a stone in the humidity and heat and eventually we subdued them – they'd fought themselves to a standstill. Jiffy came on late in the game and danced in for a try untouched, and said he couldn't work out why we'd made such heavy weather of it. Cheeky beggar.

It was about, now, though, that I realised that I didn't figure prominently in coach Mal Reilly's plans for the Test matches. In fact, I seemed to have unwittingly made an enemy of the coach, which is never good. I just couldn't get on his wavelength all tour. Perhaps he just didn't rate me and felt I'd been foisted on his squad, or perhaps it went back to an incident when we were sitting around the hotel swimming pool in Papua New Guinea. And before you make any false assumptions, I'd like to add that we did very little sitting around swimming pools – Mal flogged us on the training ground twice a day every day. This day must have been the exception.

Anyway, an unofficial underwater swimming competition spontaneously got underway. A few of the lads managed two or three lengths: it wasn't a huge pool, but it wasn't small either – I'm guessing 15 yards long. I really fancied it, dived in and with strong push-offs at each end managed five-and-a-bit lengths, which I was pretty sure would make me top dog and earn bragging rights. But I hadn't counted on Mal's manic competitive streak. He'd been looking on, got up from his sun lounger and said he could piss on that. He dived in and, bloody hell, eventually came up for air after six lengths. He was absolutely blue and to my eyes looked close to death – I've never seen a man look so ill and take it so close to the limit physically. He was shattered but totally triumphant and after he'd finally recovered his breath, he pumped his chest out and strutted around a little. Fair play, though it was an insight into what had made him such a feared player. At 40+ years old, those fires still obviously raged.

This, though, was a red rag to a bull: the gauntlet had been thrown down. All eyes turned to me. I took three or four deep breaths and plunged in again. I might have been carrying a few injuries around this time, but aerobically I was the fittest I'd ever been, and I was on a mission. I got to six lengths and considered stopping there so it could be honours even, but I still had a bit of breath left so turned again, pushed off and did another half-length before popping up and punching the air victoriously. I probably wasn't the most modest winner.

It was a nice moment personally and increased my status in the group, but actually it was incredibly dumb on my part. Mal's moment of glory and triumph – of domination – within the group had been ripped away from him. The gobby Taffy from the Second Division had upstaged him and I felt, from that moment, he was on my case. If there were any 50-50 selection calls, I wouldn't be getting the nod. These things matter; they gain an importance out of all proportion. You move around in this small tight-knit group: you're in your own bubble where you have to see everybody every day – breakfast every morning, training twice every day, travelling together all the time – and it's completely different to being at home, where you can sometimes put some distance between yourself and somebody you're not getting on with.

The chickens really came home to roost when we arrived in New Zealand, and I was picked against a particularly strong Wellington team at Porirua Park. I'd paid for my dad to join us for the final three weeks or so of the tour. He'd just arrived a couple of days earlier, so I was on edge to do well and maybe put a run of decent games together.

I'd had trouble sleeping all tour. I'm nocturnal by nature anyway and a series of new, strange hotel rooms and the heat at night in Papua New Guinea didn't make it any easier. It was tricky because we used to share rooms on tour, and I didn't even have the option of just watching the TV or prowling around my room because that would keep my roomie awake, so I used to take myself off for walks or sit around the hotel lobby.

Anyway, the night before the Wellington match, I knew I wouldn't be able to sleep and I knew Jiffy and a few of the boys were planning to head off into town to find a sports bar. The time difference was such that you could watch all sorts of sports action from around the world late at night in New Zealand. I slipped out with them, and we had a good night. They were enjoying a couple of quiet beers – no more – but I behaved myself and drank juices. Well, maybe I had one beer, tops.

We got back about 2 a.m., which doesn't even count as a night out in my books, and headed for the lift. There was a crowd of us, including 'Chariots' Offiah and our prop Keith England from Castleford – 'Beefy', as we called him. Beefy was in good form and I copped the usual good-humoured banter us Welsh have to suffer about bloody Taffies, coal miners and sheep – all the normal stuff – and we started messing around with a mock fight. It was good natured horseplay but as I swung Beefy round, his head crashed into one of those ridiculous big standing ash trays that some lifts had back then. Blood everywhere from a nasty cut on his head – I think he needed 12 stitches when we took him to see the doc, Forbes Mackenzie.

That was a bit of a mood dampener, and to make it worse I then bumped into Phil Larder, our defence coach and part of the management inner circle. I got on well with Phil – great bloke – but this was putting him in an awkward position. "Get off to bed, Bish. I haven't seen you, right?" he whispered.

Next morning I was woken up early by banging on the door from Phil Clarke, who'd been rooming with the skipper, Mike Gregory.

"Bish, wake up! You're in big trouble, mate," said Clarkey. "Mal and Maurice Lindsay want to see you ASAP about this incident with Beefy. They're hitting the bloody roof. They're waiting for you now. Put your tin hat on."

Forewarned was forearmed. I presented myself to Mal and Maurice, the tour manager. Phil Larder was there as well, although he was trying not to catch my eye and said nothing. Mal tore into me. I was the naughty schoolboy in the dock again. For Mal, it was an open-and-shut case. I'd been out late drinking the night before a match, against team orders, arrived back drunk and had got into a fight with Beefy, causing a really nasty cut. It was all totally unacceptable. I was a disgrace to my country, and I'd let the team down and my family down. Worse than any of that, I'd let him down. Maurice was quieter and just kept asking detailed questions as to exactly what had gone on. At least he was trying to get to the truth of the matter.

The Bish

I had to admit to myself that, written down in black and white, it didn't look good, even though I still felt it was totally accidental and essentially harmless. Mal's assumption of complete guilt was really annoying me and I wanted to tell him his fortune, but I bit my tongue. I also wanted to tell him that his flogging us day and night on the training ground in that heat had drained the tour of all fun and spirit – that it was counterproductive, and we weren't producing it on matchday because all the lads were knackered and heavy-legged. But I resisted the temptation. This was all about me, so I needed to defend myself and not get distracted and go off on one.

Yes, I'd been out with the boys – because I couldn't sleep and I didn't want to disturb my roomie. No, I hadn't been drinking and I most certainly wasn't drunk. And no, I hadn't attacked Beefy, it was a bit of innocent high jinks that went wrong, all initiated by his quip about the Welsh... It was an accident. If he hadn't stumbled into the ashtray, nobody would have been any the wiser. There was much less to this incident than met the eye.

I was dismissed from their presence. They were going to have a short meeting amongst themselves, but I was pretty sure that their conclusion would be that I should be on the first plane home. I can't remember how, but a few of us ended up in Mike Gregory's room, at which point Joe Lydon and Jiffy stormed in. Joe in 1990 was at the height of his powers and was probably the biggest name on that tour – he'd just joined us, having missed the Papua New Guinea leg. He's also an incredibly switched-on, bright bloke, and if ever you want a defence lawyer, Joe's your man. Anyway, he was on the warpath on my behalf even though I didn't particularly know him that well. I think he just thought the whole thing was being blown up out of all proportion, and at heart he was bit of a rebel himself.

Joe went straight up to Mike and said, "If they send Bish home, I'm going home as well. It's not on."

"Bloody hell, Joe. You only got a here a few days ago," joked Mike, trying to lighten the mood.

Joe turned to me. "You won't be going home, Bish, take it from me."

Then Jiffy joined the conversation: "I'm going home as well if Bish is sent back."

Sweet Jesus, we now had the start of a players' revolt. That had escalated quickly. Greggers went to report back to the management, and I suspect the gist of it was that Joe and Jiffy's rebellion might only be the tip of the iceberg. It had been a brutally hard tour and, if they really forced the issue here, they might not have a squad left to finish it.

After a seemingly endless wait, I was called back in to see the bigwigs. This was decision time. I looked for a sign, like I'd done with judges and juries before, but there was none. They were all deadpan. What then happened was that I got given a hell of an official dressing-down by Mal, fined two weeks' wages, dropped from the team to the bench for the game that night, but allowed to stay on tour. I sensed he saw it as another 'defeat' after the swimming contest. Left to him, I'd have been halfway home by now, but others such as Maurice Lindsay and Greggers – reporting back on the players' feelings on the matter – had held sway.

I was relieved. Everybody had been overreacting, but these things can get dangerously out of control unless somebody puts their foot on the brake and applies some common sense. I remain eternally grateful to Joe for his crucial intervention and to Jiffy for backing him up. I had all sorts of demons and hang-ups as a player and as an individual, but I really cared at all times, and being sent home in disgrace from a GB tour a few days after Dad arrived would just about have finished me off on a personal level.

As for the Wellington match that night, my head was all over the place and I was shaking a lot – with shock, I suppose – at the events of the day. When I came off the bench, GB were well in the lead but I played like a dog for 40 minutes and we ended up losing. It was comfortably the worst game of rugby I ever produced at any level. I was embarrassed and annoyed and ready to explode.

Afterwards in the bar, Clarkey came up and warned me to go nowhere near Mal; he was fuming and wanted my head again. It was a well-intentioned warning, but I'd had enough and told Clarkey to tell Mal that if he wanted to sort things out, I'd see him in the car park in five minutes, man to man. Let him say what he wanted to say to my face. There was a gasp from some of the lads at the bar – nobody messed with Mal like that – but Jiffy then injected a touch of much-needed humour by immediately offering to open a book! He was backing me against Mal all the way and was willing to accept any bets on Mal, no matter how big.

That seemed to defuse things, and my offer of a meeting in the car park was never transmitted to Mal.

All of which left the players' court. I was ordered to sing 'Pretty Woman', the Roy Orbison song which had been getting a big airing again as the Julia Roberts film had been showing everywhere we went. I protested that I didn't know the words, but a Walkman with it on tape was produced and I had to comply.

I'm not a fan of this on tour humiliation stuff – remember Lake Garda? – but I owed the lads for their support and solidarity. I seem to be the only Welshman in history who doesn't have a note in his head, and the following three minutes were torture for all concerned. But at least I was still on tour.

I never did get anywhere near a Test start. In fact, I only played once more, in our win over Taranaki in New Plymouth. Somehow the lads came through at the end of a long tour to narrowly win the first two Tests against the Kiwis to ensure a series win. We nearly made it 3-0, but they pipped us 21-18 in the last Test. Coming strong at the end of the tour to take the series was yet another example of how tough mentally and physically Rugby League guys are, and all the members of the tour party went up in my estimation. They were proper warriors, and I was proud to be a member of their squad. Personally, though, I remained disappointed at being a fringe player.

After the incident in Wellington, I kept my distance from management as much as possible but, right at the end, in the week of the third Test in Christchurch, Maurice asked me to call by his room and we had a frank but not unfriendly chat. He said that obviously it hadn't gone as I'd wanted, and I'd started on the back foot with the injury, and that I must be disappointed, but nonetheless he wanted to thank me for my efforts throughout. I'd brought energy and optimism to the tour and had pushed harder than most in training, and I'd probably deserved to get more game time. That's what he said, anyway.

For once, I opted for the diplomatic approach. Maurice was being genuine and unguarded, and I opened up a little. I told him it had been privilege and an honour; throughout my Union career I'd missed out on tours with Wales and the Lions, and I'd been denied the opportunities I felt were due to me. I'd always be immensely grateful to Great Britain for picking me from a Division Two side and allowing me to tour with them. Maurice was a little taken aback at my conciliatory approach, but we shook hands solemnly and ended the tour on very good terms. I meant what I said. I wasn't far off my 30th birthday but had more miles on the clock than that. I had a deep feeling my rugby-playing days were coming to a close.

I came back off the GB Lions tour and rested up a bit. The ribs healed, I got married and I was in reasonably good shape for the new season. But things still didn't go smoothly. The big final stand-off with Roger Millward was regrettable, but these things happen. Some see it as a knee-jerk reaction on my part and, as ever, I'm the first to put my hand up and admit my immaturity at the time – I could and probably should have handled myself differently – but the truth of the matter is, it was the final straw. Everything finally got to me and I snapped.

The opening Championship fixtures of the season were an encouraging 20-14 win over Warrington and a discouraging 42-10 defeat against St Helens, who were in rampant form at Knowsley Road. I was half back in both games and wasn't best pleased when I was moved to full back away to Oldham. Roger cited an injury crisis, which was true enough – we'd been struck down by a load of early-season knocks. During that game I got involved in a tackle incident with Charlie McAlister, Oldham's Kiwi second row. Slightly off-kilter and tackling players from a position I hadn't played in very often, I basically jumped into a smother tackle and we went tumbling down. To my eyes, it was a rugby incident, the kind of challenge you see a dozen times every weekend in Rugby League games, but it seems McAlister broke his jaw and for

48 hours or so, history seemed to be repeating itself. Oldham were calling for me to be banned for life, which was plainly quite ridiculous – you'd literally have no players left if every League player got banned for such a challenge. I protested my innocence – because I was innocent – and a load of big names in the sport did likewise, but the disciplinary hearing hung over me like the Sword of Damocles. Would I get a fair trial, or would it become another David Bishop circus?

I should have trusted League more. They're much more grown up when dealing with such matters, and the case against me was kicked out. No case to answer, no ban, no fine, nothing. There is a God! But then after my moment of euphoria and optimism, I was brought crashing down at training the next day when Roger told me I wouldn't be starting the next game despite the ongoing injury crisis. I pleaded with him, begging him to let me loose – I'd stick two fingers up to the critics and really show the world what I could do – but he was not for turning.

Now, as an old bugger in my sixties, I can vaguely see his point. He probably just wanted to let the fuss die down and keep me out of the limelight for a week, a bit like Pross after the Jarman incident. If you remember, when he'd insisted on resting me for the next game against Neath, I went off the deep end and contacted Bridgend to see if I could join. Except this was ten times worse. My deep personal affection for Pross meant we soon kissed and made up, but I had no such relationship with Roger. I also felt one or two in the club had been lukewarm in their support of me in the days between the incident and the disciplinary panel. And now this from Roger. I was raging.

I badly needed to get out there straight away, show my worth and stop the negative publicity which so often surrounded me. I'd done nothing wrong, and I wanted – needed – my moment in the sun to shine again as a player. But Roger wouldn't do that for me. Over the previous two years, I'd done everything he'd asked of me. I'd gone above and beyond. I'd played in every position he asked; undertaken every role; I'd played countless matches when I should probably have been in a plaster cast or indeed in hospital having an operation. I'd trained when I should have been at home resting. Every time, I'd bitten the bullet and fronted up, putting my mutilated body on the line. I'd done it out of a sense of loyalty to him and in particular the fans. And now this. He wouldn't meet me halfway by doing something *I* wanted and needed, just this once.

That was my hot-tempered take on things, and I flipped. I erupted into a ball of indignation and fury. I've owned up to being immature throughout my career, but all these years later I still think I had a point about this. And, in truth, it was much more complicated than that. There was so much anger and frustration building up inside of me, this was the straw that broke the camel's back. I hadn't got what I wanted out of my Union career, and it gnawed away at me and played with my mind every single day. Then I'd turned professional too late to really make the impact or money I wanted. Despite everything – injuries and then playing in Division Two – I'd fought my way into the GB squad but had then never been fit enough to do myself justice. Everybody at Rovers had apparently forgotten about the £20,000 bonus I'd been promised if I won a GB cap. That was also narking me big-time, and I summoned John Fieldhouse – the Rovers man for the *Hull Daily Mail* – and gave him one of the bigger exclusives of his life. I was off: I would never play for Hull KR again under Roger Millward. And I didn't.

I drove back to Wales that night a bit shocked at what I'd done – newly married, remember, with responsibilities – but I refused to back down. It seemed pretty well-known that Roger would be leaving by mutual agreement at the end of the season, so I decided to wait it out. I tried to keep ticking over fitness-wise and even played a couple of charity Union matches on the quiet, but it was a difficult period. Was my career over or not? I wasn't quite sure. At the end of the 1990/91 season, I had one more season on my contract to see out. With Roger gone, I reported for early season training and found George Fairbairn, a playing colleague when I'd started, in charge. I was thrown in with the youngsters and A team players and ordered to do a 10-mile run.

It was a test of wills. George was a decent enough player, if a bit long in the tooth, when I arrived at Hull KR. I thought we'd got along OK, but here he was trying to make a rather infantile point in front of everybody. I wasn't in the mood for such mind games. Come the first match I'd be fit – I was working away nicely in my own fashion, thank you very much, George, but I wasn't going to play silly beggars to satisfy his ego. So I walked the ten miles, which was very pleasant – I strode out at a good lick but got stopped halfway round by a bunch of friendly supporters, who took me into a café, where we shot the breeze for a good while. It was interesting to hear all the gossip about the previous season. Finally, I made my excuses and walked quickly back to the ground, which was deserted save for George, who was hopping mad. He let me have it with both barrels and made it clear I would be playing over his dead body at the start of the season. I can see that many people might think I was being unreasonable, and we're back to my insistence earlier in the book that I didn't grow up until the age of 40.

It was probably a needless confrontation but the truth is, I wasn't really bothered either way. Emotionally, I was done with Rugby League, that was the underlying feeling. I should have retired after my bust-up with Roger. I was going through the motions now, just fulfilling my contractual obligations. Funnily enough, I started playing really well for the As and scored a couple of crackers in a narrow defeat against Wigan A – they had a youngster on the wing called Jason Robinson, who looked pretty useful. I've seen a lot of hot steppers over the years, but Jason was unique – his was more of a high-speed shuffle, the sort of thing you see in the NFL. If any rugby player from Britain could have made it at gridiron, it was surely Jason.

When I got home after that Wigan game, one of the directors, Len Casey, phoned me up. It was ridiculous I wasn't playing for the Firsts, and he wanted me at the ground the following morning, when he'd sort it out with George Fairbairn. He'd call the press and announce peace in our time. Except behind the scenes, George was still adamant he didn't want to play ball; he wanted a full apology from me before he'd consider picking me. I dug my heels in, he dug his heels in and eventually an exasperated Len brokered a deal of sorts. George would pick me if his objections were officially minuted in the club records and his views properly recorded for the press. He'd only select me under protest.

My career was coming to a sorry end... yet, amidst this doom and gloom, my short but enjoyable Test career with Wales got underway. So many big-name Welsh Rugby Union players had converted to League that Wales could resurrect their League side and be pretty competitive. We attracted a decent crowd, with Union fans getting a frustrating glimpse of those who'd gone 'missing'. Wales RL hadn't played for seven years, but there seemed a demand for it. Big Jim Mills – a great bloke – was appointed manager, Clive Griffiths served as coach, and over the next year or so I played in four Tests for Wales, two at lock and two at hooker. It was a case of simply filling in where our need was greatest.

The first match, in October 1991, promised to be a bit special. Papua New Guinea had proved tough nuts to crack a year earlier on their own patch with Great Britain, and we prepared for a rough encounter at the Vetch Field in Swansea. But, as it happened, the Kumuls (as they were known) proved to be terrible travellers and we romped home 68-0. I was surrounded by familiar faces, past friends and foes from my Union days. Phil Ford, Jiffy, Rob Ackerman, Allan Bateman – what a player he was! – John Devereux, Jonathan Griffiths, Kevin Ellis, Dai Young, Mark Jones, Paul Moriarty, Adrian Hadley, Gary Pearce and Rowland Phillips. Bloody hell, that was some talent right there, and I don't care how bad Papua New Guinea were on the day – that Wales side, if it ever clicked, was tidy. A few weeks later, France struggled to put the Kumuls away. We were unstoppable that night in Swansea.

As if to underline the fact that we were in good nick, we were again back at the Vetch Field a few months later, beating France 35-6. France can blow hot and cold, but they'd beaten GB two years earlier, before we went on tour. But we got a bit of a reality check later in the new year when England put their big guns out and beat us 36-11, again at the Vetch Field. By then, I'd finally left Hull KR for good. I'd started four games for them under George Fairbairn (two wins, two losses), but it wasn't working and I'd picked up another chronic injury – knee this time – which would eventually require an operation. I really did need to bow to the inevitable and call time, but there was just enough in the tank for one last Wales appearance: a hard-fought 19-18 win over in France in Perpignan. There was some regulation stating that I couldn't play for Wales unless I was attached to a club, so I joined Second Division London Crusaders for a couple of weeks and made one appearance – a 40-10 defeat against Featherstone Rovers – to qualify for my Wales swansong.

For better or worse, my League career was over, and at the time I was pretty sure it would be my last serious game of rugby full stop. Little did I know.

CHAPTER 18

Baseball

TIME FOR A little tangent here, because I haven't really talked about the other sport I represented Wales in. If rugby and boxing are my sporting passions, baseball was my diversion. I really enjoyed cricket but baseball was my summer sport. I'd give rugby and boxing my full attention and 'relax' by playing baseball. That was enough to be getting on with.

For non-Welsh readers, there used to be a big baseball scene in Wales, based around big league structures in Cardiff and Newport. I think it started as a Cardiff Irish thing at the end of the nineteenth century, as a way for dockers to blow off steam without hurting each other. The version of baseball that emerged was essentially a more dynamic and muscular version of rounders. It's 11-a-side, and the bats used are halfway between cricket bats and the long, smooth baseball bats used in America. Our bats have a flat hitting surface, not rounded – and legend has it that they were originally fashioned out of spare planks of wood from crates in the docks. Sounds very possible.

The bowling is underarm, but don't be deceived by that. It can, once you master the technique, be at high speeds – they can touch 100 mph, which is as fast as the fastest bowlers in cricket – and it hurts plenty if the ball hits you instead of the bat. The fielding is very athletic – you have a helmeted backstop as in American baseball, four bases, and, unlike American baseball, you can score in any direction. Another big difference from mainstream baseball is that you don't get the luxury of 'three strikes and you're out'. If you miss a legitimate delivery, that's it – no more deliveries. Unless you reach first base ahead of the ball, you're out.

Liverpool – another big 'Irish' city – is also a stronghold and, for more than 100 years, there have been annual Wales v. England Test matches, with the England side essentially being a team selected from the Liverpool leagues.

I learned the game at St Cadoc's and captained Cardiff U11s as a 9-year-old but we didn't play it at St Illtyds, despite many of the students coming from Irish neighbourhoods, where baseball was played in the streets and parks and in the primary schools. Cricket was the summer sport at St Illtyd's, along with athletics, so in my teenage years I played baseball at Llanrumney and captained Cardiff U15s. One of my proudest achievements was to eventually win four Wales senior caps and play in that annual fixture with England. It might sound small fry, but baseball's always loomed large in in my life, and not just for purely sporting reasons.

When I came out of prison in the spring of 1981, my life was all over the place. I badly needed some friendly faces and support to get back on track. The Old Illtydians rugby club had, about ten years earlier, decided to branch out and form their own baseball section, and had risen through the five divisions of the Cardiff leagues. They were beginning to shape up and get ambitious, with the desire of earning promotion from Division One to the Premiership and taking on the big boys. Ken Poole from the club phoned me one evening soon after I got out of Aylesbury, and asked if I'd like to come out of baseball retirement and give it a crack.

Baseball

It was perfect timing. What could be better than to decompress a little and spend some quality sporting and social time with friends, familiar rugby faces and old schoolmates. We'd play hard but would always enjoy ourselves. I could top up the fitness I'd managed to achieve in prison and be ready for what I thought would be my breakthrough season in rugby in 1981/82. I look back on those baseball days as amongst the happiest of my life. Pure, unadulterated fun.

There was a core group of what I'd call specialist baseball players at the club, but we also had an entire phalanx of rugby players enjoying their second sport and our big games would draw very decent weekend crowds to the parks of Cardiff and Newport. At our peak, we'd get 3,000 fans to our big final in Roath Park, and you'd spend half the time signing autographs and posing for pictures for rugby fans.

Apart from myself, there was Mark Ring (who also went on to represent Wales at baseball), Brendan McAloon (who played rugby for Cardiff and Newbridge) and the one and only Pablo Rees. Then there was Kevin Trevett, who you might remember from the days when we did the Ray Williams book together and were members of the same Wales Youth Squad. Kevin won his Youth cap a year after me. David Barry, meanwhile, was a Cardiff stalwart and another Wales B cap, while the great Terry Holmes needs no introduction and was a keen player when available. Mike Murphy, Terry Charles (son of footballing legend John) and Gerard Meehan were also at Cardiff while Mike Jennings, Simon Williams and Ken Poole – the club's official historian – were more than useful rugby players with the Old Illtydians.

We could have put out a hell of a sevens team and, in fact, most of us didn't get round to playing baseball until the end of May or early June because we were involved in the end-of-season sevens circuit. There were a few footballers as well, headed up by David Giles (the Swans and Wales star), who was very useful and one of the best singers in the team in the pub afterwards. The inter-sport, inter-club banter and craic was fierce all summer.

Ringo, as you might expect, was a brilliant ground fielder and catcher and a pretty classy batter as well. Being Ringo, he tended to do his own thing in the field – a *libero*, as he liked to call it – but it was uncanny how often he would pop up in an unorthodox position to make an important catch, having read how the batsman was shaping up. I'm very proud to say that I played rugby and baseball for Wales with Ringo, a rare honour with such a good mate.

Kevin was a very fine all-round baseball player; in fact, he was a terrific all-round sportsman who could have been a professional footballer, in my opinion. He was a clever batter who had a wide range of shots, including a very difficult ramp shot which most cricketers seem to have just discovered 40 years later. He could play backstop or bowl too, although we used him mainly in the outfield. Kevin captained our side for a season or two. He only got capped the once, was Wales' best player with 26 runs, but never got picked again. Welsh baseball's one-cap wonder! I know the feeling.

Pablo came from a baseball family. His mum Lil was a Wales cap, and his sister Maxine starred for Llandaff Ladies. Pablo was a safe pair of hands anywhere and was rock solid at first base, where his physicality dominated the area, while as a batter he had two distinct gears. He could be very steady, playing tap shots, but he could go big once he had his eye in or the situation called for it.

Brendan McAloon was our best backstop, which is a vital position and, as I was usually the main bowler, we had plenty of interaction, as they call it, with him signalling and miming all sorts to me as he took his place behind the batter. We were both pretty fiery characters and if it went wrong, words were sometimes exchanged – but really, we were just egging each other on and would always make up with a drink afterwards. Holmesie was rock solid, a great puncher to leg when he batted and a very good fielder. Ken Poole dines out on the day he "saved the life" of Wales' finest, who'd been fielding out in the deep, directly under a massive tree. Terry started complaining that he was wasted there, nobody was hitting in that direction and Ken eventually gave in and had literally just moved him to another part of ground when the tree randomly came crashing down, in spectacular fashion. It had been raining heavily and there'd been storms in the days before the game. Anybody under that tree would have done well to escape serious injury.

And what sort of player was I? To start with, I was a batter – right-hand bat – and backstop, but at some stage in my first season with the club, we were warming up between innings and Ken was impressed with my left-arm bowling. He brought me on during the innings, I did well, and from that moment on I was our main bowler. I was involved all the time, which was perfect as direct confrontation in sport is what does it for me.

In that first 1981 season, we got promoted from Division One to the County Division. Then, in the summer of 1982, as I upped my participation during my comeback from the broken neck, I helped the team finally win promotion to the Premiership, while we also had a great run in the Silver Bowl, a cup competition. In the quarter-final, we beat favourites Llanrumney, at one stage I managed to take six wickets in six deliveries, and Terry Holmes hit consecutive fours off legendary bowler John Smith – who never conceded fours – en route to victory. In the final at Roath Park, we chased down Llandaff's big total of 135 and won with three men left, with Pablo leading the scoring.

1983 was bittersweet. We struggled in the Premiership and got relegated, but enjoyed a great run in the Welsh Brewers Cup, the most prestigious cup competition – the FA Cup of our baseball world. We called it the Telly Cup because the final was televised by the BBC, with Alan Wilkins presenting, although, alas, in front of a big crowd on a sunny afternoon at Roath Park, we failed to do ourselves justice and lost by four men to bat. But we were in good spirits and retired first to the Three Brewers pub, where the sponsors were laying on unlimited food and booze, before moving on to John Scott's wedding reception at the Bristol Hotel on the Penarth Road.

Our Cup run had brought me to the attention of the Wales selectors and that summer I got the call to make my Wales debut against England. At the time, I was busting a gut trying to get in the Wales rugby team after a great comeback season which had seen Pooler win the WRU Cup, with me named as Man of the Match in both the semi-final against Bridgend and final against Swansea. So not getting selected for Wales in rugby was weighing heavily on my mind. Before the England baseball game, I suddenly felt the need to deliver a slightly OTT pre-match speech about the pride and honour of playing for Wales; we were doing it for the jersey and the nation. I was virtually in tears at the end but it was all to no avail: we got soundly beaten. We were to enjoy better days, though.

In 1984 Old Illtydians earned promotion back to the Premiership and we consolidated our position over the next

Baseball

two seasons before we made a few waves in 1987. With my 11-month ban from the WRU in October 1986, I was officially barred from playing almost any sport, including baseball. But as we moved into the summer of 1987, everybody realised the complete absurdity of that and I played regularly for the Old Illtydians. A cup highlight for me was clean bowling 16 of the 22 batters in our big win over Grange Catholic, and we also reached the final against Llanrumney – although, come the big day, we got absolutely hammered by 90 runs.

1988 was my best-ever season. I skippered the Old Illtydians to the Welsh Brewers Cup final, which was again televised on BBC Wales – who made a big thing of it when we beat the strong favourites, Caerau, at Roath Park. That final was a strange one. I'd made my Hull KR debut the previous evening against Salford and I was pretty banged up, with a broken rib and ankle ligament damage, not to mention a couple of loose teeth, but I'd promised I'd be available and as skipper needed to set an example. I misjudged the drive down a bit in heavy bank holiday traffic, and arrived in my flash new BMW just 15 minutes before the start. After that, though, we soon settled and I was pleased with my bowling performance, which included twice bowling their star man, Brian 'Dubber' Richards, Wales' most-capped player and the best baseball player I ever played with or against. We won comfortably in the end, and the worry was only whether we could finish off the job before the increasingly heavy rain intervened. Accepting the trophy was one of the proudest moments of my life. I loved it.

Also that year, in one golden spell, I bowled England out for 20 in 17 minutes in the first innings of our Test. I was voted the Welsh baseball player of the year so, on top of a record-breaking season with Pontypool, it was some sporting twelve months. 1988 might have been the year my Rugby Union dream died and I finally cashed in my chips and went North, but it had its moments.

I played one more season the following summer, although Rugby League commitments – and injuries – were making it increasingly difficult and, me being me, there was also an unfortunate incident to deal with. I was up in Liverpool playing for Wales against England in the annual baseball International. After the match, there was some drinking and horseplay in the hotel, which resulted in the fire alarm going off and one of those emergency fire extinguishers coming off the wall. I, of course, had to milk the moment and picked it up and aimed it straight at Dubber – who, frankly, was minding his own business and entirely the innocent party. It was a regrettable but pretty bog-standard boys-on-tour sort of scenario, but the arrival of not one but five fire engines answering the alarm upped the stakes. This was now serious, and somebody needed to step forward and take responsibility. I happily did that, but for some reason the innocent Dubber, covered in that strange dry powder that some extinguishers dispense, was also hauled in front of the WBU. I explained his innocence, but nobody wanted to listen and we both copped a ban and a fine, which was more serious for him than me as I'd already decided that my baseball playing days were almost over.

I say 'almost', because there was an unlikely swansong in 1990. For some reason that I can't really explain, the Old Illtydians baseball club had suddenly imploded and didn't play for a few years. I was spending a couple of weeks in Wales before departing for Papua New Guinea and New Zealand with the 1990 Great Britain Lions when Tony Sweatman – a great friend of my dad's – phoned up and asked if I fancied coming back to play baseball for Llanrumney. I told him I'd be away on tour for nearly three months but he signed me up anyway. I got back from the tour on a Monday, and on the Tuesday he rang again to see if I could play two big games against Caerau that coming week. I'd completely forgotten about our arrangement. There was a midweek league fixture and the WBU cup final at the weekend. It seems my ban had run its course – or been lifted, I can't honestly remember, but nothing was said.

So on the Wednesday night I turned out, with my bowling really rusty. I got smashed around the park as they amassed 150-plus and we lost by an innings. As we came off, a good mate of mine – Jeff Pike, one of their Wales Internationals – jokingly said, "It's time to give up, Bish." I wasn't having that and I immediately bet him £300 (a considerable amount in 1990) that we'd win the Cup match at the weekend. He was up for that and even wanted to give me odds of 3 to 1, but I said, "Let's keep it simple and stay friends." Come the weekend, we won handsomely – and fair play to Jeff, he paid up promptly, straight after the game, saying, "Thank God you didn't take those 3 to 1 odds... now fuck off back to Rugby League-land, Bish." I left for Hull with a fair few quid in my back pocket.

It pains me to report that baseball in Wales is really struggling these days – the men's game anyway. The women seem to have picked up the baton and their version is flourishing. Good on them.

CHAPTER 19

Return of the Prodigal Son

OK, BACK TO the rugby. I know that's what you're all here for! My League career, if we're being brutal, just fizzled out – I was left feeling frustrated and unfulfilled as I mulled it all over during my ample leisure time. I didn't get to join St Helens, which was my original intention; I made it into the GB squad but after one Test that was it; and I enjoyed four games with a cracking Wales team but was too old and knackered for the 1995 World Cup, when the lads covered themselves in glory and made it to the semi-finals. I shone brightly during Hull KR's Second Division title-winning year and became the only player from that division to play on the GB tour to Papua New Guinea and New Zealand, but my League career was mostly *what ifs* – and most of that's down to me. I'd turned to League reluctantly because I felt my route to a regular Wales place was artificially blocked in Union, and I wasn't in love with the 13-man game. I didn't particularly follow it as a Union player. Money was my motivation – at least to start with, anyway, although that did change a bit.

Then there were the injuries. Other than my near cataclysmic neck injury, I prided myself on my fitness and consistency as a Union player. I was always good to go, whether it be with Cardiff Youth, Ebbw Vale, Pooler, Monmouthshire County, Public School Wanderers or in scores of sevens tournaments over the years. And if I did take a knock, I was a quick healer. But everything seemed to catch up with me overnight when I turned to League. I was targeted more than ever – well, that automatically happens when you arrive from Wales with a big price tag – but I kept on picking up shoulder, groin and ankle injuries. I seemed to spend my life on the physio couch or rehabbing in the gym.

Then there were the problems with Roger Millward, and no matter how right I might think I was, there was only going to be one winner there. He was a Red and Whites legend and a Rugby League great; I was an upstart from Wales with an unproven record in League. He'd never seen me play before the club signed me, and I never felt he believed in me no matter how hard I tried and how much my game improved.

Finally, there were the pure playing issues. Although I was confident of my all-round rugby skillset, it was difficult to identify my best League position. If I'd gone earlier in my career and enjoyed time to really learn the game, I suspect I'd still have been a scrum half, even though there wasn't much need for my kicking skills there. But Hull KR seemed to concentrate on my running and tackling game, not my ability to marshal proceedings as the main playmaker. In League, I could make a decent forward and that's where I often ended up, playing hooker or lock, which of course is unthinkable in Union terms.

All this sounds a bit negative and I don't want to paint that picture, because there were loads of pluses. I gained massive respect for the hardness, fitness and endurance of all those stalwart League professionals, many of them working-class guys from northern England – basically labourers earning a few bob to supplement their income. Many had other jobs and I was impressed that they managed to fit in the training and become so fit as part-timers. Over many decades, but particularly during this era, when League was flooded with Welsh Union talent, the critics and fans have rightly noted what an incredible Union team Wales could have put out if all those who went North had been available, and that's certainly true. But when you looked at the sheer talent and physicality of those northern lads, I have to tell you that – my God! – England would have been pretty tidy as well if they'd ever tapped into that talent pool!

The best thing about my move to Hull was that I very quickly grew to love the fans and the family spirit they created. They were the best. I loved them then and I love them now, and I look forward to my regular visits back to Hull to watch a game, yearning for and recalling big nights down the Crown. In League, there didn't seem to be a big clubhouse scene after the game; there wasn't much drinking and shooting the breeze with your opponents, even though there was a bar at Craven Park. What happened instead most nights is that we'd all pile down the Crown to drink and mingle with the fans. Many times, you might have plans to go on somewhere else, but the atmosphere was infectious and you ended up spending the whole evening there with the Red Army. The club meant everything to them and I gave my all when I played. I like to think they recognised that. Not unlike Pooler, I sometimes seemed more popular with the fans than with some elements inside the club itself. I made some great friends and memories, and remain in touch with many back in Hull.

But when it all ended, I was at a loose end. Typically, I hadn't made any plans for the future and although at first I didn't have many financial worries – we'd invested in a couple of houses to rent out, and there were still a few media bits and pieces and appearances – that cashflow soon reduced to a trickle. I'd squandered most of the money I'd earned, and it was hardly a life-changing amount anyway. Although I was only in my early thirties, my body was shot to bits and Union was still a couple of years away from going open, so there wasn't even the option of playing a couple of last seasons for Pooler on one leg. Or so I thought. And, actually, I didn't want to be one of these sad cases who doesn't know when to quit – that punch-drunk boxer who comes back for one last payday, with disastrous consequences.

Initially, I satisfied my rugby needs and scratched that itch by getting back in touch with the Old Illtydians – always a place of refuge for me – in the summer of 1994, and it was quickly agreed I'd coach them. I ended up putting in a two-year stint, and hugely agreeable it was, one of the happiest periods of my career and life, with people whose company I enjoyed. We had an inexperienced but keen group of lads, and they worked really hard, did pretty well, and we all had a good time. I was amongst friends and the Cardiff Irish community, which I felt part of, and we ticked over nicely together. I like to think I left them stronger and better than when I joined, and I was particularly proud of playing a small role in the development of Martyn Madden – a terrific natural talent, who Wales never really understood and managed poorly. He'd be gold dust nearly 30 years later, now we fully understand professionalism and how to condition certain athletic types. Martyn was a considerable athlete and preferred playing in the back row – he certainly had the running and handling skills to operate there – but I looked at his body shape and physical attributes and was convinced he'd be better suited to the more unglamorous role of prop. I convinced him and he made the switch, and after a year with me at Pooler – more of which shortly – he got snapped up by Llanelli, where he enjoyed a very fine career, even though he should have won closer to 50 Wales caps than the five he did receive.

The move back to Pontypool happened very quickly and wasn't at all planned. It started in the summer of 1996 when the club and Ringo parted ways – Ringo had been player-coach during his second spell there and seemed to be doing OK, but quite suddenly that summer it all ended. I have no idea what really happened, but had learned by then that rugby politics and finance is a very messy arena in both codes. Anything can happen. The point was that there was suddenly a vacancy as coach.

They weren't advertising for a replacement, but I heard on the grapevine it would be a salaried appointment. I thought maybe I could do that job and I certainly needed the money so I phoned up Perky, who was chairman of the Pooler committee, and said I'd like to apply. He sounded interested and an interview was organised at the Elm Road clubhouse with Perky and three or four other committee members. It went well enough, although it felt a bit weird having to go through my rugby CV with them as if I was a complete stranger. In fairness, I suppose it needed to be all above board and minuted. I outlined the work I'd been doing with the Old Illtydians for the last two years and mentioned I had some ideas, fitness-wise, to bring to the club from League, plus the defensive systems we used up north, and left feeling pretty good about myself.

Return of the Prodigal Son

A couple of days later, Perky phoned and apologised and said I hadn't got the job. Well, not as such. I was pretty stunned for a moment or two because, although I'd tried not to make any assumptions, I doubted if there was anybody better-suited for the role at Pontypool. It was a very particular club and it demanded somebody who knew how that club worked. And then Perky really confused me. He suggested we meet up to discuss something the committee wanted him to run past me. OK, no problems!

We met at a pub – the Six Bells in St Brides, if I remember correctly – and Perky came straight out with it. They hadn't yet made the appointment... because there'd been a rethink and what they really wanted was for me to return as player-coach. They could put together a really good package for me if I agreed to play as well as coach. A generous sponsor had made it known they'd pick up most of my wages.

I was surprised and shocked: I thought I'd made it clear my playing days were over. But also, deep down, I was a little bit excited and exhilarated. I'd beaten the odds before and defied my broken body to come back. Could I do it again? It was the kind of challenge that always fired me up. And, frankly, we needed the money. When I spoke to Kate about things, it took about five seconds to decide the obvious. This was an offer on the table and I had to accept. I agreed to a three-year contract.

Considering it was the very dawn of professionalism, the money was really decent for such a cash-strapped club and, with win bonuses and a few odds and ends thrown in, it wasn't far short of £30,000. Trevor Finn of Pendragon Motors – a Hull man, as it happens – was the generous sponsor who was going to foot most of the bill, with £10,000 at the start of the season and £10,000 in the New Year, and I can only thank him for his support during a rollercoaster three years back at the club. He was thoroughly professional at all times, as you'd expect from such a successful and innovative businessman. Sport can be full of charlatans promising this and that, but Trevor delivered in full at all times. He joins the list of those I need to thank properly in print.

Despite my good fortune in the appointment, I still didn't quite see how it made financial sense for Pooler, although a committee man told me I put between £1,000 and £1,500 on the gate every time I played, so I suppose I did at least increase the cashflow a little, with a few more through the turnstiles and in the club bar. What I didn't know until I clocked on in the pre-season was that we'd lost 18 players from the previous season's squad, with most of them joining 'smaller' Gwent neighbours such as Ebbw Vale, Abertillery and Newbridge. How the mighty had fallen, and how quickly. And we only had £5,000 to recruit a few players, paying just pocket money, really. Looking back, it was a farce, but what people forget is that in 1996 nobody had any idea what professionalism in Union looked like. I reckon most thought it just legitimised the old brown-envelope system and 'generous expenses', i.e. all that murky business was now officially legal and there'd be no comeback.

Only a few enlightened, richer clubs realised straight away that what it actually meant was that going forward, players would have to be on a retainer and eventually a salary. Pontypool, predictably, took the most conservative view. They had the reputation of never paying any players – although, as I've explained, they bunged me generously on the quiet – and as far as they were concerned, all they'd do would be to make £5,000 available for sweeteners, over and above legitimate expenses. It was madness, really. They turned a blind eye to the new reality, not understanding that from this point, players would ruthlessly follow the money. Old loyalties, connections with junior clubs and schools would go straight out the window. Pooler couldn't expect talented players or even seasoned old warriors to come flocking to the Park just for the privilege and a bellyful of free beer and sandwiches. We quickly learned there were clubs three divisions beneath us paying some players £100 a week.

To my amazement and slight discomfort, Pooler's reaction to professionalism was to put all their eggs in one basket and invest mostly in a single individual. Me. Which really cranked up the pressure. I was effectively Director of Rugby, coach and star player, even though I could scarcely walk to the newsagent's. That was their limited take on professionalism.

I put these concerns on the back burner for a while. My immediate priority was to lose some weight, coax my body back into action and get as fit as I was able. With the depleted squad I'd inherited, the only way I could begin to justify Pooler's investment in me was to at least get on the pitch and entice the fans back to the Park. It might have had the feel of a tribute band but some tribute bands are still worth watching, in small doses.

I reverted to my tried-and-tested Rocky Balboa routine. On with the headphones. Long, quick walks to start with, then jogs, followed by punishing sessions down the boxing gym. My legs might be creaking but I could still work my upper body and I went at it very hard. It took a while, but gradually I became less of a blob and was again vaguely recognisable as the professional sportsman I'd once been. And I was enjoying the challenge – I'd missed the buzz.

Of course I had. Returning to some kind of playing career would help keep the old man at bay.

I was also conscious of the need to set an example at twice-weekly training at Pooler. In my pomp, I did that totally on the pitch: I asked to be judged solely on my performances. But now a new group who knew me only by reputation, not deed, was looking to me. With a sense of dread, I started taking part in some of the Grotto Runs. I hated every moment, but it had to be done. What a turnaround! Much to the surprise of many, I backed that up by demanding a few basics from the boys: punctuality at training and wearing club blazers on matchday, which caused a certain amount of guffawing from those who knew me and my dress code of old... Pross had always wanted us to attend matches in blazer and tie and although I'd bucked the trend on occasion, as I got older, I began to appreciate what he was getting at. At least turn up looking like a team singing from the same hymn sheet. Arrive as a collective, not a gaggle of individuals. Dress smart, play smart. It's only a little thing but it helps, and frankly we needed all the help we could get.

I was determined we shouldn't try to run before we could walk, and took care of the basics first. At one training session our skipper Dai Lynch, a good centre, reported back that the lads were getting a bit bored and could I mix our sessions up a bit more, make them more fun. Dai's point was well-intentioned, but I was the wrong person to have that debate with. Mastering and perfecting the basics was the bedrock of my rugby philosophy.

"I'll tell you what, let's ask the ref on Saturday if he could mix it up a bit for us and cut out scrums and line-outs, and blow ten minutes early before we get too tired," I replied, pointedly.

Return of the Prodigal Son

It was a bit of cheap shot from me but I think the lads got where I was coming from. Train Hard, Play Easy.

We were a shoestring operation, make no mistake. I remember one time I was chasing a player I thought Worcester might let us have on loan and phoned up Les Cusworth – 'Knobhead' – who I knew from the sevens circuit of old, plus a few XV encounters with Tigers. Les told me that the club was being bankrolled by a multi-millionaire, Cecil Duckworth, and he had his own well-appointed office, while I had to shamefacedly tell him I was using the public phone on the wall by the Pontypool changing rooms. My midweek office was the broom cupboard of a referee's room. I remember putting the phone down at the end of our conversation that day and thinking the game was moving at 1000 mph and we at Pooler weren't moving nearly quickly enough.

My God, that was a tough season, but I enjoyed it, nonetheless. It had been eight years since I officially played Union, save for a couple of crafty games for the Old Illtydians when I was in dispute with Hull KR, and three years since I'd played League. Even in the second tier of Welsh rugby, I noticed the hits seemed harder and bigger than when I was playing at the top level back in 1988 and, of course, I still had a target on my back. In fact, even more than ever. There was a bounty on my head – I'm convinced some players were on a bonus if they took me out of the game!

We were gutsy and keen but desperately outmuscled and outclassed upfront. I tried to get Madman involved in coaching but he had a prior commitment with Blaenavon, so we soldiered on, and to finish fifth in the table was about as good as we could have expected. I was in no position to play 80 minutes every week, so I had the constant dilemma of whether to start or to come off the bench. Coming off the bench appeared to work best as it seemed to raise the energy level of some of the lads when we most needed it. I certainly remember one game against South Wales Police when we'd gone 22-0 down before I came on, and suddenly we started clicking and came back brilliantly to earn a 22-22 draw, with my good self nipping over for two tries. In fact I scored 11 tries in 14 games, so the old try-scoring knack hadn't deserted me entirely, which was gratifying, but it took most of Sunday and a good part of Monday to get over my cameo appearances. I wasn't remotely the David Bishop who'd played for Pooler in the 1980s, but I gave 100% every time I put that jersey on. The feelgood factor was immense: I was enjoying myself again.

To my delight, we put a bit of a Cup run together, which is never bad for the momentum with a side. I enjoy everything about the Cup. Away matches against absolute minnows down west somewhere in the pissing rain and mud, to sell-out games at the Park against the big names of Welsh rugby – it's got a bit of everything. This time I had to reconcile myself to the fact that, if not absolute minnows, we were one of the small clubs, even though it was less than six years since Pooler had reached the 1991 final. That's how quickly and how far we'd fallen in the pecking order.

It was fun. We beat Dolgellau 12-3 in the fourth round and then Pencoed 21-9, both new opponents for me. Next it was Whitland – riding high near the top of Division Four – at the Park, and what a game they gave us. They were leading 24-23 going into injury time with me on as a replacement and we didn't seem to be going anywhere with our last 'Hail Mary' play, when I had a chance to drop a goal from 35 yards out. It was game over if I missed, but they're the situations I relish, and I managed to smash it over to earn a quarter-final place. I was hoping for Cardiff at home, which would be a big crowd at the Park and a decent payday for the club but certain defeat; or South Wales Police at home, which would have given us a fighting chance of being shock semi-finalists. In the event, we copped Llanelli away and predictably took a 59-17 hammering at Stradey. I twisted my knee early in the week and probably shouldn't have played – I went in for small operation the following week – but I couldn't resist one final trip down there and a tussle with Rupert Moon, who I've always got on with since his Abertillery and Monmouthshire days. They were three yards quicker than us, a fully professional outfit already, but we fought gamely for the full 80.

I was genuinely moved when I was finally forced off after 57 minutes and, to my surprise, got a huge ovation from the crowd as I limped back to the dugout. A fair few Llanelli fans also came up afterwards and requested autographs, which again touched me. They guessed, correctly, that it would be the last time I'd ever play at Stradey and, what with the knee playing up, it seemed like this might be curtains for me, full stop. Heaven knows, I've given west Walians and their clubs the sharp end of my tongue over the years – partly it was just me playing up to a stereotype, but mainly because I perceived the WRU back then as being run by vindictive and preachy west Walians – but to realise they rated me as a player and to receive that generous ovation meant a lot, and I immediately felt guilty for some of my comments over the years. Me and my mouth.

So that first season, in my mind, was as good as we could have expected. We'd benefitted massively from the emergence of two very promising players, although it was bittersweet because they clearly had to move on as soon as possible to further their careers. Professionalism meant there was money to be made at the top and we couldn't expect promising kids to hang around. Martyn Madden had come up from the Old Illtydians with me and gave me a season, while Pooler themselves had unearthed a real good 'un in local boy Iestyn Thomas, who was a young prop a little in the Pricey mould. Iestyn was another good athlete, very quick over the ground and comfortable with ball in hand, who was beginning to learn his trade technically in the front frow. Like Martyn, he put in a great shift for us before he moved up the valley to Ebbw Vale – who by this point were playing a division above us – and then on to Llanelli and Scarlets, where he played for the next decade or more, winning 33 Wales caps during his time there. He joined Martyn down there. Martyn had enjoyed a stormer in adversity in the Cup game, helping to make two of our three tries, and Llanelli didn't waste time coming in for him. I don't blame them.

I knew the lads needed to leave ASAP if they weren't to miss the boat with Wales, but I couldn't see how the Pooler team could develop without significant recruitment. It was Catch-22: I couldn't make a silk purse out of a sow's ear, and my fears came to fruition when, without our two mainstays up front, we really struggled in the reconstituted Division One (with the Welsh Premier Division now above it) the following season. It was a bitch of a league – 30 dog-eat-dog matches through autumn, winter and spring. I managed to rehab my knee and, after thinking for the umpteenth time I was done, I miraculously appeared in 23 of those league games. It nearly killed me, but we limped home in 14th position with just 11 wins, narrowly avoiding relegation right at the death.

Return of the Prodigal Son

That second season was bloody hard work. We lacked any kind of stardust. I tried my best when I came on, and was as effective and dangerous as anybody we had, but I struggled to provide the spark we needed. To borrow from golfing terminology, sometimes you need somebody who can shoot a birdie most matches, an eagle with some regularity and – praise be to the Almighty! – an albatross every so often. That's what lifts a team and gets them playing 10% better than they were 30 seconds beforehand. Without being falsely modest, there was a time when I was that man for Pooler, and there were others, like Shaft or Madman, and of course Ringo, who could produce amazing moments of one sort or another. By this stage of my career, though, I couldn't really do that any more, and it grieved me a bit, although I never stopped trying. I felt a responsibility to the fans: I needed to justify those wages. I wouldn't short-change Pooler.

At the end of the season, I went to the committee and pleaded with them: "I'm David Bishop, not Paul fucking Daniels. I'm not a magician. Please give me something to work with." It seemed to fall on deaf ears – Pooler's interpretation of professionalism was still at odds with reality – but soon afterwards Snooty, a busy man with his media career at the time but trying to do his best by the club behind the scenes, asked me exactly what I needed. The absolute priority, I said, was a couple of big ball-winning forwards who could keep us in games and guarantee some quality pill for the backs. And personally, if I, in my rugby dotage, could be served up some decent possession, there was more chance of me controlling the games better tactically and having more influence on proceedings.

Eddie went off and worked his contacts and the next thing I knew, we had four boys join from Bath on what appeared to be an almost permanent loan. Bath were one of the strongest teams in Europe during this era and some of their lads – really good players – were struggling to get game time, so I think that was the basis of whatever deal Eddie brokered. Anyway, the long and the short of it was that Pooler were soon to benefit from the services of two top young English locks in Alex Brown and Will James, Alex for a season and Will for the best part of two years. Alex was a great line-out operator, lean like the All Black Ian Jones, and a real prospect. I'm surprised he only got a handful of England caps – although they always seem to have locks coming out of the woodwork over the bridge and he also started to pick up injuries at the wrong time, which never helps. Will, who was basically a Devonian but boasted a grandfather from Pontypool and felt a real connection with the town, was an old-fashioned workhorse in the tight and around the park – a tractor, we call them – and eventually earned a few Wales caps as well. Both were terrific for Pontypool and really perked the place up. They did us proud.

Other quality players started to appear at the club. My old mate Phil Ford, my Cardiff Youth colleague before his very successful career in League, reappeared and was still in good nick. Matt Silva was another Welsh guy who went North with Halifax only to return when Union went open, and he provided experience and quality kicking. Matt McCarthy and Ben Jeffries were useful backs and up front we had experienced Tongan hooker Fe'ao Vunipola, the father of Billy and Mako. I'm not sure he understood anything I said, with my strong Cardiff accent and his English at the time, but we seemed to be on the same rugby wavelength so rubbed along famously. A very talented ball-handler and tough lad. Richard Field was a former Wales Schools skipper and promising flanker; David Brier was a useful Kiwi back-rower we discovered working locally in the area. I made contact and to be honest all the persuasion he needed to get him to come was the promise of a new pair of boots. Will James skippered and was available all season, Alex Brown most of the season. We were a cross between Dad's Army and the local Youth Club, but we were up for anything.

We had something about us that season and it was an immensely enjoyable last hurrah for me, playing-wise. We won 23 of our 30 league games but were pipped to second place by Bonymaen – who won only 22, although they did draw two games. They, however, had mastered the art of garnering try bonuses and actually finished 11 points clear of us in the table. I was vocal against the introduction of bonus points from the off, so it wasn't just sour grapes when I had a whinge at the end of the season. Sport is about winning – it's why you keep the score! – and winning pure and simple. Scoring tries in defeat is no great achievement for me: it feels like you're getting points for artistic impression, like in ice skating. You've lost the game, end of story. You get situations nowadays where teams go into a league game and their priority is scoring four tries, not winning. It doesn't matter if they lose by 40 points as long as they score their four tries and get the try bonus. I hate that. That can't be right. It warps the game. Anyway, rant over – I've been proved to be on the wrong side of history on that one. Bonus points quickly became a fact of life and part of every league structure in the world.

We put a bloody good league campaign together that season and, what's more, we rolled back the years and enjoyed a bit of fun in the SWALEC Cup again. We started off with a straightforward 64-6 win over Rhigos and then sneaked a 15-13 victory over Whitland away, in a classic tight, nervous Cup encounter. Then came our biggest result in a long while – an unexpected 15-14 win over Neath in the seventh round, our first win over the Welsh All Blacks in six years. They were a division above us and on paper a much stronger side, but there was a little bit of magic in the air at the Park and a decent crowd of 4,000 or so roared us home. There was just a hint of what it used to be like. That day we had both Will and Alex in the second row and they bossed the line-out and restarts and gave us that base we needed to at least be competitive. Possession is everything in rugby – nothing ever changes in that respect.

Unfortunately, Alex had to sit out the quarter-final, which was at home against Cardiff. Our dream fixture – a guaranteed big crowd and a chance for me to give Ringo, who was one of the coaches there by this time, a bloody nose. Well, theoretically. I knew we'd need to sneak at least 30 men on the pitch to have any chance, but we vowed to go down with all guns blazing.

I can't deny that I thoroughly enjoyed all the media attention and hype ahead of our clash with Cardiff, although I'd forgotten that, for a while, their participation in the Cup that season had actually been in doubt. In August 1998, Cardiff and Swansea were both expelled by the WRU for the 1998/99 season for refusing to sign a 10-year Loyalty Agreement with the WRU, arranging their own unauthorised games against English opposition instead. In the end they were allowed to play in the Cup due to pressure from the sponsors, and reached the quarter-final against us.

That Cardiff side was rammed with Wales Internationals and there was no realistic chance of a Pooler win, but we approached the game with a positive determination to enjoy

Return of the Prodigal Son

ourselves, and for me it was definitely my final sniff of the big time as a player. Every press and media outlet bar none was on the phone for an interview, and myself and Mark indulged in a lot of pre-match banter. We even agreed to meet in a Cardiff bookies the day before to film an interview with BBC Wales. We laughed and joked our way through the morning, which was natural for the two of us, although I'm not sure you'd get rival coaches doing it today.

The match was entirely predictable but fun, nonetheless. We gave it a good lash for 50 minutes and I think were only 19-12 down at that stage. We went close to scoring a try that might have seen us draw level, but from then on it was almost all Cardiff, with their superior fitness and firepower. They punished us ruthlessly, although I was delighted that we had enough ticker to hit back with two late tries to give the score a veneer of respectability. 52-26 to Cardiff.

I came on early in the second half for Neil Hope, and immediately felt my age. The game was being played at a pace I hadn't experienced since my League days, but I dug in and contributed as best I could. I personally remember the game mainly for two things. Firstly, Cardiff's Canadian flanker Dan Baugh – a rough, tough case – hit me with a latish high shot as I kicked the ball, which would have landed me in all sorts of grief if I'd been the perpetrator. In today's climate it would be totally unacceptable, and even back then it was a marginal shot by Dan.

It hurt like hell but I just shrugged it off, which probably saved Dan a spot of trouble with officialdom. I've never been one for milking it when I was on the receiving end. I couldn't, however, have our Canadian friend telling his grandchildren that I was a soft touch, so I bided my time. I was older and wiser. I didn't intend to do anything really stupid, but there had to be a little payback so, when we were attacking in their 22 and he was loitering close by the ruck on the blindside, I put in a big body check as he attempted to come round. It winded him and he was mad as hell, but by that time the ref had come round and the ball was there to be played and he had to suck it up. Like I did when he clobbered me. We laughed about it afterwards.

And then, with about ten minutes left and the game won, Rob Howley went off, to be replaced by Robert Jones. Our final head-to-head, and it was poignant, really. For all our supposed rivalry, it was amazing how few times we actually played against each other over the years.

The day was done and the game was gone, and I took a few moments during the closing exchange to look around and soak it all in. A big crowd had been basking in the sun on the bank and generated a great atmosphere. The old chants of 'Pooler, Pooler, Pooler' rang round. Not as threatening and meaningful as of old, but they still brought a tear to my eye. This was it, the last time I'd ever experience that in a big game, and the buzz it gives you. I'd been so privileged and, for all my grievances with Wales and all those moments I shot myself in the foot, I'd been so lucky. Nothing beats being a player performing in front of a crowd, and I knew with some certainty that afternoon that I was going to miss it all horribly.

A successful season came to a close and, although that was it from the playing point of view, I felt I was only just getting started with the coaching. It was the summer of 1999 and I was feeling pretty good and optimistic about life – which should have served as a warning, really, because that's when things normally go pear-shaped for me. I could envisage only good things for Pooler as we entered the new

Return of the Prodigal Son

millennium. I knew deep down that I'd done an outstanding job making Pooler competitive again; I'm not sure anybody could have done better given the circumstances, and that was just the start of things. Another couple of seasons and we'd be back with the big boys on a long-term basis.

But unbeknown to me, there were a few dark clouds on the horizon. In fact, I'd got an early warning at the start of the season, when the club's new chairman and benefactor Jeff Taylor phoned me up and arranged a meeting at the Celtic Manor Hotel outside Newport, where he tore up my contract, saying that the club couldn't afford me. That might well be the case, although strictly speaking it wasn't the club who paid most of my salary, but a contract is a contract: that's one thing I'd learned as a professional. Fair play to Trevor Finn and Pendragon, they continued to keep their part of the bargain for the rest of the season. But that three-year contract was now coming to end. What next for me and Pooler? Playing-wise, I couldn't drag my sorry carcass through another season, but I believed I'd more than proved my suitability to coach and run the rugby side of things. I was good at maximising our potential, spotting underutilised talent, doing loan deals and keeping the players motivated. We were only going in one direction.

I was up at Usk in the summer of 1999 doing my Level 3 coaching certificate when a throwaway remark from John Bevan – the former Wales and Lions wing – sounded the alarm bells. "Are you going to bother with pre-season training?" he asked.

What? Why wouldn't I bother with pre-season training? I got John – who was very well-connected and knew everybody in the game – to tell me what he knew. He said he'd heard that Junna was going to be coaching Pooler next season. He apologised profusely – he assumed I'd known and was OK with it.

I was furious and phoned Taylor that night.

"What the fuck's going on?

He sounded a bit flustered but if I understood him right, he was arguing that they couldn't afford me any more and that some people were saying that I was becoming bigger than the club.

"Excuse me? 'Bigger than the club'?" I was absolutely livid. "There is – and only ever will be – one Mr Pontypool. And that's Ray Prosser. And if you think money's the issue, I'll happily do it for nothing. I'll even waive the testimonial game I was promised, which you think I've forgotten about."

I was working up a fair old head of steam, but he was unmoved. He was not for changing and repeated that he'd already offered Junna the job and Junna had accepted. He started muttering something about maybe working as an assistant to Junna and perhaps something could be sorted out over the testimonial game if I really insisted, but I didn't believe him any more. If he wasn't man enough to talk to me directly about keeping me on or not before making the appointment with Junna, how could I trust anything he said? This wasn't a man I could work with any more.

My time with Pooler was over, and it depressed me greatly. Another stolen dream, and this time I'd been pretty much blameless. I was really disappointed that Junna hadn't contacted me personally to say what had happened, and I got him on the phone and let fly. He claimed that Taylor had said he'd phone me and explain everything, but I wasn't appeased. As a long-time old playing colleague, Junna should have had the courtesy to phone and talk things through with me first. It was all bloody messy, but the rugby world was changing. It gave me no pleasure to read a few years later that Junna had in turn been shafted and ended up having to take Pontypool to court for constructive dismissal after being forced out by Taylor. I should have bitten my lip: Junna was just trying his best, we all were. It was still very early days in the brave new world of professional rugby and we were all still getting to grips with how things would work. We were all gettng our fingers burnt. But it broke my heart to leave Pooler like that, after such a good season and such a wonderfully enjoyable and enriching time representing the club and the town.

CHAPTER 20

Coping with Charlie

LIFE BECAME VERY rough and problematic very quickly once I finally retired for good as after being ousted as player-coach at Pooler in 1999. With hindsight, you can see all the dangers and pitfalls but, at the time, you just lurch from crisis to crisis, assuming something will come good for you. With a sportsman's confidence and ego, you assume you can fight your way through and put things right, but I spiralled out of control and hit rock bottom before, with the help of family and good friends, I bounced back up a little. But it's a daily fight. When you have an addictive personality, you go into the ring every morning to fight off those dark forces and it can make your late middle age and early old age pretty challenging. I could fill a small notebook with the names of the ex-sportsmen and personalities who, to a greater or lesser degree, have gone through the same problems as me. Even through the haze and confusion, you start realising you're seeing the same old faces at the same old dives. Drug addiction doesn't discriminate, and nor does clinical depression.

So how did it all go wrong for me? Not that life had ever been a smooth ride. First came the depression of no longer being a player – and don't underestimate that: it can be crushing if you're not prepared for it. To use the old cliché, rugby was my life. It really was. I knew nothing else, I was qualified for nothing else; it was my world and there was an actual physical pain when I woke up one morning and it was no longer there.

Suddenly you have no structure to your day or week. No training sessions you have to attend, no meetings and, above all else, no games in midweek and on Saturday. The release on matchday, the much-needed high from physical exertion and competition and the feelgood factor of fans cheering, or even booing and jeering – I loved that as well – was my first addiction. I couldn't get enough of it. It fed my ego and made me feel a complete man, not a failure. It was my high, but it was also my comfort zone. Being on a rugby pitch was the only time I ever felt completely at peace with myself and the world. Take that away and there are bound to be repercussions. I can see that now.

So I just wasn't prepared for the absence and loss; nor did I realise how much I'd miss the lads who'd surrounded me for much of my life. You do become family; you grow really close on the pitch and of course enjoy all the good times and high jinks off the pitch. And then it's scattered to the winds, as if deep down it meant nothing at all. Rugby's no longer the priority for anybody – life becomes all about chasing jobs, earning money, supporting your family – and that new life can take you anywhere in the world. You have to start growing up, and some of us found it difficult. The band splits up, so to speak, and although a very long way down the line there may be a big emotional reunion or two, you're suddenly flying solo. You may stay in touch with two or three particular mates if you're lucky – I always kept in touch throughout everything with Doc and Snooty – but mainly you feel empty and alone.

Another very practical problem is employment. What do you actually do to earn a living? Objectively, I'd done a fine job with almost no resources during my time as player-coach at Pooler and thought there'd be plenty of offers when that ended in tears. In fact, there were a couple but, me being me, I held out for the big one. I thought I'd be walking into a big well-paid job with one of the regions. I'd served my apprenticeship: the time was right. It didn't happen, and I ended up missing the boat altogether. Then I turned to the media. I had spells with both S4C and BBC Wales as a pundit and I remain grateful for the opportunity, but it was an awkward marriage because I'm incapable of not speaking my mind. I have no filter. If a player's having a rubbish game, I'll say so, regardless of how big a name he might be. If a pass is forward, I'll say so; if a referee's made a totally ludicrous decision, I'll call him out. If the WRU is destroying the game in Wales, I'll speak out. If I think Wales are going to lose by 40 points, I won't sugar-coat it when we preview the game. I won't give false hope when there is none. I've never understood why the truth is considered controversial. If you owned Nijinsky or Shergar, would you ever bet your own money against those horses? Anyway, I got pulled aside quietly on a couple of occasions and was asked to be more positive and, although we didn't fall out, I realised that perhaps this wasn't for me.

Instead, I got an amazing opportunity to co-host a nightly sports phone-in programme on Real Radio, which was much more up my street. It featured vigorous and hopefully amusing debate about the big sporting issues of the day, with myself taking the lead on rugby and chipping in on other sports. I have David Giles to thank for putting a word in for me on that one and, for six or seven years, that was my mainstay. We really got stuck in. One time, I helped set up a fantastic debate/argument between Leighton James and Robbie Savage, who went at it hammer and tongs. Another time I had David Moffett lined up to defend his decision to take Wales down the regional route, but he dropped out on the morning of the programme. So we climbed into the plan in his absence and dismantled his ideas.

The money wasn't massive, but it was my only regular income and much more needed and appreciated than anybody could guess. I hadn't come out of my Rugby League years as a wealthy man, and the need to keep abreast of what was going on in the sporting world meant the programme helped keep my head above water in terms of morale as well as financially.

So far, I'm painting a picture of quite a normal story, which was probably replicated by scores of my playing contemporaries and those retiring from other sports in south Wales, such as football and cricket. And don't forget – with rugby, anyway – we now know that a history of past concussions may have contributed to our mental health issues. I certainly believe that may be part of my situation, and have joined the group that was founded to seek legal redress after Alix Popham made his early-onset dementia situation public. I've done all the tests and spent the best part of a day, or so it seemed, in one of those MRI scanners having my brain monitored, being set certain mental tasks or having electric pulses sent through my grey matter to test my reaction. I wouldn't want to do it again – that narrow tube is scary. The results were depressing. In terms of visible brain deficit – they use some funny terms! – I'm amongst the worst they've examined. There appears to be a lot of damage, in layman's terms.

But there were already other factors in my situation. I always knew I had an addictive personality. I had to do everything to the nth degree, and if you've made it this far in the book you might well, correctly, think that was inherited from my father. I was so addicted to playing rugby and the buzz it gave me that I ignored specialists and overcame a broken neck to continue my career. I literally gambled with my life at the top of that diving board at the Empire Pool. I was addicted to winning and sometimes struggled with defeat. I was addicted to getting my own way and controlling situations, sometimes with my fists. I could be hugely volatile. I was up one minute, down in the dumps the next; the Antichrist one minute, good as gold and Mamma's little boy the next.

What would happen to that Jekyll and Hyde aspect of my personality when I had fewer highs and more lows? The answer, I now know, is that I went chasing artificial highs.

I had no trade other than as a casual labourer and driver on building sites, helping my brothers or father-in-law. I had no skills and I'd made a fair few enemies on the circuit. I wasn't going to be besieged with offers of jobs which involved little more than turning up at 9 a.m. and occasionally chatting up clients. Although sports mad, I didn't have a relaxing hobby. I wasn't a golfer then, although it's been fun to discover the game in late middle age, and I hadn't thought about channelling my energy into something completely different such as, I don't know, surfing or skiing, to maintain that physical buzz. Very quickly I was struggling – although of course, like all sportsmen, I became a master at disguising it.

As a player, I made no secret of the fact that I smoked the occasional spliff, more for appearances' sake than anything else, because weed did little for me. But I'd crossed a line, I suppose, and now in retirement I started looking for something a bit stronger. In the circles I moved in in the late Nineties and Noughties, cocaine was quickly becoming the recreational drug of choice, so I started dabbling. Although, of course, you can never really dabble with cocaine because it grabs you by the neck and never lets go.

The first time you take cocaine, the euphoric high and the release of energy is off the bloody Richter scale. You wonder why you hadn't discovered it much earlier. It seems like a wonder drug – you feel like you've scored the winning try for Wales at Cardiff Arms Park and all is well with the world. For a few hours, sometimes quite a bit longer in the early days of your addiction, you're back on top of the world. You feel like the master of all you survey and invincible again, just like you did in your playing pomp. Confident, optimistic, clever – well, that's how you feel. But to the rest of the world, you're manic, talking nonsense and often acting like a complete arse.

Cocaine is a heartless, sly bastard and please, if you're reading, don't ever go anywhere near it. The depths you plunge to when you come down off a cocaine high just can't be imagined unless you've been there. You end up in a situation which feels ten times worse than the depression that tempted you to take the drug in the first place.

And because those first few highs were so high and so desirable, you need it again to climb out of the depths of your new depression. And again. And again. The cycle is endless and life-destroying. The highs become shorter and shorter and more difficult to reach; you need more and more cocaine; and you'll do anything to get it, because you feel you can't survive without it, and can't face the depression which crushes you when you come off the highs. All the time, by the way, you think your relationship with cocaine is your little secret that nobody's noticed, but you can't hide the signs of cocaine addiction. You just become too weird and unreasonable. Eventually, family and friends start clocking what's happening.

Feeding the habit becomes more expensive and you start doing crazy things to pay for your addiction. You empty your joint account with your wife. You have to get your hit, whatever it costs. You beg off friends and family, then you steal off friends and family, or sometimes people you've just met. The most I ever paid was £3,000, but that was for barely a fortnight's supply at the time. Do the maths. It really doesn't add up unless you're a multi-millionaire.

You can't sleep, you don't eat properly, you get palpitations, you feel cold all the time, then you feel hot and clammy all the time, your body twitches, you develop a tremor and generally struggle to function as a human being. You feel like death. So you live only for your next hit. Just one more time. If only I can start feeling a little better, I'll give it up. I promise. But no. It just doesn't happen like that. You live like a hermit in a cave during the day, withdrawn from the world, unwilling to talk to family or engage with friends, and then trawl various ratholes and dives at night, looking to score. You start noticing the same old faces, all being eaten up by their cocaine addiction. I've lived that life and crawled home at some ungodly hour and said my prayers – out of habit, rather than hope – and gone to sleep not knowing if I'd wake up the following morning. And, frankly, not caring much either.

And then you start on crack cocaine, which is the lowest of the low – even more dangerous. Crack cocaine is stronger and more expensive, the highs are even higher but are they're very short-lived and over before they've really started. They also mix all sorts of shit with crack cocaine – baking soda, talcum powder, caffeine, laxatives, all sorts – to bulk it out and make more money for the dealer. It can be very toxic.

My situation was even more fraught than some. I 'enjoyed' a certain celebrity status, if you like – I'd been a creature of the night most of my adult life and knew a lot of people, as the saying goes. If push came to shove, I didn't have to go through a dealer, I could go direct to the main men. They'd sometimes even give me drugs on credit or very occasionally gift a hit. Even though my funds were fast diminishing, there was a while e when I still had instant access to drugs.

That was my life for much of the Noughties. I fought it in my own way, and there were periods when you might have thought I was doing OK, but I wasn't. It cost me my marriage and in 2002, Kate and I divorced. She'd stuck with me, loved me, tried everything she knew, but there came a point when she just couldn't take it any more. She had to think of her own sanity, and who could blame her? It was totally my fault. My self-destructive tendencies were in full flow. I had just enough grip on reality to not really contest the divorce and came to a simple arrangement. When I'd signed for Hull KR, and had money, Kate – being clever as well as beautiful – had insisted that we buy a couple of properties to let, by way of a life investment for us. Thank God she did, because with my cocaine habit I was soon going through our available cash like a knife through butter. When it came to the divorce, I said she could have everything: our house, the rental properties and everything, if I could just have £20,000. Kate was aghast. She knew that wasn't the way forward for me, but at least that way she and the two girls would always be provided for and as far as I was concerned, I just needed that £20,000 to relaunch my life. It would all be different after that.

Well, of course it wasn't – not for a good while, anyway, but I kept fighting the good fight. I wanted to get better for Kate, the girls and then my grandchildren as they came along. And there has been an improvement. It was slow at first but then came in big leaps. A big moment came when I signed up for a month at the Priory in Roehampton in an attempt to detox and reset my life. In one way it was a complete failure but, in another way, it was the first step back to relative normality.

I hated the place on first sight – I'd had enough of hospitals and institutions in my life – and was well out of my comfort zone as I checked in, was shown my sparsely furnished room, and was told the first meeting of the group was at 3 p.m.

I got there last – old habits never die – and it was the classic chairs-in-a-circle scenario you see on TV dramas, with about a dozen people present and one counsellor in the middle. I sat down and the person on my right was invited to introduce themselves and explain why they were there.

"Hi, I'm Don. I was a dentist but I got divorced, became a chronic alcoholic and I need help."

"Hi, I'm Jan. I was an intensive care nurse for 20 years but the stress got to me and I started drinking too much and then turned to cocaine. I can't cope any more. I want to quit but don't know how."

"Hi, I'm Terry. I'm a police officer. I've somehow manged to hide my addiction and keep my job, but I'm addicted to booze and cocaine. I need my job – I love my job, but the reality is, I'm a danger to the public and my colleagues. I need help."

"Hi, I'm Julie. I've been a GP for 25 years. We're understaffed and the stress is massive. I can't cope and I'm hooked on cocaine. I've referred my patients for help in the past when they present with my symptoms and difficulties, and now I must seek help myself."

And on it went, with me the last patient due to talk. It took quite a while, because some didn't just content themselves with their opening comments but started to give more details and got emotional as their anguish started to unwind. I was emotional too, but in a different way. I could feel something boiling up inside of me. Partly the old rage that used to drive me, but I was also beginning to think clearly for the first time in many years. These were proper professional people, with real responsible jobs, and here they were, sitting in a confessional circle with me. I didn't belong here; it didn't feel right. I was having a bit of a road-to-Damascus moment. This wasn't going to work for me. Eventually it came to my turn and boy, was I ticking.

"Hi, I'm David. I used to be a rugby player. I'm a cocaine and crack addict and I'm leaving. I'm out of here."

There was a sharp intake of breath followed by a few embarrassed coughs, and as I got up from my chair to storm out, I stopped. I felt I owed them a bit more explanation.

"Listen. There's only one person who can get me out of this mess and that's me, the person who caused it in the first place. I wish all of you the very best. You're deeply impressive people and, believe me, I know exactly how you feel and share your anguish. But, as from today, I'm declaring war on cocaine. It's my fight and I need to get busy winning the war. Good luck to you all – I love you all."

And with that, I headed back to my room, packed, checked out and was back in Cardiff for supper. In many ways, it was a big waste of money, but in another way, it worked. Just being at the Priory provided that elusive moment of self-awareness and self-loathing – the bucket of freezing cold water over the head – that I needed in order to start addressing my addiction in earnest. I learnt subsequently that it's not at all unusual for somebody to have this lightbulb moment early in the first week at the Priory.

I felt much stronger mentally, driving home, and since that day have never been near crack cocaine. As for cocaine, that took longer, but my periods between hits became longer and longer. No addict will ever say they are 'cured', even though it's a long time since I succumbed. You go into the ring every morning and fight the fight afresh. The temptation never goes away – in the back of your mind, you know you could, and the temptation is to just grab that short-term fix.

And of course, unless you're blessed with the happiest of lives and perfect good health, you still get down and depressed on occasion. It's perfectly normal for anybody to have periods when they don't feel themselves, or when they're stressed by their personal circumstances. When you've taken cocaine previously, you know for certain it'll make you feel better for an hour or two. Life throws up temptations. Covid was hell for everybody and, as a singleton in a flat – a singleton who'd also just suffered a stroke – my God, I was tempted. I had to physically fight that desire, that temptation, but that's the battle many of us find ourselves in. And the way out is to keep busy: don't become isolated, mix with your old mates – in fact, actively look up old mates and start engaging again. For all you know, they might be suffering as well.

One of the few upsides of this period in my life and the ongoing fight is that you learn who your real friends are. Family and loved ones, obviously – they've been through

Coping with Charlie

hell, coping with my moods, and are still there in my corner – but also old mates and new friends. It was the latter that surprised me. They've been some of the most loyal, supportive and understanding, and amongst them I'm proud to count Wales football legend Craig Bellamy, who, as I write this, is making a fine start to his term as Wales coach – a job he was born to do.

It was a bit odd how we became mates. I used to be a regular at Ten Mill Lane, which was a very 'in' spot in town, and I'd got to know some of the Wales footballers who'd adopted the place. I'd clocked Craig there a few times with the guys – of course, I knew who he was: a brilliant young footballer and a big name in Welsh sport – but we hadn't been introduced or anything.

Then one night I had to go to the toilet in a rush, as you do occasionally, dashed into the cubicle and was going about my business when Craig rushed in and started banging on the door. He'd been caught short as well and it was an emergency, so to speak. I was just finishing up, opened the door and there was a heavy with Craig – there used to be a minder or two looking after the Wales boys when they were out and about – ordering me to get out. I didn't much like the tone of his voice, told him to piss off and mind his own business and dragged Craig back in the cubicle, put him against the wall and informed him I going to smash his head in, although I had no such intention, I was just playing up to my hard-man reputation. I worshipped the bloke as a footballer. At that moment Mark Hughes, Ryan Giggs and a few others came in and it all calmed down, everybody started laughing and we went back to the bar and got a few drinks in. It was a bizarre introduction to a guy who quickly became, and remains, one of my very best friends, but life can be like that. Tempers having cooled, we started chatting and we got on like a house on fire. Bellers is a very genuine, no-nonsense bloke, and he seemed to like it that I always speak straight from the heart and kowtow to nobody... I don't know if my life story somehow touched a nerve with him. But I went on to be best man at his wedding, and he's got my Wales shirt in his collection alongside Messi's and Ronaldo's, which I regard as probably the greatest compliment of my sporting life. I'd lent the shirt to the Old Illtydians to hang in their clubhouse, but for some reason Craig really wanted it, so I asked the Old Boys if that was OK, and they were really cool about it.

I'm 20 years older, so perhaps I'm an older brother figure, although there are times he's looked after me, I don't mind admitting. We've never analysed our friendship – it's just there – but I suppose we have a lot in common. I wouldn't say we're peas in a pod: Craig has none of my wilder dark side, but there are definitely crossovers. Bellers was originally from a pretty tough part of town in Splott, got in trouble quite a bit as a youngster, wasn't academic, left school early, never wanted anything other than to excel at football, to which he's devoted his life. As a player, he was very fiery and dynamic – intense and inspirational – and was incapable of giving less than 100% for any team he ever represented. He played more than 450 games, nearly 300 of those in the Premiership, and won 78 Wales caps despite some pretty serious injuries and surgeries. He was utterly dedicated to his sport and profession, almost manically so.

Like me, I think he found the mental side of sport difficult on occasion, such as when he was injured and sidelined or going through a quiet patch, not scoring many goals, and his confidence was dipping. Yes, Premiership footballers get paid an extraordinary amount of money, but as a sportsman I look at that and think of just how much pressure they must be under all the time. You're being paid to be brilliant and win all the time. He wrote about his depression, how he was on medication at one stage when he played and how he stepped down as Vincent Kompany's assistant at Anderlecht because of a recurrence of his mental health difficulties.

Craig, though, is real trooper, a warrior and a very good man to boot. He's fought to be the best version of himself and, although we haven't often talked directly about depression, the truth is, I probably admire Craig more than anybody else I know. He fought the odds and fulfilled his sporting dreams, and continues to do so.

He's generous to a fault. I've lost count of the number of times over the years that the phone would ring unexpectedly.

"What you up to, Bish? Do you fancy a week on the beach down in Cape Town? Bloody lovely this time of year – we could do some shark diving." Another time it might be a week in Dubai at one of the six-star hotels the football guys like staying at – he tried to buy me a ridiculously expensive watch there once, but I talked him out of it – while other times he'd be on the blower suggesting a golf weekend. "Where shall we go, Bish? Where do you fancy playing this week?"

We were great company for each other on these trips and they were fantastic fun, but much more importantly, Bellers is generous with his time and emotions. He had, and still has, this habit of phoning me when he somehow knows I'm down, as I fight my depression. He just seems to know the signs when I'm struggling. He'll be on the phone just chatting, upping my mood, while other times he might suggest a trip to shake off the blues and to show he cares. He knows how much I miss the buzz.

His friendship with me, by the way, automatically extended to my family: my dad; my ex-wife Kate and our kids; my former partner and now very close friend Jane – anybody in my close orbit. For Bellers, friendship is unconditional. My dad adored the bloke. Apart from just being good company, Dad also admired the way he'd worked at his skills and fitness for his entire life to make himself pretty much the complete footballer. There was no role Craig couldn't undertake on the pitch – defence, midfield, attack – and no skill he hadn't mastered. In Dad's book, that made him not only the perfect sportsman but the perfect sporting pupil.

Anyway, I was honoured when he asked me to be his best man, and he even laughed when I told him it was only because no other beggar would do it! That was a special day at St Bride's Church at St Brides-super-Ely, with the reception at their house nearby, and I kept the best man speech as sensible as I could. Most of the big Welsh football names were there, from Sparky to Robbie Savage, and on more than one occasion I've read that one of Bellers' big mates from his Celtic days, Rod Stewart, was there as well. I don't remember that at all – sorry, Rod – but I was pretty nervous, doing my best man duties. Perhaps I missed him.

I was able to repay a little of this friendship, I hope, on the day Gary Speed died. He and Bellers were very close mates; in fact, at one stage, I knew Gary fairly well myself. I saw him around Cardiff quite a bit and, like everybody, liked him. I had a good catch-up with him in Cardiff two weeks before his death, when Wales beat Norway 4-1, and I bumped into him again briefly about a week before he took his own life. He seemed fine, everything perfectly normal, but pretending to be happy and OK is part of the condition when you become depressed – a defence mechanism and a coping mechanism as well. Telling people you're sad and not OK is the difficult bit, especially for men.

Myself and Jane were driving up to Liverpool for Bellers' first game against his old club, Manchester City, after he returned to Anfield. It was a Sunday and we had plans to hook up with him afterwards, but halfway up came the news on the radio of Gary's death by hanging. It hit me like a physical blow. I had to pull over at the next services and minutes later it was Craig on the phone. He was in bits, devastated. Kenny Dalglish had already told him that he was to take the day off, and Bellers said to drive over to his apartment in Sefton.

We arrived, and Jane said she'd wait outside for a while because Craig needed a few minutes with his buddy first. She was right, of course. He opened the door and literally fell into my arms and sobbed his heart out, and I wasn't much better either. It was a very private moment, as Jane had known it would be. He'd looked up to Gary like no other footballer or indeed sportsman, from their Newcastle days onwards. After a while, Jane came and we spent the rest of the day thinking and talking about Gary, and supporting Craig. A couple of days later, I think it was, he went out and played an absolute stormer for Liverpool in a League Cup win over Chelsea, creating their two goals. As I knew he would. It was his tribute and, as he came off with ten minutes to go, he dissolved into tears.

Craig's reaction to Gary's death gave me quite an insight into how tight-knit and supportive the Wales football guys were. From the very first moment I started mixing with them in Cardiff, I was struck by the fantastic camaraderie they had, across the generations, and how they all supported each other. They're a real band of brothers. Rugby has this reputation of being the great bonding game, where team spirit can conquer all – and there's a bit of truth to that, no question – but I never encountered a tighter unit than that group of Wales footballers. They were there for each other and enjoyed each other's successes.

There were others I got to know – notably John Hartson, who's a gem of a human being, with a warm, gregarious nature that appeals to me. John, who's had his own struggles to overcome, always seems to be on great form and having a good day, and he automatically lifts the mood of anybody in his orbit. I used to go up for a weekend in Glasgow when he was playing up there and that was lively, I can tell you. We remain close and it's a rare week when we don't have a catch-up on the phone. I get very down on myself sometimes – where did it all go wrong? etc. – and then I'll think: how lucky am I to count people like Bellers and John as proper friends?

CHAPTER 21

Walking My Way Back to Fitness and Sanity

LIFE BECAME EVEN more challenging with the arrival of Covid in March 2020. And I wasn't in great shape to start with. I still felt I was drifting, my weight had ballooned and I'd recently been diagnosed with type 2 diabetes and prescribed a load of pills. Now, I know this might sound odd from a bloke who's ingested industrial amounts of cocaine in his time, but I actually have a morbid fear of medicines/chemicals and the harm they can do. Or perhaps it was my cocaine habit which accentuated it, because that certainly brought home to me what harm chemicals can wreak on the body. Even with those designed to do good, there are almost always side effects.

There's probably no logic or science in that, but they're my views and I reacted to the news of my diabetes by deciding to heal myself. Bugger the doctors and conventional medicine; I'd treat diabetes like a sports injury – a broken neck, if you like. In the old days, I'd go full pelt at the rehab and would expect to rid myself of the condition. In this case, it'd be achieved by shedding three stones in weight and getting fit again, and that would involve much more sensible eating, cutting right back on the booze – wine, mainly: in middle age I'd cultivated a taste for decent red wine – and getting active again. I'd become a lard-arse. When sport's literally your life – playing, coaching or commentating – you can lose the plot when it no longer dominates your life, and you let everything go.

Depression leads to you becoming very demotivated, and that's just the start of it. You're normally aware of what's happening and you start reaching out to friends and family, but then there comes a point when you say, "They have their own problems and responsibilities, you can't go running to them every time you feel low." So you step back, go in on yourself and a vicious cycle can set in.

At the end of 2019, early 2020, I'd started my regime – with modest results – but, to be honest, I was already beginning to lose a bit of motivation. I thought the improvement would be instant, but it doesn't work like that. But then came Covid and lockdown, which bizarrely turbocharged my bid to get healthy and hold back the years.

Covid was grim, don't get me wrong, and as a single, divorced bloke with limited income living in a flat on his own, who 'celebrated' his 60th birthday at the height of the pandemic, it was no picnic. But it did have its compensations. The gyms might have been shut, but the streets and footpaths were empty and, as you'll recall, in the spring and summer of 2020 we enjoyed miraculous weather. It was like living in the south of France.

There was nothing to do except get outside and walk. "Walking is the best medicine" is something you'll often hear older people say but, frankly, I thought all that was a little beneath me. I was a proper athlete, a strong guy: rugby player, boxer, baseball player, swimmer, judo player and all the rest of it. I didn't need mere walking.

My God, I got that wrong. I started walking every day and, increasing my workload, began looking forward impatiently to my next walk. That'll be my addictive nature, I suppose. The release, the fresh air, the feeling of getting fitter, slimmer and healthier every day. The freedom of it and the time to think and put a few things in perspective, amongst other things. It was out on one of my long walks that I decided that I'd put up or shut up, and finally commit to writing this book – whether you call it an autobiography or just my analysis of events in my life. Unlike my 'get fit' phase after the broken neck, I didn't put on the headphones, *Rocky*-style; I just walked free. I wanted to escape all the hassles that were worrying me, and roam mentally as well as geographically. I'm so obsessive about some things, endlessly playing over past situations and grievances, that my brain needs to rest and go into neutral sometimes, or to be redirected to other thoughts to get a bit of perspective.

So through those early months of Covid, I was walking with the enthusiasm of the recently converted. I'd get up early, have a quick breakfast and head out, a small rucksack on my back with my phone, a bottle of water and perhaps an apple or banana. I'd go from my place in the old docks down the eerily empty streets of the ghost town Cardiff had become. If it was early, there'd be literally nobody about, and I could walk down the middle of St Mary Street and Westgate Street as if I owned them, which was good for morale. Past the Principality Stadium (although I still call it the Millennium), past the Angel, on to Castle Street, over the bridge and right down the footpath into Sophia Gardens and the banks of the Taff. It was then that my walk proper started – a physical and also a mental journey. I only had my thoughts for company, and the River Taff to guide me. As I followed its banks, there was almost never anybody around, certainly not on the mornings when I was up with the lark.

I'd walk on, ticking off the bridges on my right: the Millennium Bridge, Blackweir Bridge, Llandaff Bridge, the Radyr Footbridge and up to the M4 and the Iron Bridge. It was an odd mix of built-up areas and countryside, but seemed to match the surreal times we were going through. Some days I'd retrace my steps, others I'd cross over to the eastern bank and come back that way. When I got back into Cardiff, I'd go for a bit of a tour around the deserted city, checking out old empty haunts, looking for signs of life and perhaps hoping to bump into somebody for a chat. It felt as if I was in some strange apocalyptic TV drama... there was almost nobody around, but that didn't alter my mood. I was always in good spirits by the time I got back and, after that, the rest of the day didn't drag so much. I'd completed my 'effort' for the day, so I could veg and watch the TV with a clear conscience. I rarely did less than 18 km on these daily walks, often quite a bit more if I roamed around the city. They occupied most of the morning and I didn't linger. I'm no race walker, but I walked as fast as I comfortably could to give the old ticker a workout and work up a sweat.

The weight fell off me and a lot of my diabetes symptoms eased. I was winning that war, at least, and I was also calmer and less fretful. If you have a short temper, go for a long walk, as the old saying goes.

Then came a huge setback. The world was gradually finding a way of co-existing with Covid and it became possible to fly down to Australia again, and I badly wanted to visit my daughter and grandchildren. There was a problem, though. There could be no admittance unless I had proof that I'd been fully vaccinated. I wasn't happy – as previously discussed, I now very much distrust medicines and vaccinations – but this was a Catch-22. If I didn't get the jab – in fact the Aussies needed evidence of two – then there would be no trip down under. I bit the bullet and presented myself at my local clinic.

I didn't feel quite right for a few days, but nobody else was complaining so I told myself to stop being a wimp. I took it easy for another couple of days and then on day six after my jab I started walking again. For my first walk, an old mate, Andrew 'Spadgie' Barrett, came along for company. We didn't do my full loop, but it was a fair old walk and we were going at a decent clip when I started to feel a bit odd as we headed for home, returning down the eastern bank of the Taff. The lower part of my right leg suddenly wasn't working properly: it didn't hurt, as such, but it felt strange, and I kept tripping up over non-existent kerb stones or losing my balance a little. Some bits of my leg didn't seem connected with the rest of the leg – I felt uncoordinated. It wasn't particularly dramatic or agonising, and I just assumed it was some random muscle cramp or trapped nerve or something. An old war wound. But it was really annoying, and Andrew could see I was struggling and asked if I was all right. I, of course, said there was no problem.

I made it home OK and optimistically thought everything would have cleared itself after a few hours' rest and a bath… but it kept coming at me. The numbness – or lack of feeling, if that makes sense? – crept all the way up the leg and into my hip and lower back and then up my torso and into my arm. Again, there was no pain, but it was requiring more and more effort to move around. My body wasn't doing what my brain was telling it to do. It was time to get myself down to A&E, and you know how much I hate hospitals.

They were straight on the case, treating it more seriously than I'd expected. CT scans, MRIs and other scans I'd never heard of before. Within no time, a Professor Hughes was informing me I'd suffered a stroke, and that the road back to full recovery would be long and would have to start now.

I was in denial. Strokes are what other people get, not me. I looked around the ward and there were people seriously ill after strokes, unable to talk or use various limbs – to all intents and purposes paralysed, at least in the short term... A few days earlier, I'd been the fittest I'd been in probably 20 years. People who walk 18 km a day every day don't get strokes. There had to be another reason – some other diagnosable disease, some other cause. I opened up with the professor about my considerable cocaine habit of former years, and he conceded that might have been a factor, and I also mentioned that I'd reluctantly agreed to have a Covid jab just six days earlier. He didn't dismiss that either, although he warned me that, given my medical history and past drug habit, there was no way objectively that anybody could conclude my stroke had been just the side effects of a new vaccine. I was probably overthinking things. People have strokes. Some young, some old and some in between. Some outwardly fit individuals, and others not so.

I listened but continued to struggle with the diagnosis. I had to fully understand it before I could accept it and fight my new reality. I wallowed for a few days, felt depressed and lethargic and could feel the weight piling back on.

Part of the trouble was that it was described as a 'minor' stroke. In fact, on the original scans, it had initially been missed altogether and it was only on a second scan that it had been picked up. My false logic told me that a 'minor' stroke couldn't put a tough, hard-man athlete like me out of action to such an extent, and it needed Peter Lewis to give me a pep talk and spell it out to me.

Doc explained that the workings of the brain were a million times more complicated than the workings of the most intricate and sophisticated Swiss watch but, as with such a watch, it only needed some very small, minor malfunction to cause a lot of trouble down the line. Yes, there are degrees of strokes, and the big ones can obviously be immediately life-threatening, but even the much smaller ones can cause significant damage. I needed to take that on board ASAP and get cracking with the rehab. There was no time to waste.

Message received and understood, so the fight back to fitness – well, something approaching normality – began. The NHS offered some useful rehab physio, but they were still overwhelmed with Covid and I wanted to go at the rehab full-bore, 24-7. That's how I roll.

Rugby's unofficial freemasonry kicked in. There's normally somebody who'll lend a hand, and I must at this stage also acknowledge that my old adversaries the WRU have a former players' fund to help with medical issues after retirement, and they put a few quid in the kitty for treatment. One of the first people to get in touch after my stroke was an old mate, Steve Cannon, who'd been one of the scrum halves trying to nail down a spot at Pooler when I joined. There was every reason for myself and Steve to be wary of each other, but actually we immediately became big buddies and lifelong friends. He was one of the first players to come and see me when I broke my neck. Steve had trained as a physiotherapist and was highly respected around Cardiff and, in no time, he was on the phone asking how he could help. It was a big boost: somebody willing to support and monitor me on a regular basis – somebody who knew my ways and knew I'd be inclined to take things to the limit, but who, as a mate, would command me to step back a bit when I overcooked the rehab.

So I started the walking again. Slowly at first, but building up gradually. I changed my route to start with – I didn't want to do my familiar River Taff routes because that would be a daily reminder of how far I was from what had been possible physically just a few months earlier. That would have been depressing.

No, this time I headed south to the Old Custom House down by the Cardiff Bay Barrage. There and back is 8.5 km, and I average about 90 minutes. On a good day it's an hour and twenty, on a bad day it's an hour and forty. I try not to time myself, but as a sportsman you can't help yourself. The OCD kicks in… I do it pretty much come rain or shine and, although the numbness and feeling of loss of power down my right-hand side never really goes, it keeps the body moving, the blood pumping and the spirits high. Some days I feel really good and go on down to Penarth to complete a good, long round trip, but there's always a price to pay for that. You can't cheat your body like you can when you're younger… I've learned it's much better to stay within my limit every day than to open up the taps fully one day and be unable to move for the next two or three days.

I've added the gym back to my routine as well now, often in tandem with my lifelong mate Terry Borley, who I haven't mentioned enough here. Another guy who's always been there for me.

My philosophy with the gym these days is short and sharp. No phones, no coffees and no hanging about gossiping afterwards. In and out. 30–40 minutes top whack. Time to go home or get out there in the fresh air. The gym is a job of work for me. I come out with a great sweat. Back home for something to eat, and then I'll get ready for my walk. 'Keep the old man at bay, keep the pensioner away' is my maxim.

It's funny. It's only now that I'm writing all this down that I realise that, the health issues aside, what I've actually been doing in recent years is replicating the busy routine of a professional sportsman or full-time rugby player, which is how I would term my 'amateur' Union days. My days are filled with allocated slots for training or conditioning, resting, family time, 'doing this book' time... The days pass quicker that way, which is no bad thing for me.

And if anybody's reading this and looking for encouragement: yes, for the record, there have been many times I haven't wanted to go for my walk. When it was rainy or cold, or just when I was feeling particularly lethargic and the right-hand side of my body felt like it had gone to sleep or suddenly filled with wet sand or concrete, which it still does on a bad day. And there have been times when I've been walking when I still felt cranky and was cursing – "Has my life really come to this?" – but I can tell you this with compete honestly: there's never been a time when going for a walk hasn't made me happier. You get back, have a shower, put the kettle on, stretch out on the settee, have a nap, watch some television, phone a few friends. Nothing seems so bad.

A good walk's better than any drug I've ever taken. It straightens your mind out. As does the occasional chat with my mate Wobbley, a severely disabled Hull KR fan who I mentioned early on in the book. He's always full of gossip and good cheer. His calls always leave me thinking, 'What the fuck have I got to worry about?' I'm blessed. I can go to the gym every day and twice on Christmas Day if I want. I can walk every day, roaming the city and the coast. I can walk down to the pub and enjoy a glass, or wander over to a café and meet mates for a coffee. You bastard, Bish – stop whingeing and get on with it. Enjoy what you've got, rather than focusing on what you haven't got, or what you've thrown away.

That lesson came home sharply recently when I was finishing the first draft of this book off. I was playing in a charity golf day and it was lashing down. We were playing off an elevated tee and, after hitting my drive, I unwisely decided to jauntily skip down the bank as if I was in my twenties again. One leg slipped away from me and the other caught underneath me as I came down with all my weight. There was an audible twang. Everybody thought I'd done a knee ligament or an Achilles tendon, but it was my quadriceps that had gone twang and ripped away from my knee joint. I haven't got the words to tell you just how painful that particular injury was and, for a while, it seriously slowed me down. You sit at home and the demons start showing their heads again, but I've learned to stay patient. I won't be defeated.

CHAPTER 22

Absent Friends

I'M NOT THE only one whose health has been an issue in the last few years. I think most people of my vintage are starting to slow down and most former rugby players are quite creaky by their sixties, but recently too many good friends, former colleagues, feared opponents and nominal 'enemies' – but deep down, mates – and just fellow travellers have been meeting their maker. A couple of journalists who were generous in their words and fair in their comments – Robin Davey and Steve Bale – have passed during the latter stages of pulling this book together. My long-time solicitor Bernard de Maid – an Old Illtydian by the way; I'd forgotten to mention that – died suddenly. I'd spoken to him a few weeks before, when I think he was on holiday down in South Africa, and he was slightly alarmed at the prospect of this book coming out. Actually, that's not fair: he was very supportive generally, but strongly advised me to let sleeping dogs lie on one or two specific issues. Out of deference to a very good man who always did his best for the underdog or those he felt had suffered a miscarriage of justice, I've taken his advice – from the grave, so to speak.

I mentioned Alun Carter previously and, even as I sit down to start this little chapter, I'm hearing that Haydn Willmott has gone and Mark Jones, the fine Tredegar, Neath and Wales forward, as well. Haydo was one of those who were the heart and soul of the club at Pooler, a local lad who arrived as a centre before Pross converted him to flanker. He was as tough as old boots, not far behind Madman in that respect, and although he wasn't an automatic First XV starter, I was always happy to have Haydo reporting for duty – he always had my back. I'd heard he'd become very ill and thank goodness myself and Doc managed to get up to the hospital to visit him just a few days before he passed. I sensed he was going and very deliberately said my farewells while trying not to depress him too much. Doc was much more optimistic and thought he had a few months to go, but we Catholics, alas, sometimes have a sixth sense with these things.

Not knowing exactly when somebody's going to exit this world is the best reason I know for keeping in touch more, and I wish, more than anything, that I'd been given the chance to say a proper goodbye to Eddie Butler. His unexpected passing hit me harder than any death in my life, outside of family. When he died, I got a real sense of how Craig Bellamy must have felt when he heard the news about Gary Speed.

I haven't spoken enough of Snooty; it's all been a bit raw, and I need to rectify that now before I sign off. You might think we were an odd mix, unlikely mates, and perhaps you're right, but sometimes that's what makes a friendship. Cardiff street fighter, jailbird and – according to the WRU – public enemy number one meets Cambridge scholar, man of words, BBC graduate and Wales rugby captain.

Snooty was a huge supporter of mine, both on and off the field. As Pooler skipper, he always believed in my ability and would defend Pooler's uncompromising physical approach to the hilt. Although he missed the game though injury, he instinctively knew that nothing particularly unusual went on that night in Newbridge, and backed me through thick and thin. It was a raucous Gwent derby, they were getting tasty upfront and I decked their lippy lock with one freakishly good punch. He didn't waver once and would go into battle on my behalf whenever the question arose.

Eddie's support really counted. He was respected and nobody, absolutely nobody, could tell Eddie what to think: it was impossible for him to be bullied into a prevailing or 'popular' opinion. He'd look at the facts, assess the individuals concerned, and make own his mind up, thank you very much... The cleverest man I knew and am ever likely to know. When Eddie went in to bat for you, it carried some weight – although not, alas, with the so-called Big Five. He spoke up for me in court one time as a character reference, and I know that he knew that, deep down, I was OK and not the devil incarnate, as some people painted me. Eddie rated me, and at a time when my confidence and self-esteem was low, that was a big boost.

Eddie would often just phone up, for no reason, really. "I just fancied a chat with David Joseph Bishop, the Bish, rugby player and mate," he'd say when I asked him what was up and if there was anything wrong. As if something being wrong was the only reason you could ever phone an old mate! We'd shoot the breeze, reminisce about old battles won and lost; I'd give him my lowdown on any new players I'd seen and give him the benefit of my thoughts on Wales, the Lions and rugby in general. He always seemed to attach some importance to my opinion. Then, when we'd been getting a bit too serious and sounding like old blazers in the clubhouse, we'd finish off by taking the piss out of each other for five minutes before agreeing when next to meet up.

I last heard from him just before he set off to Peru with his daughter Nell on a Prostate Cymru charity trek, and we arranged to hook up as soon as he got back. In fact, I wanted a few words of advice on this book, as it happens, on whether or not to leave out one or two things... He sounded great on that call – healthy, full of life and not as worried about the state of Welsh rugby as I was. The glass was usually half full with Eddie.

News of Eddie's death in his sleep on the trail to Machu Picchu broke on a Thursday afternoon, and I was too stunned and choked to make any public comment. Other than phone my condolences to his wife Sue, there was nothing I could do, nothing I could say that would begin to do him justice. Coincidentally, I was also right in the middle of a small and very odd personal odyssey in which Eddie unwittingly loomed large. It was uncanny and it's a bit of a shaggy dog story, but bear with me.

A few months before he died, Eddie persuaded Mark Ring and me to get up to the Rolls of Monmouth course to play some golf with him. Any time spent with Eddie was a bonus so we hacked around, enjoying the fresh air, before retiring to the 19th hole. Eddie was in cracking form and started to relate some incredibly long and sad story about the Rolls family, with all three sons of the 1st Baron of Llangattock being killed long before their time. Eddie went into schoolmaster mode – he used to be a teacher – and was a fount of all knowledge, speaking on the subject without pausing for breath. I'll admit – with a glass of wine in my hand and feeling pleasantly knackered and windblown after our golf, and with one or two people making my day by coming up for a selfie or a quick chat – I only caught half of it. I distinctly remember, however, that he compared the

Rolls family with the Kennedys in the USA for all their bad luck, and having a sort of curse that had settled over them. And that one of them, the youngest son, who founded Rolls-Royce, had died in a plane accident. After that, I didn't think any more of it. In one ear and out of the other.

Then, just before Eddie died, Great-Uncle Evan Rhys Lewis Bishop suddenly came into my life. I'd been vaguely aware of a great-uncle who'd lived in Swansea and worked as a miner before emigrating to Edmonton in Canada. Cousin Justin, one of the west Wales Bishops, decided to do some digging, and we learned that he'd returned to Europe as a Private in the Canadian Army during World War I and had died in Boulogne on 26 June 1916, 11 days after receiving shotgun wounds to the head in the Battle of Ypres, during fighting in the Mount Sorrel region. Further investigation revealed that he was buried in the Eastern Cemetery in Boulogne. No modern-day family member had ever visited it, and we badly needed to rectify that.

My brother Terry, his wife and I had planned to visit Boulogne that weekend, just 24 hours after news of Eddie's death far away in the Andes broke. Frankly, I was glad of having something to do to divert me, otherwise I'd have been a complete mess. After a late night and too many drinks on the Saturday night in Boulogne, when I got very emotional talking to Terry about Eddie, we were up early on the Sunday and went down the cemetery, which was huge and beautifully kept. We were booked on a lunchtime train home and were too early for the cemetery office to be open, so we needed to split up to find the grave ourselves. About 30 minutes later, I was the lucky one to strike gold and gave the family whistle to summon Terry. It was an unexpectedly emotional moment.

We paid our respects, laid our flowers, shed tears for our own flesh and blood and then it was pretty much time to head home. We walked back to where we'd parked the car via another block of graves, and suddenly Terry stopped by the grave of the 2nd Baron of Llangattock. Terry didn't know who he was, but stopped because of the mention of Llangattock, where he'd been doing building work at the village school most of the summer.

He shouted over and I joined him. "Bloody hell. That must be one of the Rolls sons," I told Terry. I explained that Eddie had been telling us all about them a while back. I leant down and had a further look. He died on 31 October 1916: Halloween, my birthday. Bit odd.

We were in a rush now, and as we drove back to the Eurotunnel, Terry started googling like there was no tomorrow.

"Jesus, David: the Rollses lost another brother during the war – Henry Allen – and he's buried at that cemetery back there as well. Let me look him up. Sweet Jesus, he died in 1916 as well, on 26 June. That's the same day that Great-Uncle Evan died."

We stopped the car.

"So what about the third brother, who died in the air crash?" I asked.

More googling from Terry. "That was Charles Stuart Rolls, died aged 32 in a plane crash in Bournemouth – first fatality from a plane crash in the UK, it says here. Buried at St Cadoc's Church in Llangattock." St Cadoc's school in Cardiff was of course where we all went to primary school.

This was all a bit much to take in – coincidence running wild in northern France. I reached for my mobile to phone Eddie and tell him, before remembering he'd gone. He'd have loved all this stuff and would have laughed at me suddenly getting into history, and the magical mystery tour we were embarked on. He'd have come up with some erudite thoughts or a phrase summing up what it all meant. I have no idea myself; perhaps it means nothing at all, but I believe in little signs and coincidences. They usually mean something. It felt just for a few minutes as if Eddie was still with us, as if my mate was still alive... but of course he wasn't. In fact, at that very moment, his body was probably still being carried off a mountainside in Peru. I turned the phone off and for a few minutes felt distraught and utterly bereft.

CHAPTER 23

In My Opinion...

Best Rugby Union player I encountered?
Mark Ring. Different class, another planet, Paul Daniels in boots. He had no gas whatsoever but it didn't matter because he just unpicked defences with his magic and vision. He'd mastered every skill. Fly half was his best position, even if he ended up at centre much of the time. He made everything appear to happen in slow motion. Every sport has the odd player like this. Everything looked perfectly choreographed with Ringo, even if he was making it up on the hoof most of the time, amongst all the chaos. I loved it that he had the spirit and skill to back-heel drop-goal conversions for Cardiff, even if he did cop a match ban for it. Love you, Ringo, and thanks for the memories.

Best League player faced?
Tricky, but I'm going Martin Offiah, who I first encountered playing Union at the Amsterdam Rugby 7s and other tournaments. He's right up there with Ellery Hanley, Joe Lydon, Shaun Edwards and the other pure Rugby League talents I encountered, but the thing about Chariots is that he was from a boarding school down south and played for Rosslyn Park. There's nothing in his background that suggested he'd become a League legend – he wasn't even one

of the Taffia, taking the well-worn road from south Wales. He was a phenomenal athlete and try-scorer. Jiffy also became a cracking League player. His gas on the break was unreal.

Best uncapped player?

It's insane, defies belief, that Mike Budd didn't ever get capped by Wales. At least I got one cap, and – as we've discussed at length – that haunted me. Fancy being as good as Mike and getting none. I can't think of any back-rower in Wales at the time who should have been capped ahead of him, except for Madman, Chris Huish. Mike was brave as a lion for Bridgend and Cardiff. Too brave for his own good, sometimes – he used to pick up a lot of injuries. He cut easily, in boxing terms. A St Joseph's boy from Cardiff, from memory. It was with great sadness and disbelief that we heard he'd taken his own life at the age of 46. The unspoken battles and demons some people are fighting are scary, as I know all too well.

Best scrum half I encountered?

Terry Holmes, by a distance. Terry had everything, including the strength and power of a flanker, but also read the game very well. A superb all-round player before injury struck. Behind Terry, it would be Bath's Richard Hill, who was a fiery, passionate, bloody annoying sort of scrum half behind a good pack, who was never cowed by Welsh opposition. Llanelli's Jonathan Griffiths was a very decent, strong player in both codes too.

A shout-out also for veteran Aussie John Hipwell, who taught me a lesson or two when Pooler played the Wallabies in 1981, when he looked old enough to be my father. He must have been some operator in his pomp. Of the modern brigade, Mike Phillips was out on his own – a Terry Holmes sort of player. A lively character as well. I've enjoyed our few meet-ups.

Best fly half I played with or against?

Fly half is the only other position I'm qualified to comment on, having spent most of my life partnering them at half back. Obviously, it's Ringo for me, for the reasons already stated, with Wasps' Huw Davies as runner-up, just ahead of Jiffy. Huw was a phenomenal player with pace and skill, and pound for pound was one of the strongest, toughest, hardest blokes I ever played with or against. England should have built an entire back division around him. Jiffy was a blazing attacking talent with Neath and went on to really make a splash in League. Of those I didn't play with or against, it's Neil Jenkins.

Best coach I had?

Thomas Raymond Prosser... closely followed by David Joseph Bishop Senior! Roy Agland, my boxing coach, should get an honourable mention too.

Best sporting advice I can give?

Confront your weaknesses and master them. If you can't pass off your left hand, practise all day passing off your left hand. Ditto if you can't kick off your left foot. If you haven't got a left jab, practise your left jab. If you lack pace, practise sprinting; if you lack stamina, put in the long miles. Don't concentrate too much on the things you've already mastered. It might make you feel better, but it won't improve you as a performer. My dad understood this better than anybody.

Best boxer I faced?

My old schoolboy and Youth rival, Paul Lewis from Newport, who stayed amateur and won a barrowload of Welsh titles and appeared in all kinds of ABA Finals. Technically very good, strong with two good hands and plenty of ticker. Paul leads me 3-2 in our personal duals and, as we won't ever be stepping into the ring again, he wins on a split decision. Well boxed mate, you were class.

Best boxer ever?

I would have to be Sugar Ray Leonard. Brilliant footwork, great athlete, astute tactician, warrior. The full bag of chips. If not the best there's ever been, he's certainly the best I've seen and studied. As with Ringo in rugby, when I watched Sugar Ray, I got the impression of somebody who'd somehow slowed the fight down. Everything looked scripted and inevitable, yet it wasn't. Of course it wasn't – that's not how it happens in boxing... unless you have a genius like Sugar Ray in the ring.

Best baseball player I faced?

David 'Dubber' Richards from Newport, who could do the lot – bat, bowl and field – and with style. He was a big character to boot, and I'm still mortified that I managed to get the legend of Welsh baseball banned for a while, after the fire extinguisher incident in Liverpool, in which he was completely innocent. Sorry, Dubber. Everybody: it was me, not Dubber!

Best bloke in rugby?

We lost Eddie Butler a while back, but I still have Neil Jenkins in my corner, for which I give thanks. We've spoken most weeks for decades now. We come from different eras, but we just hit it off. He keeps me abreast of the modern-day scene and I tell him how it was back in the day and make him laugh at the madness of it all. He's an absolute gent – his friendship is a joy. Neil is the very best of Welsh rugby, which is why he's so loved and admired in other countries as well. Great Lions tourist.

Best training exercise?
Let me tell you a secret. Some people are just naturally fit and don't have to train that hard. It's a complete bastard, it's bloody unfair and coaches hate to admit it because they feel it undermines them, because some players can just turn up on match day and turn it on. But if you need to get fit in a hurry, I strongly recommend you get down to the boxing gym and learn to skip properly like the pros. Stick with it, master it. There's no better all-round exercise.

The best of times?
I never felt better than when I won my Wales Youth cap against France. Pre-prison, pre-broken neck, pre-the crushing disappointments and controversies that chequered my career, pre-mental health and drug issues. I was fit, bloody good and going to take on the world. In a way, I still did, but not in the manner I planned. Everybody was so proud, I was so excited and I can see it still in the picture of me in the jersey for the first time. Hope and optimism are everywhere. Enjoy those moments when they come around, because they disappear quickly.

Best nightclub in Cardiff back in the day?

I loved them all, but for a while there was nothing to touch the scene at Jackson's, just along from the national stadium.

Best patron saint?

As a good Catholic boy, I go nowhere without the St Jude pendant Mamma gave me after I broke my neck. The patron saint of lost causes, he's got me out of a few scrapes, and I'd feel naked without him!

Best place visited in Wales?

A day away from Cardiff is a day wasted in my book, but I've got a soft spot for Aberaeron, way out west. I've been there plenty of times, but spent the entire time either playing sevens or getting hammered in the pub afterwards. I always had a brilliant day, though; the sun always shone and they tell me the coast nearby is lovely. I might go back one day.

Best all-time Pooler XV?

I'm tempted to take the fifth here. This is nigh on impossible, because I'm full of admiration for everyone who put their body on the line for Pooler, and I want to keep the friends I still have in my life! So I'm going to sidestep this a little, and pick two teams. To play a mythical World XV, there's the very best Pontypool side of all time, which would clearly include, for example, the likes of Galacticos Terry Cobner and Jeff Squire in the back row, despite the intense competition. And there's the David Bishop XV: a slightly more free-wheeling attack-minded team that I'd be honoured to captain on tour – let's say on a two-match end-of-season trip to Ireland, where the rugby would be hard and the socialising off the Richter scale.

All-time Pontypool XV, to play World XV
15 Peter Lewis
14 Malcolm Price
13 Roger Bidgood
12 Lyndon Faulkner
11 Goff Davies
10 Mark Ring
9   David Bishop
1   Ray Prosser
2   Bobby Windsor
3   Graham Price
4   John Perkins
5   Steve Sutton
6   Jeff Squire
7   Terry Cobner (c)
8   Eddie Butler

David Bishop XV, to make some noise
15 Paul 'Pablo' Rees
14 Phil Ford
13 Roger Bidgood
12 Keith Orrell
11 Bleddyn Taylor
10 Mark Ring
9   David Bishop (c)
1   Ray Prosser
2   Bobby Windsor
3   Graham Price
4   John Perkins
5   Eddie Butler
6   Chris Huish
7   Mark Brown
8   Frankie Jacas

CHAPTER 24

It's All About Me

Bobby Windsor: Pontypool, Wales and Lions legend

"David Bishop is the greatest Welsh scrum half I ever saw at club level, and by a distance. He was better than Gareth at club level because he was brilliant all the time, and he played every week: come rain, come shine, home and away, midweek and Saturday… Unfortunately, we'll never know at Test level, although he looked very good in the one Test he was permitted. Gareth was brilliant around the world, no question, but I'm convinced if just given the chance, the Bish would have equalled him. The game was denied something special by the refusal of Wales to pick him."

John Perkins: Pooler captain and Wales lock

"The two best players I ever saw or played with or against were Terry Cobner and David Bishop."

Paul Lewis: 14-time Welsh Amateur Boxing Champion and 5-time ABA Champion

"Bish was a formidable opponent who unquestionably would have gone on to win Welsh and British titles as an amateur at senior level, and would have been in line for big competitions like the Commonwealth Games and Olympics. He was a stick insect when we first started boxing at the age of 13, but by the time of our last fight when he was 16 or 17, he was filling out. If he'd stuck with the boxing, he would almost certainly have gone up a few weight divisions from me. He was rough as hell to handle and with his big knock-out left hook, he might have gone a long way as a professional. Bish had plenty of X factor: he could damage any opponent with his big shots. Bish would have needed to work on his defence but that was his next step as a boxer if he'd stuck with it. He was only 17 when he turned to rugby full-time. I was really disappointed because our rivalry had spurred me on – I felt we were reaching for the stars together and the two families had become friendly. Everybody concerned with Welsh boxing could see his potential."

Mark Ring: Cardiff, Pooler and Wales centre and fly half

"How can I describe The Bish? He was Dupont 40 years before Dupont. Same build, maybe an inch taller; solid as hell; half gymnast, half weightlifter; kicked off both feet; incredibly dangerous on the break; natural try-scorer. The Bish did special things and he dropped goals direct from line-outs, which I haven't seen Dupont do yet – although you suspect it's in his armoury. People talk about The Bish's pass, which was sound as a pound, in my opinion. Was it, technically speaking, as quick as the Robert Jones pass? No, not quite; but as a back you had much more time playing with The Bish at nine because he had so many tricks up his sleeve, was so strong on the break, had such a varied kicking game that he terrified opposition back rows. They would constantly be on the back foot, trying to deal with his threat. Playing outside The Bish, you had the ultimate armchair ride.

"The most incredible single passage I've ever seen in a lifetime of playing and watching rugby at the highest level came from The Bish at the height of his powers at the Nazareth Sevens, a big charity event. All the Catholic schools put in old boys' teams plus ringers, and it was nothing to see three or four Internationals per team. The Old Illtydians were playing Saint Albans and Adrian Hadley was on the wing for them. They chipped from their own 22 and Adrian – a bone fide Test wing whose forte was the longer sprints, so he could get up to speed – had a three- or four-yard advantage on David. It was a try all day every day. Bish wouldn't give up, though. He was a mind-over-matter player, but he still had no right to beat Adrian to the touchdown. But here's the thing: he didn't just win the dive to the ball touchdown, he didn't touch it down. Instead, he just slid along with it off the ground, popped up, and then ran another 110 metres upfield, beating three defenders to score at the other end. Incredible. It's virtually impossible to imagine anybody running further, quicker, to score a try in the history of rugby. And then, would you believe it, Old Illtydians collected the restart, fed Bish on the blindside and he ran another 70 yards to score a second try. He was a comic-book hero sort of player.

"The Bish was utterly convinced, every time he took the field, that he was the best and his side would win. And those players and characters are very rare indeed, even at the top level. When Wales started hitting difficult times towards the end of my career, I looked around the dressing room and asked myself where The Bish was. We needed him. He might have transformed us, because we had a decent amount of talent, just very little self-belief and attitude."

Mark Jones: former Wales baseball captain

"Bish was the Paul Gascoigne of Welsh sport. He was an outrageously gifted, quirky and exceptional baseball player those summers he was able concentrate on the game – one of the fastest bowlers Wales have ever produced. He spread his stardust when he played. He and Ringo and some of the other rugby boys would attract a big crowd and media reports, and baseball never had it so good in Wales. The Bish has a huge heart: he really put himself out to be available for the big baseball games and he's never turned down a request for help with any event or fundraiser."

John Actie: schoolmate and friend

"Life throws you some curveballs and it's then that you learn who your true friends are, and The Bish is rock solid. We had the occasional ruck over trivial matters, but he's always been there for me, always had my back. Bish was a half-decent scrum half at St Cadoc's but he knows I carried him until he was about 11! God bless you, Bish."

Brian Thomas: Neath (player & coach) and Wales

"Bishop is the best player in the northern hemisphere. He is a very strong man both in mind and physique. Sometimes, a player can be strong in physique but weak in mind. He is strong in both. He has many strings to his bow. He has been criticised in the past for not being a team man but he is a team in his own right, and that says it all. I have seen him play when he has effectively played in five positions in the side, not just scrum half. He knows where to be when our kicks went astray; he snapped them up. He's magic. The one game Pontypool have lost this season, he wasn't playing. He has got everything and I find it surprising that Wales keep ignoring him. They would be fools not to take him to New Zealand. Pontypool would have lost to us twice this season without him."

John Billot: *Western Mail* rugby correspondent and *Welsh Rugby Annual* Editor

"David Bishop is the best scrum half in Welsh rugby since World War Two. Surely there has never been a more dynamic and deadly attacker among scrum halves than David Bishop? He is to Pontypool what Wild Bill Hickock was to Abilene, the complete one-man army."

Peter Jackson: veteran *Daily Mail* rugby correspondent

"The best one-cap wonder in the history of Rugby Union or Rugby League. Or probably any other sport, for that matter. His display against Gloucester in 1982 was the best example of a one-man team performance I have ever seen on a rugby field."

Roger Bidgood: Pontypool and Wales

"Bish, it turns my stomach every time I think back to what the selectors did, with your non-selection. I and everyone else who played with you knew you were the best scrum half by a country mile. I loved playing rugby with you, Bish, and having you on the pitch made players of average ability into good players, because there were things you could do on the pitch that made life so much easier."

Eddie Butler

"David Bishop singlehandedly carried the weight of the nation's attention on foul play. There lurked throughout the land a horde of players guilty to a man of sins far more heinous than the punch thrown by David Bishop."

Samara Bishop: daughter

"David Bishop is the kind of man who can't be explained – only felt. A whirlwind of talent, violence, charisma and contradiction, he's burned through life with a fire that's mesmerised crowds and terrified rivals. On the field, he was electric – a once-in-a-generation player with a pulse for the game and a will that refused to be broken, even by a broken neck or broken rules. Off the field, he's an enigma: fiercely loving and dangerously volatile, both hero and hurricane in the same breath. To know him is to be changed by him. And while his legacy may be tangled in controversy, what can't be denied is this: as a player, David Bishop was unforgettable. A soul too big for the system, too wild to tame, and too human to ever be easily defined."

Sean Bishop: brother

"Thank God you didn't tell the story about the puppies."

APPENDIX 1

Mamma's Stew

Ingredients
shin of beef (although in my old age, I splash out on a cut)
2 vegetable stock cubes
2 lamb stock cubes
3 onions
7 carrots (4 grated, 3 sliced)
1 parsnip (grated)
potatoes to taste (peeled)
4 leeks (chopped)

Instructions
1. Put the meat in cold water and bring to the boil. Simmer for 45 minutes.
2. Add stock cubes, onions, carrots and parsnip.
3. Stir and simmer for another 45 minutes.
4. Throw in the peeled spuds. Cook for another 25 mins.
5. Add leeks and simmer for another 25 minutes.

APPENDIX 2
Playing Record for Pontypool

Pre-switch to Rugby League

Season	Apps	Tries	Cons	Pens	Drops	Points	Notes
1981/82	7	3	1	0	0	14	Club & WRU Cup
1982/83	35	33	2	0	4	148	Club & WRU Cup
1983/84	34	39	35	5	5	256	Club & WRU Cup
1984/85	30	20	1	0	3	91	Club & WRU Cup
1985/86	24	11	0	3	0	53	Club & WRU Cup
1986/87	5	2	0	2	1	17	Club & WRU Cup
1987/88	37	35	0	7	1	226	Club & WRU Cup
1981/88	172	143	39	17	14	805	**Club & WRU Cup**

Post-switch to Rugby League

Season	Apps	Tries	Cons	Pens	Drops	Points	Notes
1996/97	1	1	0	0	0	5	Friendly
	2	0	0	1	0	3	Anglo-Welsh
	14	11	8	3	0	80	League
	4	0	0	0	1	3	WRU Cup
	21	12	8	4	1	91	**SEASON TOTAL**
1997/98	23	7	1	0	1	40	League
	0	0	0	0	0	0	WRU Cup
	23	7	1	0	1	40	**SEASON TOTAL**
1998/99	21	9	1	0	1	50	League
	4	0	0	0	0	0	WRU Cup
	25	9	1	0	1	50	**SEASON TOTAL**
1996–99	69	28	10	4	3	180	**TOTAL**

Appendix 2

Season-by-season summary

Season	Apps	Tries	Cons	Pens	Drops	Points	Notes
1981/82	7	3	1	0	0	14	Pre-League
1982/83	35	33	2	0	4	148	Pre-League
1983/84	34	39	35	5	5	256	Pre-League
1984/85	30	20	1	0	3	91	Pre-League
1985/86	24	11	0	3	0	53	Pre-League
1986/87	5	2	0	2	1	17	Pre-League
1987/88	37	35	0	7	1	226	Pre-League
1996/97	21	12	8	4	1	91	Post-League
1997/98	23	7	1	0	1	40	Post-League
1998/99	25	9	1	0	1	50	Post-League
ALL	241	171	49	21	17	986	GRAND TOTAL

Note: 1981–1988: 4 points for a try; 1996–1999: 5 points for a try

APPENDIX 3

Rugby League Club Appearances

Note: DB = David Bishop; T = try

Championship 1988

Date	Opponent	For	Against	Result	No.	Position	DB
28 Aug	Salford	14	24	L	#6	Five-eighth	–
25 Sep	Halifax	12	4	W	#7	Halfback	T:1
2 Oct	Oldham	16	30	L	#7	Halfback	–
9 Oct	St Helens	22	30	L	#7	Halfback	–
16 Oct	Bradford Northern	24	22	W	#7	Halfback	–
23 Oct	Leeds	8	21	L	#7	Halfback	–
6 Nov	Wakefield Trinity	38	18	W	#7	Halfback	–
20 Nov	Widnes	6	43	L	#7	Halfback	–
11 Dec	Wakefield Trinity	12	6	W	#7	Halfback	–
2 Jan	Hull	12	15	L	#7	Halfback	–
15 Jan	Oldham	34	6	W	#7	Halfback	–
22 Jan	St Helens	0	29	L	#7	Halfback	–
5 Feb	Warrington	7	17	L	#7	Halfback	–
19 Feb	Halifax	12	12	D	#7	Halfback	–
5 Mar	Wigan	18	19	L	#12	Second row	T:1
12 Mar	Featherstone Rovers	6	28	L	#7	Halfback	–
15 Mar	Leeds	13	18	L	#7	Halfback	–
19 Mar	Salford	18	24	L	#7	Halfback	–
24 Mar	Hull	2	26	L	#13	Lock	–

Appendix 3

Second Division 1989

Date	Opponent	For	Against	Result	No.	Position	DB
3 Sep	Keighley	50	16	W	#7	Halfback	T: 1
24 Sep	Trafford Borough	48	8	W	#7	Halfback	T: 1
1 Oct	Oldham	4	12	L	#7	Halfback	-
8 Oct	Nottingham City	54	4	W	#12	Second row	T: 1
22 Oct	Swinton	38	16	W	#11	Second row	T: 1
29 Oct	Fulham	44	0	W	#7	Halfback	-
5 Nov	Halifax	20	6	W	#7	Halfback	T: 1
26 Nov	Dewsbury	54	6	W	#7	Halfback	T: 2
17 Dec	Fulham	60	6	W	#7	Halfback	T: 1
26 Dec	Ryedale-York	12	0	W	#7	Halfback	-
31 Dec	Hunslet	36	10	W	#7	Halfback	-
1 Jan	Nottingham City	58	0	W	#7	Halfback	-
17 Jan	Oldham	6	9	L	#7	Halfback	-
21 Jan	Workington Town	40	6	W	#7	Halfback	T: 1
4 Feb	Bramley	60	2	W	#7	Halfback	T: 3
18 Feb	Runcorn Highfield	36	6	W	#7	Halfback	-
4 Mar	Keighley	66	10	W	#7	Halfback	-
7 Mar	Whitehaven	46	2	W	#7	Halfback	T: 1
18 Mar	Whitehaven	92	10	W	#7	Halfback	T: 3
8 Apr	Runcorn Highfield	38	12	W	#7	Halfback	-
11 Apr	Dewsbury	2	3	L	#7	Halfback	-

Championship 1990

Date	Opponent	For	Against	Result	No.	Position	DB
16 Sep	Warrington	20	14	W	#7	Halfback	-
23 Sep	St Helens	10	42	L	#7	Halfback	-
30 Sep	Wakefield Trinity	12	18	L	#7	Halfback	-
7 Oct	Oldham	28	25	W	#1	Fullback	-

375

Championship 1991

Date	Opponent	For	Against	Result	No.	Position	DB
20 Oct	Halifax	8	76	L	#14	Bench	–
10 Nov	St Helens	15	38	L	#15	Bench	–
15 Dec	St Helens	24	14	W	#6	Five-eighth	–
22 Dec	Salford	28	7	W	#6	Five-eighth	T: 1
26 Dec	Leeds	8	22	L	#6	Five-eighth	–

Championship 1992

Date	Opponent	For	Against	Result	No.	Position	DB
18 Oct	Featherstone Rovers	10	40	L	#7	Halfback	–

Cup competitions

Competition	Date	Round	Result	Opponent	For	Against	No.	Position	DB
Yorks. Cup 1988	18 Sep	1	W	Keighley	28	22	#6	Five-eighth	–
Yorks. Cup 1989	17 Sep	1	W	Bramley	54	12	#7	Halfback	T: 1
Yorks. Cup 1989	27 Sep	2	L	Castleford	12	28	#7	Halfback	T: 1
Yorks. Cup 1990	19 Aug	Prelim	W	Nottingham	100	6	#7	Halfback	–
John Player Special Trophy 1988	13 Nov	1	W	Keighley	40	0	#7	Halfback	T: 1, G: 1
John Player Special Trophy 1988	4 Dec	3	D	Wigan	16	16	#7	Halfback	–
Challenge Cup 1988	29 Jan	1	W	Rochdale H.	28	24	#7	Halfback	T: 1
Challenge Cup 1988	12 Feb	2	W	Chorley B.	28	4	#7	Halfback	FG: 1
Challenge Cup 1988	26 Feb	3	L	Warrington	4	30	#7	Halfback	–
Challenge Cup 1989	28 Jan	1	L	Wigan	4	6	#7	Halfback	–
Regal Trophy 1989	2 Dec	1	L	St Helens	26	40	#7	Halfback	T: 1
Regal Trophy 1991	17 Nov	1	L	Castleford	10	22	#7	Halfback	–

APPENDIX 4

Rugby League Career Summary

Competitions

Competition	Apps	Tries	Goals	Field Goals	Points	Win	Loss	Draw	Win %
Tour matches: GB	6	1	–	–	4	4	2	0	66.67%
Tour matches: Wales	1	1	–	–	4	1	0	0	100.00%
Challenge Cup	4	1	–	1	5	2	2	0	50.00%
English Championship	28	3	–	–	12	9	18	1	32.14%
Regal Trophy	4	2	1	–	10	1	2	1	25.00%
Yorkshire Cup	4	2	–	–	8	3	1	0	75.00%
UK Second Division	22	16	–	–	64	18	4	0	81.82%
OVERALL	**69**	**26**	**1**	**1**	**107**	**38**	**29**	**2**	**55.07%**

INTERNATIONAL

Test matches by team

Team	Apps	Tries	Goals	Field Goals	Points	Win	Loss	Draw	Win %
GB (1990)	1	–	–	–	–	0	1	0	0.00%
Wales (1991/92)	4	1	–	–	4	3	1	0	75.00%
OVERALL (1990–1992)	**5**	**1**	**0**	**0**	**4**	**3**	**2**	**0**	**60.00%**

CLUB CAREER

By season

Season	Apps	Tries	Goals	Field Goals	Points	Win	Loss	Draw	Win %
1988/89	25	4	1	1	19	9	14	2	36.00%
1989/90	25	19	–	–	76	19	6	0	76.00%
1990/91	5	–	–	–	–	3	2	0	60.00%
1991/92	6	1	–	–	4	2	4	0	33.33%
1992/93	1	–	–	–	–	0	1	0	0.00%
OVERALL	**62**	**24**	**1**	**1**	**99**	**33**	**27**	**2**	**53.23%**

By club

Team	Apps	Tries	Goals	Field Goals	Points	Win	Loss	Draw	Win %
Hull Kingston Rovers	61	24	1	1	99	33	26	2	54.10%
London Crusaders	1	–	–	–	–	0	1	0	0.00%
OVERALL	**62**	**24**	**1**	**1**	**99**	**33**	**27**	**2**	**53.23%**

Note: In 1988/89, 1989/90, 1990/91 and 1991/92, David was playing for Hull Kingston Rovers. In 1992/93, he played one match for London Crusaders.

APPENDIX 5

Sendings-Off – The Facts

CLUB	1980/81	1981/82	1982/83	1983/84	1984/85	1985/86	1986/87 to date	TOTAL
Aberavon	1	1	1	3	2	–	–	8
Abertillery	–	2	1	1	2	–	–	6
Bridgend	–	2	–	–	2	–	–	4
Cardiff	–	2	1	3	–	1	–	7
Cross Keys	1	–	2	3	1	1	–	8
Ebbw Vale	–	1	1	2	–	–	–	4
Glamorgan Wanderers	1	1	1	2	1	–	–	6
Llanelli	1	1	–	2	3	–	–	7
London Welsh	1	–	–	1	–	2	1	5
Maesteg	–	–	2	–	–	–	–	2
Neath	–	1	3	1	3	1	–	9
Newbridge	4	1	3	1	4	1	1	15
Newport	–	2	3	1	–	3	–	9
Penarth	1	1	1	1	1	–	–	5
Pontypool	2	–	1	4	–	1	–	8
Pontypridd	–	–	–	4	3	2	–	9
South Wales Police	1	1	1	–	–	–	–	3
Swansea	1	–	1	1	1	1	–	5
Tredegar	1	–	2	1	1	–	–	5
TOTAL BY SEASON	15	16	24	31	24	13	2	125

Note: Table compiled by the *South Wales Echo* from official WRU figures. The sendings-off for the 1986/87 season are only up to its publication on 4 October 1986.

Acknowledgements

ONE OF THE reasons I wanted to write this book was to say thank you – as well as sorry – to the people who have been part of my life and helped me along the way, and hopefully I've done that. Topping that list always is my family, followed by the many sporting friends I've made over the decades and the faithful fans – of Pooler and of Hull KR – who keep in touch and kindly remember the good days rather than the bad ones.

I've tried to faithfully record what they all mean to me – that's my acknowledgement – but as we approach publication, I do lie awake at night wondering if I've missed anybody out. It would grieve me greatly. So if you'll indulge me one final time – I have no intention of ever writing any sort of book again, so you won't be hearing any more from me – I just want to namecheck a few people I should have written about more.

I'd like to dedicate this book to my family, especially my daughters, Samara and Natasha, and my grandchildren, Thalia, Joseph, Amara and Ezra. I hope you know how much I love you all. It's for my ex-wife Kate too, as an apology for being such a prick when we were married – I'm truly sorry.

I'd like to thank Jane Blackburn for all her friendship and support over the last 11 years – she really is an unbelievable person. The only thing wrong with her is that she's a Black

Acknowledgements

and White! Likewise, a huge thanks to Craig Bellamy for writing the foreword to this book, and for being there for me in so many ways over the years. I really appreciate it, mate.

Early school days were vitally important for me, so thank you to Jerry Dawson at St Cadoc's, who spotted a natural scrum half and moved me off the wing. Thank you also to both Miss Head and Mr Hillier, who were in charge of the baseball team and insisted I played a sport which was to give me so much pleasure and fun. Re-reading my baseball chapter, I should also have highlighted what a brilliant player Paul Cross was and lavished more praise on the Llanrumney duo of John Smith and Stephen Haines. Legends.

My Old Illytdians rugby mates played a bigger role in my life than I seem to have conveyed. Paul 'Pablo' Rees, obviously, but others like Kenny Poole, Jed Meehan, Michael 'Spud' Murphy, Stephen Franks – 'Potter', of boxing fame – and Mike Catris. Mike used to captain the club and is a huge character, and another one of my mates who became a massively successful businessman. Yet again, I wonder how I'm completely lacking that particular gene or why none of their entrepreneurial genius ever rubbed off on me. What did rub off was their friendship and sense of fun. We all remain tight 40, and in some cases 50, years on.

Looking back and viewing the bigger picture, which is what writing a book allows you to do, I can see now that Cardiff Youth played a bigger part in my life than I've possibly acknowledged. They were great days: a brilliant side where winning and playing good rugby was the norm and optimism reigned. I'm thinking of Peter – 'Pedro' – and Jose Souto, Andrew Gilham, Chris Collins and his brother Tim, who passed away before his time, Tim Carruthers, and Kevin Trevett, also a sporting talent who departed too early.

Terry Charles was another friend from that era who also crossed over into the baseball group.

The bigger picture I've been painting has also shown me how much I owed to Ebbw Vale for taking me on when I was kicked out of Cardiff, slipping me a few quid 'travel expenses', giving me first-team rugby against the very best in Wales and standing by me when I had to spend a year in HMP Aylesbury. A great club run by good folk, and I come out in a cold sweat to this day at the memory of leaving them for Pooler. It was the right move, but it felt so wrong.

Much more recently, one guy who deserves a huge mention is Steve Smith, a busy and successful businessman with Concept Fire and Security, who I bumped into at Valentino's restaurant one time. You don't make many new friends when you get to my age – well, blokes don't – but we hit it off and Steve offered to organise a charity golf event in my name, which is quite an undertaking and needs somebody with that businesslike attention to detail and a willingness to just grapple with the nitty gritty. Steve's great company and organises everything with a smile, even when I know he's nursing a hangover, and right from the off 'got' me and my sometimes difficult, cranky ways. As well as raising a few quid for charities, these golf days are a great way of reconnecting with old friends and rivals, which, as we now know, has an important role to play in improving your mental health in retirement. Thanks so much, Steve.

Thanks also to everybody involved in making this book a reality. Only now, right at the end, have I really believed it would happen. I thank the publishers, Y Lolfa, for their belief in the project, and in particular editor Carolyn Hodges. Thanks to Seimon Williams, who made a number of helpful suggestions at the draft stage; to Geraint Powell,

Acknowledgements

for his help with the Pooler playing stats in Appendix 2; and to Wobbley and to the Rugby League Project for the League stats. A big thank you also to Brendan for all his hard work and patience, and for acting as my unofficial shrink during our many conversations as I've tried to piece things together and make sense of it all, and to all those who have shown an interest and offered encouragement. If nothing else, it kept me sane during Covid and a few very difficult years, health-wise.

Finally, particular thanks to those who contributed a few choice words about me – my daughter Samara, Ringo, Bobby, Paul Lewis (the boxer), Perky, John Actie, Mark Jones (the baseball man, not the rugby player), Roger Bidgood, veteran journalist Peter Jackson and, from the grave, Eddie Butler, John Billot and Brian Thomas. Words like that keep me going on the bad days: thank you.

It's not been the life I envisaged – not remotely – but there's no denying it's the life I've lived, and there's no denying either that for all my bitterness over many things, I've been blessed with my family and friends. I subtitled this book 'It's all about me', but really, it's about them as well. I thank you, one and all.

David Bishop
August 2025

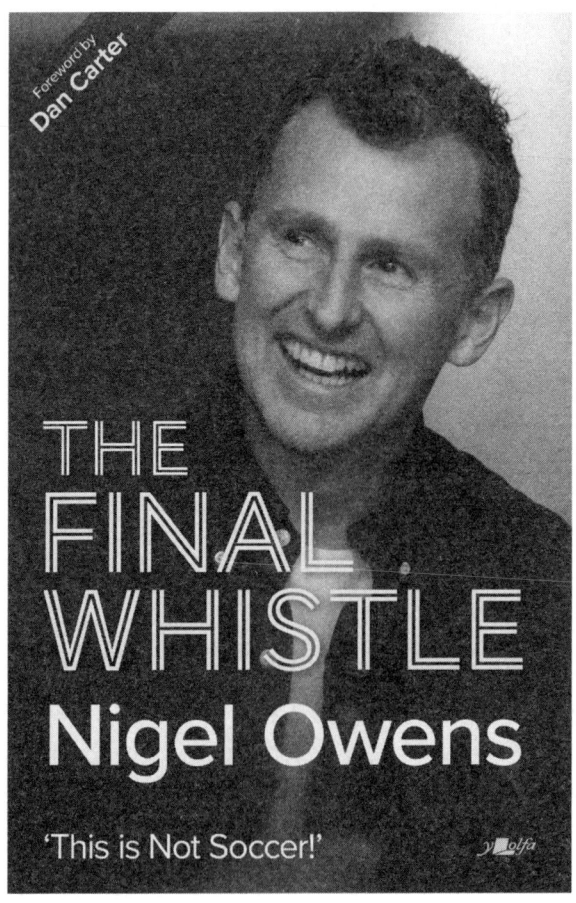

NOW IN PAPERBACK!

Nigel Owens is one of the most famous referees in World Rugby and one of only two Welsh refs ever to officiate at a Rugby World Cup Final. In his bestselling second autobiography, he reveals all about the second half of his career, including the full story of his last Rugby World Cup in 2019.

£12.99